797,885 Books

are available to read at

www.ForgottenBooks.com

Forgotten Books' App
Available for mobile, tablet & eReader

ISBN 978-1-5277-0980-5
PIBN 10883124

This book is a reproduction of an important historical work. Forgotten Books uses
state-of-the-art technology to digitally reconstruct the work, preserving the original format
whilst repairing imperfections present in the aged copy. In rare cases, an imperfection in
the original, such as a blemish or missing page, may be replicated in our edition. We do,
however, repair the vast majority of imperfections successfully; any imperfections that
remain are intentionally left to preserve the state of such historical works.

Forgotten Books is a registered trademark of FB &c Ltd.
Copyright © 2017 FB &c Ltd.
FB &c Ltd, Dalton House, 60 Windsor Avenue, London, SW19 2RR.
Company number 08720141. Registered in England and Wales.

For support please visit www.forgottenbooks.com

1 MONTH OF
FREE
READING

at

www.ForgottenBooks.com

By purchasing this book you are eligible for one month membership to ForgottenBooks.com, giving you unlimited access to our entire collection of over 700,000 titles via our web site and mobile apps.

To claim your free month visit:

www.forgottenbooks.com/free883124

* Offer is valid for 45 days from date of purchase. Terms and conditions apply.

English
Français
Deutsche
Italiano
Español
Português

www.forgottenbooks.com

Mythology Photography **Fiction**
Fishing Christianity **Art** Cooking
Essays Buddhism Freemasonry
Medicine **Biology** Music **Ancient
Egypt** Evolution Carpentry Physics
Dance Geology **Mathematics** Fitness
Shakespeare **Folklore** Yoga Marketing
Confidence Immortality Biographies
Poetry **Psychology** Witchcraft
Electronics Chemistry History **Law**
Accounting **Philosophy** Anthropology
Alchemy Drama Quantum Mechanics
Atheism Sexual Health **Ancient History**
Entrepreneurship Languages Sport
Paleontology Needlework Islam
Metaphysics Investment Archaeology
Parenting Statistics Criminology
Motivational

The *City of Norfolk* leaving Baltimore. (Photo by Hans Marx)

Steam Packets
on the
Chesapeake

A History of the Old Bay Line Since 1840

By Alexander Crosby Brown

Foreword by Walter Lord

TIDEWATER PUBLISHERS

Centreville, Maryland

Copyright © 1961 by Tidewater Publishers

All rights reserved. No part of this book may be used or reproduced in any manner whatsoever without written permission except in the case of brief quotations embodied in critical articles and reviews. For information, address Tidewater Publishers, Centreville, Maryland 21617.

ISBN 0-87033-111-6

Library of Congress Catalog Card Number: 61-12580

Manufactured in the United States of America

In 1940 an Account of The Old Bay Line was
Dedicated To
A.C.B., Jr., and *B.J.B.*

With the Expressed Hope that they Would Grow Up
To Follow a Long Line of Forebears in a Love of
Salt Water and Ships

To Them are now Added
S.B.B. and *J.H.B.*

With the Hope that They will Grow up to Become
Sailors' Sweethearts

Other Books by Alexander Crosby Brown

WOMEN AND CHILDREN LAST

MR. HARDY LEE: HIS YACHT (Edited)

THE MARINERS MUSEUM: A HISTORY AND GUIDE

NEWPORT NEWS' 325 YEARS (Edited)

THE OLD BAY LINE: 1840-1940

HORIZON'S RIM

Contents

Introduction

I N 1940, The Baltimore Steam Packet Company, then and still the oldest shipping line in the United States, marked an anniversary celebrating its first hundred years of smooth sailing on the Chesapeake. The Old Bay Line, for this is the familiar title earned by the company in the maturity of its years, was chartered by the States of Maryland and Virginia in 1839 and, the following year, began to provide a dependable steam packet service between the ports of Baltimore and Norfolk at opposite ends of the Bay.

With the United States ringed by thousands of miles of navigable coastal waters and the services of the Old Bay Line confined merely to some two hundred miles on the Chesapeake, naturally it is not claimed that the attainments of this little company is by any means world-shaking. It is significant, however, that this venerable organization, which has been in the transportation business under the same corporate name for almost a century and a quarter, may be considered a microcosm of the entire field of American steam navigation. As such, the Old Bay Line's record takes on unexpected importance as typifying all American steamboating.

To survive storms and water hazards, wars, depressions, sometimes cut-throat competition, and to keep abreast of ever-changing economic and political conditions has not been an easy task. The Old Bay Line is to be congratulated for meeting these innumerable challenges and so earning the right to claim the status of an institution well worthy of perpetuity.

One of the observances of the Centennial was the publication of a book of limited distribution tracing the company's story from its inception down to the centennial year. This work, printed by the Dietz Press of Richmond, Virginia, was issued under the joint auspices of the Baltimore Steam Packet Company and of The Mariners Museum in Newport News, Virginia, of which I was then Corresponding Secretary. Since 1940, however, the Old Bay Line and the Nation at large have passed through another World War deeply affecting the destinies of all. So much has happened to men and ships in the interim, that it was logically decided a new edition of the book, brought up to date with additional chapters covering these more recent events, would prove a useful contribution to the literature of the sea.

In revising and enlarging the text, the author was given, as on the initial occasion, the unstinted help and encouragement of the Company and, particularly so, from two officials who by now are to be considered old friends, Bob Dunn, president of the Line, and Ray Jones, passenger traffic manager.

The following passages, excerpts taken from the preface of the first edition of *The Old Bay Line: 1840-1940*, are still applicable to this revised work.

"Although one often encounters an unfortunate tendency to forget those forces which most tellingly combined to create and unify the United States of America into a nation, nevertheless sober analysis points to the development of transportation as being the most vital single factor which permitted this to take place. In the field of transportation the role of steam propelled craft is of paramount importance and Roger Williams McAdam truthfully acknowledged that 'the American steamboat knit the East and built the West.'

"This country had been richly endowed by nature with broad, navigable rivers and deep, protected sounds which, like sparkling beads on a giant necklace, are dotted along the coast from Maine to Florida. At the beginning of the Nineteenth Century with no highways worthy of the name and settlements linked together only by sailing craft, pawns of wind and tide, it may be readily seen that the evolution of the steamboat as the *only* reliable and swift means of communication proved an inestimable boon. The meteoric development of steam-driven craft was in direct answer to the pressing need which first called them into being.

"Rivaling Long Island Sound in importance as a water link along the eastern seaboard, Chesapeake Bay, fed by more than a dozen broad rivers penetrating deep into the hinterland, had been from early times the theater of spectacular developments in the maritime history of the nation. In 1607 into the Chesapeake sailed the three little ships seeking to establish the first permanent English Colony in the New World at Jamestown. A century and three quarters later by its waters was fought the conclusive contest of Yorktown which insured at last the independence of the American Colonies. Then, in 1812, Chesapeake Bay and its tributaries again were the principally contested areas during the second struggle with the Mother Country. Again, and tragically so, the Civil War brought the Chesapeake and its rivers into the limelight. The Great War saw the Hampton Roads Port of Embarkation a bulwark of the nation's war effort. [History was to be repeated in World War II.]

"No less important has been the peacetime role played by the Chesapeake. Her shipbuilders and mariners spread her fame throughout the world and wherever sailors congregated the famous

Baltimore clipper became the byword for capability, seaworthiness, and speed. While her mariners on the high seas continued this splendid tradition, it is easy to appreciate why locally still another class of resourceful sailors came into being: the steamboatmen, for Chesapeake seafolk were not long in recognizing the importance of craft with 'teakettles' in them made to stem the tide.

"Much has been said of the tremendously unifying influence of the railroad in this country, and it is true that the steel rails spreading ever westward have played a vitally important part. The railroads, however, came as the second step in the history of communications. It is significant to note that they were originally envisaged not as competition to the coastwise and river steamboat lines, but were designed to extend and complement them by pushing deeper into the surrounding country. Thus, the first railroads were feeders for the steamboats.

"That anathema, speed, which first called steamboats into being, later turned on them with infanticidal fury, and steam craft today cannot compare to their heyday of a few generations ago. The original picture became reversed, rails controlled the ships and competition was to the death. For a long time the steamboat held its own until, with automobiles, buses and trucks coming into the picture, a great many of the famous old lines like the Bangor and Fall River were forced to suspend their services. *Sic transit gloria mundi:* cliché, but true!

"In Colonial days, life was necessarily stately and slow. Travel even for the wealthy had little to recommend it, for when the jolting stagecoach was mired down in knee-deep mud, passengers rich and poor alike had to put their shoulders to the wheel to get it out. The steamboat offered ease and elegance plus speeds hitherto believed impossible. With steam the great class of American tourists was born.

"For those to whom speed was paramount, the steamboat was later abandoned for the railroad, and this in turn has been supplanted by aircraft. Fortunately for those who bemoan the passing of a slower, more gracious living, the desire to retain the calm of Colonial days has not been entirely lost. Many ask themselves the need for hurry, the tempo of modern life is already geared too high for health or comfort. With this sane trend made manifest, the safe and comfortable steamboat can still find a place. Unlike any other existing means of travel, a ship affords its passengers three-dimensional space, a pleasant contrast to the virtually two-dimensional corridor of the train, or the one-dimensional seat on plane or bus.

"For any organization to have survived throughout the varying economic picture for the past century would surely indicate that it was not only well-grounded in the first place, but that those in whose charge its destinies have lain were particularly adept at meeting new situations and readjusting to conform to changing times. It is not strange that Chesapeake Bay, a principal artery of lifeblood of the nation, should have given birth to what is today the oldest active steamboat company in existence in America. The Baltimore Steam Packet Company, now familiarly known as the Old Bay Line, for a century has run steamers up and down the Chesapeake, gateway between North and South. Unique in the pageant of America's waterborne commerce, the Old Bay Line, whose history is traced in the following pages, in rounding out its centennial of faithful and constant service to the American public occupies an enviable position in the annals of American enterprise.

"Joanna C. Colcord, in her *Songs of American Sailormen*, cites an old sea chanty sung in bygone days by sailors of Chesapeake Bay's famous Baltimore Clippers, which carries the refrain:

> A hundred years on the Eastern Shore,
> O yes O,
> A hundred years is a very long time!
> A hundred years ago.

> A hundred years have passed and gone
> O yes O,
> And a hundred years will come once more
> A hundred years ago.

"Perhaps geologically or astronomically speaking, the centenary period is insignificant, but when applied to shipping it may be truly said that 'a hundred years is a very long time!' Of the many steamship operators in the United States today only a small proportion may trace their existence back into the past century. Congratulations, therefore, to the patriarch of the tribe! We trust that 'a hundred years will come once more.'

"For the historian, the compilation of a record of this kind is not as easy a task as might be first imagined. Source material has proved both scarce and elusive. Four times during the hundred year period, the Company has had valuable old records destroyed, three times by fire, once by flood. The search for material on the Line has been, however, both pleasant and rewarding. A sketch of an ancient Old Bay Liner turned up in London, details of others came in from as far afield as California and Alaska—such have proved the ramifications in tracking down the events and personalities of the Company's story.

"It would be superfluous to point out that this chronicle could not have been accomplished without the very real and generously awarded help of a great many people."

Newport News, *Virginia*   ALEXANDER CROSBY BROWN

Foreword

The Old Bay Line, as the Baltimore Steam Packet Company has long been familiarly known, enjoyed its heyday in the 1890's. Alexander Brown, author of this book and a great-great-grandson of the Baltimore banker of the same name, makes this firm contention. No statement could meet with less argument here, for my own grandfather, Richard Curzon Hoffman, had the honor to be president of the Line from 1893 to 1899.

Nor am I particularly surprised that this was such a happy period for the Company. I vividly remember the gleaming brass, the rich food, the unhurried air of well-being that permeated Grandfather's house, and it all fits perfectly with the many good things I associate with the Old Bay Line.

What I didn't realize was the nature of the relationship between Grandfather and the Line. In my innocent youth and family vanity, I had always assumed that the old gentleman had given his high standard of happy living to the ships. Actually, it was the other way around. The ships had been there long before him, and after reading this wonderfully nostalgic book, I now know that these vessels had always stood for impeccable service and that it must have been they that gave the standards to Grandfather.

Where the Old Bay Line got its qualities remains a mystery. Perhaps through some magical blending of the best in the North and the South, made possible by the Company's unique role in "bridging" the two sections. It is nice to think that the North has contributed its tradition of mechanical proficiency, making the ships so reliable; while the South has contributed its gracious ease, making the service so utterly delightful.

If this highly unscientific theory explains where the Old Bay Line got its special qualities, only a miracle can explain how it retains them. In today's desert of hideously uncomfortable transportation, the Line remains a miraculous oasis of The Way Things Should Be Done.

When I took my most recent voyage in 1958, after being far from the Chesapeake for at least twenty years, I must confess I feared for the worst. Surely, I felt, the Old Bay Line, too, must have lost its touch. How wrong I was. Everything was still there—and I'm

sure is there now—the stewards' starched white jackets, the delici-
ous dinner, the cozy bar, the air of faraway romance as we steamed
up the Bay under the stars.

Alec Brown has done an immense service in reminding us all not
only that this is the way Americans used to travel, but that in at
least one blessed corner of our country, we can still do it today.

New York City   WALTER LORD

Steam Packets on the Chesapeake

CHAPTER I

Via Old Bay Line In 1840

M ORE than a century ago an anonymous traveler was inspired to pen the following superlatively flowery description of a trip he made down Chesapeake Bay. Cautioning the reader to fortify himself well with a deep breath, here it is—verbatim:

The trip from Baltimore down the Chesapeake, in the fine steamer *Georgia*, was a delightful one. I have often heard old sea-captains, who have traversed almost every known sea, lake, bay, and river in the world, speak in the most exalted terms of the noble Chesapeake. As a bay it has no equal, not even in that of Naples, all things considered. I know of no more delightful trip, especially in the summer season. Mine, on this last occasion, was particularly so. I emerged from the confines of a hot, murky city, and was soon out upon the broad blue waters, with an exquisite breeze, which came up with invigorating freshness from the silver waves. Night came on, and her azure curtain, gemmed with myriad stars, was drawn over the expanse above. A little while longer, and the pale moon, with her round modest face, peered up the eastern horizon. She looked like a sylvan queen gently blushing to take the place of her lord and master, who had just sunk from his majestic career behind a golden halo.

A scene on the Chesapeake, thus changing from noon-day to gray eve, thence to dim twilight, and deepening into the soft azure of a summer's night, is truly inspiring alike to the poet and painter, as well as invigorating to health, and renovating to the finer feelings of sentimentality and romance.[1]

While our unnamed voyager, who may as well be referred to hereafter as "Mr. Smith," is comfortably reclining on the afterdeck of the "fine steamer *Georgia*", reveling in the sublime scene which he has painted for us and complacently permitting his "finer feelings" to have their way with him, let us go back to the beginning of his voyage and briefly consider the noble packet which is speeding him southward at the awesome rate of ten miles per hour. Mr. Smith had booked passage on the *Georgia*, flagship of the then new line plying between the ports of Baltimore and Norfolk. Although he has intimated that he had made the trip before, on that sunny day more than a century ago undoubtedly he had his carriage deliver him and portmanteau at Spears Wharf, Baltimore, well in advance of the scheduled 4:00 P.M. departure. Snugly secured to her dock, the good ship *Georgia*, elegant in her coat of white paint, glistened in the afternoon light.

With ample time to kill, our Mr. Smith must have walked down the wharf, leaned against a weatherworn spile and taken in to the fullest the animated scene before him. Heavy teams groaning under loads of bales, crates, and boxes surged through the dusty thoroughfare. Perspiring stevedores loaded piles of merchandise on hand trucks and rolled them over swaying gangways into the darkened doorways piercing the sides of the *Georgia*. Ladies in billowing dresses picked their way gingerly across the road, leaning heavily on the arms of their escorts, resplendent in stovepipe hats and flowery waistcoats of watered silk. Dusky porters in white coats and caps bearing the legend, "Bay Line", surrounded each approaching carriage, obsequiously bowed out the travelers and whisked away their luggage. In the background, "runners" of the rival "Upper Route" would hint darkly to all who would listen of the alleged dangers of steamboat travel and urge travelers to go on in safety to Washington in the "cars."

There was a constant din and the babble of many voices rent the air. Officers on the ship were calling instructions to their seamen; teamsters were shouting to the struggling horses; dock hands and stevedores lightened labor with song; small boys darting under foot yelled to one another; and hawkers impetuously cried the merits of their wares. Suddenly the shrill note of the *Georgia's* newfangled steam whistle resounded and Mr. Smith consulted his heavy gold watch and decided that it was time to go aboard. Picking his way over to the passenger gangway, he mounted in time to catch a startled "oh" from the lady passenger immediately preceding him. She had looked down to the dark strip of water separating ship from shore as she climbed the steps. At the head of the gangway, Mr. Smith nodded to a fine frock-coated figure who could be none other than that doughty mariner, Captain James Coffey, master of the noble *Georgia*.

He surrendered his ticket to another commanding individual, Mr. Wilson, ship's "clerk," as pursers were then termed, and made his way to the upper deck to watch the late arrivals come on board. Another impetuous blast of the steam whistle rent the air and white-coated stewards called, "All ashore that's going ashore."

View of Baltimore City from Federal Hill. The steamboat *Georgia*, one of the first four vessels of the Old Bay Line, is shown entering harbor at the right of the print. A lithograph by E. Sachse, Baltimore, 1859. (Courtesy of Enoch Pratt Free Library, Baltimore)

The last few passengers had hurried across the gangplank when a team of lively horses pranced up to the dock and canvas bags were tossed from the wagon and whisked aboard. The "Great Southern Mail," just arrived from Philadelphia, had been delivered and now the *Georgia* was ready to begin her 200-mile voyage down the length of the Chesapeake Bay. Lines were cast off as Captain Coffey, speaking trumpet in hand, took his command station on top of one of the giant paddle boxes—the lunette structures that covered the big paddle wheels projecting out from the sides of the vessel like packs on a burro. The gilded wooden eagle surmounting the pilothouse stood ready, poised for flight.

Crisp orders were given, the paddle wheels began to revolve and the proud steamboat slowly drew away from her dock. Gaining way, she headed straight out into the crowded channel as Spears Wharf and the waving figures ashore diminished and were gradually lost from view.

Probably Mr. Smith was still in no hurry to go down to find his cabin, as the various sights and sounds of the harbor must have held his attention. By the Lazaretto they passed the steamer *Patuxent* of Captain Weems' Rappahannock River Line. Her churning paddles marked a wake of creamy water far behind. Fleets of graceful pungy schooners, some with watermelons piled high on deck, were sailing up the Patapsco, their snowy canvas and rose pink sides forming variegated patterns against the foil of blue water and green slopes beyond.

At last Mr. Smith reluctantly tore himself from his place at the rail and made his way down to the Gentlemen's Saloon to claim his "birth," as it was generally spelled. Coming from the brilliant sunshine outdoors, he was momentarily blinded until his eyes became accustomed to the dimmer light within. Tiers of bunks lined the sides of the richly carpeted cabin and Mr. Smith, assisted by a steward, deposited his luggage in the space assigned to him by lot. By this time, several convivial spirits had assembled around the bar and, although his appetite had already been whetted by the salt air, Mr. Smith decided that he would partake of a julep as a foretaste of the hospitality of the South whither he was bound.

Supper was now in order and, although the dining saloon was below on a deck devoid of portholes, the meal was a cheerful one with white napery and silver glistening in the light cast by whale-oil tapers.

Gaining the deck again, Mr. Smith sought a chair on the open afterdeck and fell into conversation with a naval officer and his lady who, he learned, were bound for Portsmouth where the officer was to be attached to a ship then lying at the Gosport Navy Yard. He had noted on his way through the saloon that several card games were in progress and, although he would have enjoyed whiling away an hour or so at whist, he sensibly decided that playing cards with strangers, particularly on steamboats, was a little risky.

The officer and his lady retired early and Mr. Smith, stretching out comfortably in his chair, was left to the musings he outlined for us in his description quoted previously. Obviously pleased with his lot, our friend undoubtedly sat up on deck late drinking in the pleasant sights, smells, and sounds, being reluctant to exchange them for the discomforts of a narrow mattress in the stuffy cabin below. The paddle wheels continued their rhythmic slapping, waves danced in the moonlight, and the phosphorescent wake stretched out astern in a straight line. Clouds of black smoke burst from the tall black funnel that was the *Georgia's* crowning feature and occasional showers of gleaming sparks burst forth to rival the Milky Way, as Mr. Smith undoubtedly would have expressed it. Up through the fiddley wafted the smell of steam and hot oil and he could hear the distant clanking of machinery and the almost continual thud of heavy pitch-pine logs which the stokers were tossing from bunker to boiler.

By this time, most of his fellow passengers had either gone below or were sleeping out on deck with coats drawn over them. Occasionally sailors passed pursuing their various duties and, at periodic intervals, Mr. Smith could hear the lookout striking the ship's bells and reporting all well. Off on the horizon shone the lights of passing ships and, on the starboard hand, the yellow gleam of a lighthouse marked a harbor entrance.

With a sigh, Mr. Smith at last must have pulled himself from his chair, knocked out his pipe, and, realizing a busy day awaited him in Norfolk, gone down to bed.

Since we are privileged to look ahead into the future, while our friend sleeps, let us contrast the fine specimen of naval architecture called the *Georgia* with the steamers on which he might have traveled today. We are afraid that the little *Georgia*, noble steam packet though she was for her times, would be dwarfed to insignificance by her modern sisters. Today passengers have well-appointed staterooms, electric lights, and running water—a decided contrast to the *Georgia's* dimly lit cabins and crude washing facilities. If during the night the ministrations of a steward were required, Mr. Smith would have had to search the corridors in his nightshirt until he found one; today he merely would have to touch the electric bell.

These and similar contrasts being obvious, let us take a good look at the little *Georgia*.[2] John A. Robb of Baltimore had been her builder and she had been launched in 1836, four years before the Baltimore Steam Packet Company came into being and made her the flagship of its fleet. The *Georgia's* wooden hull was strongly built of tough red cedar and locust, for she was designed as a sea boat for the Atlantic Line on the exposed run from Norfolk to

Charleston around treacherous Cape Hatteras. She measured 551 tons and was 192 feet in length, with a beam of 24 feet and depth of 12.2 feet. Her planks were secured to staunch ribs with copper fastenings and her bottom was covered with copper sheathing as a protection against marine borers.

Charles Reeder had built the *Georgia's* 140-horsepower steam engine, a typical lever-beam type with a single upright cylinder measuring almost four feet in diameter from which plunged a piston with a nine and a half-foot stroke. The cast-iron walking beam which took the power from the piston and transferred it to the crankshaft was placed above on a massive wooden gallows frame. Heavy copper boilers, fired by burning logs, furnished low pressure steam. Slowly turning paddle-wheels drove her through the water, but if a breakdown occurred, she could resort to spreading sails. Modern Bay Line steamers have radiotelephones, but if a mishap occurred to the *Georgia*, she had to make her way alone. "A new and superior steam packet" was how they described her back in 1836,[3] when Captain William Rollins first conned her out of Norfolk harbor en route to the South Carolinian port, and passengers on the line were reassured by the announcement that "the captain is well acquainted with the coast and the engineers are approved practical men," and that the ship's cabins were "fitted with taste and splendor," each berth being "provided with one of McIntosh's *life preservers.*"[4]

We have seen that Mr. Smith's berth was one of a number arranged in tiers along the sides of the main saloon aft. In another part of the boat was situated the mirrored and begilded "Ladies' Cabin," from which men were excluded. A smaller cabin was situated forward of the machinery and similarly equipped with curtained berths. The *Georgia* also had four staterooms with two berths each on the main deck; the modern equivalent would be cabins de luxe or bridal suites.

Meanwhile, as Mr. Smith was sleeping soundly on his narrow shelf while insomniacs tossed to the accompaniment of their more fortunate companions' snores, the *Georgia* plowed along through the night. Her voyage half completed, she passed her running mate on the line, the smaller side-wheeler *Jewess*, commanded by Captain Thomas Sutton, northbound for Baltimore.

The first gray streaks of approaching dawn found her skirting a fleet of fishermen in sailing canoes outward bound for the day's work on York Spit shoals. She plowed steadily onward to meet short choppy seas washing over the Horseshoe, as the ebb tide ran counter to the gentle Sou'wester sweeping off the land. Soon she rounded Thimble Shoals and made her way westward toward the mouth of Hampton Roads. The dock at Old Point Comfort, lying below the guns of recently completed Fortress Monroe, awaited and some sleepy-eyed passengers who were getting off to stay at the Hygeia Hotel for the "bathing season" at the new resort were already on deck.

The clamor attendant to bringing the *Georgia* alongside the wharf undoubtedly awakened Mr. Smith and his companions and, after waiting his turn to dip his face in a basin of cold water, he quickly dressed and went on deck.

A heavy tide-rip ruffled the water and the *Georgia* tossed uneasily, straining against the hawsers which bound her to the land. Meanwhile several passengers had gone ashore, some to stay at Old Point, others to transfer to the steamboat, *Thomas Jefferson*, which was tied up ahead of the *Georgia,* bound for James River landings, City Point and Richmond.

As soon as the last piece of cargo had been left ashore, the *Georgia's* whistle blared, she fell back on her spring line, the paddles churned, and she was off on the final leg of her voyage across Hampton Roads and up the Elizabeth River to the thriving port of Norfolk. The roadstead was full of ships: lofty clippers homeward bound from South America and the Orient; sailing packets, every stitch of canvas drawing as they skirted the Rip Raps bound for the harbors of the world; glistening white steamboats, like the *Georgia* herself, belching forth clouds of gray smoke; busy side-wheel steam tugs towing strings of loaded barges.

Mr. Smith hated to miss anything that was going on, but his empty feeling inside had to be satisfied first and shortly after the boat had cleared the Old Point dock, her passengers assembled at the breakfast table.

A little over an hour later, the *Georgia* threaded her way up river and nudged in to her dock lying in the center of the busy town. Mr. Smith cast a last quick glance around the harbor. Across the water and beyond the town of Portsmouth on the opposite bank, he could pick out the tall spars of United States Navy frigates lying by the Gosport Yard. Directly opposite, he could see the wharves to which the *Georgia* would soon repair, the passenger cars and puffing locomotive of the Portsmouth and Roanoke Railway already waiting to speed on southward (at a dozen miles an hour) those of the *Georgia's* company who had booked through passage. With mixed feelings, our sentimental friend then turned his back on the scene, seized his portmanteau, and stepped down the gangway to the land. His trip via Old Bay Line almost a century and a quarter ago was completed.

CHAPTER II

Genesis

ALTHOUGH the steamboats of a hundred and twenty years ago were by no means the efficient and capable craft later developed, nevertheless, when the Baltimore Steam Packet Company was organized in 1839, steamboats were no novelty on the Chesapeake Bay. Before taking up the main thread of this account of the Old Bay Line, it would be appropriate to review the history of steam navigation on the Bay for the twenty-five-year period prior to the inception of the Baltimore Steam Packet Company.

First an attempt should be made to refute again the popularly accepted myth that Robert Fulton, though undoubtedly a genius. invented the steamboat. Many years before Fulton's *Clermont* steamed up the Hudson River, inventors had built and operated steam-driven craft both in this country and abroad. One of these men, James Rumsey, had built a successful vessel on the Potomac River in which George Washington was interested. John Fitch, misunderstood and ridiculed, at the same time built a series of steamboats in New York and Philadelphia. Fulton, however, combined mechanical skill with practical business acumen, and his North River steamboat, the *Clermont,* was unquestionably the first commercially successful steam craft. The *Clermont* made her bow in 1807, was rebuilt and lengthened the following year, and then was followed by the *Paragon, Car Of Neptune,* and other steamboats, each superior to its predecessor. Permanently established steamboat services having germinated in the waters of New York spread rapidly throughout the country. On June 8, 1808, John Stevens' celebrated *Phoenix,* debarred by the Fulton-Livingston monopoly, was taken around the Jersey coast by Captain Moses Rogers and placed in service on Delaware Bay. To get there, she made the first ocean voyage of a boat propelled by means other than manpower or the wind.

Baltimore's first steamer was the *Chesapeake*, built in 1813 at Flannigan's Wharf by Captain Edward Trippe, and she was the first commercial craft to ply the waters for which she had been named.[5] Two members of the syndicate that built her, Andrew F. Henderson and General William McDonald, should be especially singled out here, for a quarter of a century later these men were among the incorporators of the Baltimore Steam Packet Company, Henderson serving as its first president and McDonald, a director.

The *Chesapeake* was especially constructed as a link in the transportation service between Philadelphia and Baltimore. Although long planned, the Delaware and Chesapeake Canal was not completed for another fifteen years and the then accustomed routine of the southbound traveler consisted of his boarding a sailing packet at Philadelphia for the passage down Delaware Bay to Newcastle; thence via swaying stagecoach across the upper neck of the Delmarva Peninsula to Frenchtown, where he again embarked on a sailing packet for the trip down the Elk River, across the head of the Chesapeake, and up the Patapsco River to Baltimore. This region is notorious for its calms and transportation was both slow and uncertain. As soon as the builders could have her ready, the *Chesapeake* was placed on the Baltimore-Frenchtown run on what became known as the Union Line.

The dispatch with which the *Chesapeake* could traverse this route made it impossible for sailing packets to compete with her. Two years later, the rival Briscoe-Partridge Line, whose ships ran from Baltimore to Elkton, secured a little 110-foot steamboat, the *Eagle*, built in Philadelphia in 1813, which was then brought around by sea from the Delaware to the Virginia Capes. Her trip was under the command of the same Moses Rogers who was master of the *Phoenix* and who later commanded the famous auxiliary steamship *Savannah* on her epic transatlantic voyage in 1819.

The *Eagle* arrived at Norfolk on June 19, 1815, after a passage of twenty-five hours from the Delaware Capes and, following a short layover, proceeded to Baltimore. She arrived on June 25, having been twenty-nine hours under way. Although she was the first steamer to sail the length of the Chesapeake, the steamboat *Washington*, Captain O'Neale, had preceded her to Norfolk by almost a month. The *Washington* had been sent down from New York where she had been built and she was destined for service between Washington and Potomac Creek, as a link in the Southern stage route.

In traversing the route from lower to upper bay in 1815, however, the *Eagle* blazed the trail which has been followed by steamers of the Old Bay Line ever since. The latter traces its ancestry back without break to this memorable little craft—the first Norfolk-Baltimore steamer.

If the *Georgia,* first boat of the Old Bay Line, on which our friend Mr. Smith had taken passage, seemed crude compared to their modern craft, what of the little *Eagle?* It was stated that she was only 110 feet in length. Her width was less than 20 feet and her cumbersome machinery and boiler which occupied the best part of the hull were placed slightly forward of amidships so that the distance from her bow to her paddle-wheel shaft came to 46 feet. Her wooden hull was closely patterned after those of sailing packets, and she was steered by a long tiller at the stern, as they were. A tall mast from which a square sail could be set was placed forward of the machinery. Proceeding aft, next came the cumbersome paddle wheels shrouded by their protecting guards astride which stood the massive crosshead of her elementary "steeple" engine. Fireroom and boiler surmounted by its smudgy smokestack came next, while the entire after part of the deck was covered by a tentlike awning. Below this was the "great" cabin which served as dining and sleeping quarters for passengers and which was mainly ventilated by a row of windows piercing her square transom stern. There was no pilothouse and Captain Moses Rogers, stovepipe hat firmly planted on his head, conned her from the top of one of the paddle boxes, bellowing instructions to his quartermaster aft, or climbing down to stamp on deck as signal to his engineers.

Although the *Eagle* was employed mainly on the Baltimore to Frenchtown run, she made several trips down the Bay to Norfolk and in July, 1815, she steamed up the James to Richmond, making the round trip back to Baltimore in a week.

On April 18, 1824, the *Eagle's* boiler exploded killing Henry M. Murray, a discharged soldier who was a passenger, and injuring several others, including Captain George Weems, who was then operating the steamer on the route to Annapolis and the Patuxent River.[6] According to the historian, T. W. Griffith,[7] this melancholy occurrence marked the first steamboat fatality on the Bay.

Following the *Chesapeake* and a companion craft on the Union Line, the *Philadelphia,* the third Baltimore-built steamboat was the packet *Virginia.* The *Virginia* was the first steamer to have been built expressly for the Baltimore and Norfolk service and a contemporary description rated her as being a "very large and staunch boat, elegantly fitted."[8] It is interesting to note that to achieve this distinction in the year 1817, some $55,000 had been spent on her construction, a mere fraction of the cost of building a vessel suitable for the trade today.

As first built (she was later lengthened), the *Virginia* measured 136 feet in length, with a beam of 24 feet, 9 inches and a draft of 5 feet. Her arrangement and method of construction were similar to the *Eagle,* but her machinery was larger and more efficient. William Flannigan built the hull and Watchman & Bratt, the engine. This was of the low-pressure, "steeple" type and had a single cylinder of 35-inch diameter by 4-foot stroke, achieving 44 horsepower at 18 revolutions per minute of the paddle shaft. Her boiler was of shining copper and, therefore, of greater longevity than the less expensive cast iron ones, for in those days ordinary sea-water was evaporated to make steam, leaving a clogging residue of salt. In order to keep up her normal steam pressure of eight pounds, the *Virginia* burned between twenty and twenty-five pitch-pine logs every fifteen minutes. It may be readily understood that, since she took about 24 hours to make the trip, little room was available for cargo, for some 2,500 logs had to be stowed at the beginning of each voyage. Not infrequently the steamboats of this period, having been delayed by storm or fog en route, had to finish out their voyages under sail with boilers cold.

Staggering as the wood consumption undoubtedly seems, at the time there was, of course, a supply of virgin timber considered inexhaustible growing on the banks, ready for the axe. Today more trees are felled daily to provide newsprint than all American steamboats of 1820 could consume in months.

Benjamin Ferguson owned and independently operated the *Virginia*. She first arrived at Norfolk on July 31, 1817, commanded by Captain John Ferguson. She was described while coming in the harbor as "magnificent upon the bosom of her native element."[9]

By the end of August, she was operating on a weekly schedule, although excursions were conducted in between times at both ends of the Bay. One scheduled to Havre de Grace and Port Deposit on the Susquehanna, was advertised as follows:

> "This trip is offered to the public for recreation, pleasure and convenience. In passing up the river the novelist will be delighted with the various scenes of nature and art: the ingenuous limner will find employment for his pencil, the historian for his pen, and the philosopher subjects for contemplation. . . ."[10]

Over and above his poetic proclivities, Captain Ferguson was the logical man to command the *Virginia* for he had been actively connected with Norfolk-Baltimore sailing packets prior to the appearance of the steamboat on the Chesapeake. Although not definitely proven, it is suggested[11] that on September 13, 1814, Francis Scott Key witnessed the famous bombardment of Fort McHenry from the deck of "one of Ferguson's Norfolk packets" and was thus inspired to write "The Star-Spangled Banner."

Although times of departures were subject to change and delay and, of course, times of arrivals could not be predicted with the clockwork accuracy of today, the crude steamboats of this, the first decade in their history, were an enormous improvement over the sailing vessels which they slowly but surely began to replace.

Here is as good a place as any to explain what differentiated a "packet" from an ordinary trading vessel. In former times, though vessels were advertised to sail on a certain date, if weather was not propitious or cargo space unfilled, they might stay on in port for days or even weeks. Later, however, the demand for regular conveyance of passengers and mails brought about the inauguration of packet service. The vessels so employed advertised their departure for a certain day, and when it came, sail they did—regardless of weather conditions or unfilled cargo holds.

Thus regularized, it is easy to see why packets became popular for passengers and the better class of freight and also for the transportation of "packets," as the mails were then termed. Fast ships came into demand for this scheduled service and, when the steamboat arrived and it began to be possible to predict arrivals with a fair degree of certainty, the fate of the sailing packet was sealed.

In 1819, the *Virginia* was advertised to leave Newton's Wharf, Norfolk, on Mondays at 9 A. M. and to return, leaving Baltimore at the same hour on Thursdays. The *Virginia* was a fast boat and once made four passages between Baltimore and Norfolk in as many days,[12] although it was customary for her to take a week for the round trip. This record voyage gave her 86 hours elapsed time covering a distance of 880 miles, thus making her speed 7.28 knots or eight and a half statute miles an hour. Undoubtedly she was aided by good winds for, without sails, her engines were supposed to provide only 6.4 knots.

Being a novelty, these early steamboats were very popular and frequently ran summer excursions between their regular runs. One to Havre de Grace has been mentioned. Another was advertised for the *Virginia* in August of 1819 when she was scheduled to leave Norfolk "on a party of pleasure to York-Town (Va.) on Saturday next, precisely at seven o'clock in the morning."[13] Apparently our ancestors were a hardy breed, for a 7 A.M. departure would hold scant appeal for trippers today and most certainly could not be categorically classed as an excursion of "pleasure."

Although beyond the scope of this account, the later career of the old *Virginia* is not without interest. She served various owners on Chesapeake Bay until, in 1845, an announcement was made that "an old Southern passenger packet named *Virginia*" had been purchased and, renamed *Temple Of The Muses*, taken to the Hudson River to be rebuilt as a showboat.[14]

Once begun, the rise of steamboats in the United States was so meteoric as to draw world attention to the progress that was being made. One would like to ascribe full credit for this to American genius alone, but it should be stated that conditions along the Atlantic seaboard and the Western Rivers were most conducive to such development. When first evolved, the steamboat was both unsuitable and unseaworthy for use on the open ocean. America had miles of protected waterways and rivers where the water route was the only one. It is easy to see, with their well developed roads on one hand and unprotected coasts on the other, why England and France were slower to adopt the use of steamboats.

This did not cause them to overlook what was going on in America and foreign engineers were sent over by their governments to observe conditions here. One of the most celebrated of these men was the French engineer, Jean Baptiste Marestier, who visited the United States in 1818-1819, and whose invaluable *Mémoire sur les Bateaux à Vapeur des États-Unis* was published in Paris a few years later. American engineers and shipbuilders were too busy to take time out to make drawings and commit their progress to writing and it is significant to note that in many cases the only reliable drawings which have survived came from Marestier's board. Only in recent years has this rare book been rediscovered and given proper recognition. Among other things, his are the only contemporary drawings surviving of the famous *Savannah*.

In due course, Marestier's investigations took him to Chesapeake Bay and without them we would have a quite imperfect picture of the first steamboats which plied its waters. The passenger packets, he reported, offered their passengers large saloons carefully ornamented, around the sides of which were placed the double tiers of bunks, *"tenus très-proprement."*

When the ships were crowded, Marestier remarked that passengers slept on chairs or couches, the dining room tables, or even the floor. Signs requested them to remove their shoes before getting in bed. Ladies had their separate cabin, but came to the men's cabin at mealtime, for this also served as the dining room. The galley was situated close by the engine room and furnished meals which must have seemed extremely plain to the French palate; at any rate, Monsieur Marestier bemoaned the complete lack of *sauces recherchées*, and other frills. Vegetables were boiled in steam drawn from the ship's boiler and the spit was turned by a gear connected with the main paddle shaft. Forward of the engine room were crew's quarters and storage space.

Several other of the dozen odd steamboats which Marestier counted on the Chesapeake plied from time to time on the Baltimore to Norfolk run. These included the *Roanoke*, which ran with the *Virginia* in 1819, the *Surprise*, the *Richmond*, and *Petersburg*, as well as other Baltimore steamboats which made excursions down the Bay.

The *Roanoke*, built at Norfolk and intended to be used as a towboat on the Roanoke River, was commanded by Captain Middleton, and was employed mainly on the James River. She was not a particularly lucky boat and her pair of imported English walking-beam engines gave constant trouble. In 1820 she was put up at auction, but apparently continued running on the James River.

The *Surprise* had the distinction of being propelled by a rotary steam engine, forerunner of the giant turbines used on ocean liners today. George Stiles, a former mayor of Baltimore and owner of privateers in the War of 1812, operated her and she was used mainly between Baltimore, Annapolis, and Easton, Maryland. Less than a year old, she was badly burned in 1818 at her wharf at a loss of $3,000.

The *Richmond* and the *Petersburg* were primarily James River steamboats. The former made the phenomenal speed of 14 miles an hour on an excursion to City Point in 1819, the year after she was built, and apparently did not come on the Baltimore-Norfolk run until 1830. The "new, swift, and elegant" *Petersburg*, Captain Daniel W. Crocker, was used there at odd times before being converted to a towboat owned by the Virginia and North Carolina Transportation Company and used to tow barges on Albemarle Sound to the southern entrance to the Dismal Swamp Canal from 1829 to 1835.[15]

Following the *Virginia*, however, the next important regular steamboat on the run to Baltimore was the 1817-built *Norfolk*. She was the first steamboat built in the city whose name she carried and she cut the scheduled time to twenty hours. The *Norfolk* was almost identical in size to the *Virginia*, but her engine was more powerful and she was equipped with two copper boilers. The *Norfolk*, after plying the James to Richmond for a few months, was purchased by the New Bern Steamboat Company and operated on the Carolina Sounds between Elizabeth City and New Bern, North Carolina. She returned to the Chesapeake in 1818 and ultimately was put in the Baltimore run by Captain John Campbell. In April, 1820, she was advertised to leave Bowley's Wharf, Baltimore, on Mondays at 9 A.M., returning from Norfolk at the same hour on Fridays.

The year 1828 marks an important turning point in the history of steam navigation on the Chesapeake, for during this year a company was formed which absorbed the various individually-owned services competing on the Baltimore-Norfolk run. It was this organization, the Maryland and Virginia Steam Boat Company, which, in 1840, was dissolved and reformed as the Baltimore Steam Packet Company.

CHAPTER III

The Maryland and Virginia Steam Boat Company

T HE Maryland and Virginia Steam Boat Company was formed in March, 1828, with a subscribed capital of $150,000, and with the avowed object of linking Baltimore, Norfolk and Richmond with steamboats sailing "at regular stated periods."[16] The reasons causing it to fold up after operating only a dozen years are not known. But, in all probability, the financial panic of 1837 was a contributing factor. The *American Beacon* of January 2, 1839 reported that the company declined to renew its contract with the Post Office since the $3,000 it was getting proved insufficient, and the government refused the requested sum of $5,000. It should also be remembered that during the decade it spanned, a new (at first contributing but later competing) system of transportation came into being—the railroad—of which more will be said later.

In any event, the new company got off to a good start and began to furnish the public with a much needed service, namely, a coordinated system of transportation which tended to eliminate uncertainties and delays. Boats left Baltimore and Norfolk simultaneously and connections for the through traveler were afforded with the Frenchtown packets at one end of the Bay and the James River and Charleston steamboats at the other.

Steamboat travel on the Chesapeake was becoming increasingly reliable and popular. From the handful of craft noted by Marestier ten years previously, the registered tonnage had increased in 1827 to 2,207 for Maryland and 946 for Virginia. In order to present a comparative picture, it should be stated that Louisiana topped the list with the staggering total of 17,003 tons and New York followed with 10,264 tons.[17] In both states, the majority of boats used high-pressure steam boilers and explosions were a common and dis-

15

astrous occurrence. Conditions became so bad on the Mississippi that some vessels that did not use high-pressure steam had the words "Low Pressure" painted in large letters across their paddle boxes to reassure prospective travelers. It was stated in 1832 that fourteen percent of all steamers in operation were destroyed by explosions and fires in which approximately a thousand people lost their lives.

On the Hudson River, in 1828, a system of "safety trailer" barges was tried out. The steamboat *Commerce* towed behind it a splendidly appointed barge, the *Lady Clinton*, on which the more fastidious took passage. "Why sleep on the edge of a volcano?" reasonably inquired a contemporary advertisement.[18] The idea was a good one, but it did not work out, for towing the barge cut down the steamboat's speed and most travelers considered it more sporting to take the added risk for a quicker and more exciting voyage.

Fortunately, however, Chesapeake Bay was remarkably free of steamboat disaster and, proportionately, accidents were far less frequent than in other localities. Meanwhile, engineers were designing boilers better equipped to perform quietly the work they were meant to do, but no type of governmental control existed until 1838, when the U. S. Steamboat Inspection Service was founded.

The first vessels owned by the Maryland and Virginia Steam Boat Company were the 1817-built ships, *Virginia* and *Norfolk*, which by this time were veterans of the Baltimore-Norfolk line. On September 30, 1828, they were purchased together at auction from the estate of the late Benjamin Ferguson for the sum of $62,500.[19]

During this period, the company contracted with the Baltimore shipbuilding firm of James Beecham and George Gardiner for the construction of two new vessels. These two steamboats were built at the same time and entered service in 1829 as the *Columbus* and *Pocahontas*. Both measured about 137 feet long with a beam of 30 feet and a depth of 11 feet. The *Columbus* had the conventional "square" or "crosshead" steeple engine with a single 50-inch cylinder and six-and-a-half-foot stroke that gave her a speed of ten miles an hour. With the other vessels of the Line, service was three trips weekly and the fare $7.00, Baltimore to Norfolk, and an additional $3.00 for the run up the James.

Since the *Pocahontas* became one of the first boats actually to serve in the fleet of the Baltimore Steam Packet Company, it is appropriate to include here the following contemporary description of her. Do not be misled by the spelling of the sleeping accommodations—she did not carry a floating maternity department!

She is [this account stated] in all respects a boat of the first class, and being intended exclusively for the transportation of passengers, combines the most improved arrangements, as well on the score of elegance as comfort. . . . The principal cabin or dining room is below deck, it is a spacious, light and airy apartment, handsomely finished and furnished, and contains thirty-two commodious births. One hundred persons may here be accommodated at table. The centre of the boat below is occupied by boilers and machinery, the former (of copper) having been placed below in order to ensure perfect safety in navigating the Chesapeake in rough weather. The front cabin contains 20 sleeping births, a bar-room, dressing room, etc. The cabin appropriated for the use of ladies exclusively, is an elegant apartment on the main deck. It is richly furnished and decorated, and contains 20 sleeping births and two state rooms. An upper deck, the loftiness of which affords abundance of light and a free circulation of air to the main deck and lower cabins, extends the extreme length and width of the boat, and presents a safe and delightful promenade of the most ample dimensions.[20]

An interesting and slightly hair-raising navigational maneuver commonly practiced in those times consisted in transferring passengers and cargo from one ship to another under way. The celebrated Irish comedian, Tyrone Power, great-grandfather of the late motion picture star, has left in his *Impressions of America* a graphic eyewitness account of these procedures which took place when the steamboat *George Washington,* on which he had taken passage from Frenchtown to Baltimore in September, 1834, was a party to such a transfer.[21] Here are his own words on the subject:

Whilst steering through the waters of the Chesapeake, perceived a large steamer standing right for us, with a signal flying. Learned that this was the *Columbus,* bound for Norfolk, Virginia, for which place we had several passengers, who were now to be transhipped to the approaching vessel.

We were out in the open bay, with half a gale of wind blowing, and some sea on; it therefore became a matter of interest to observe how two large ships of this class would approach each other.

The way they managed this ticklish affair was really admirable; before we neared, I observed the Norfolk ship was laid head to wind, and just enough way kept on to steer her; our ship held her course, gradually lessening her speed, until, as she approached the *Columbus,* it barely sufficed to lay and keep her alongside, when they fell together, gangway to gangway: warps were immediately passed, and made secure at both head and stern: and in a minute the huge vessels became as one.

Here was no want of help; the luggage and the passengers were ready at the proper station, so that in a handful of minutes the transfer was completed without bustle or alarm. Meantime the interest of this novel scene was greatly increased by the coming up of the inward-bound Norfolk-man, which flitted close by us amidst the roar occasioned by the escaping steam of the vessels lying-to, a noise that might have drowned the voice of Niagara.

Posterity is indeed indebted to Mr. Power for being such an interested observer. Here follows a sidelight on the type of passengers who were southbound on this particular September morning:

> As we thus lay together, I noticed that the upper or promenade deck of the *Columbus* was completely taken up by a double row of flashy-looking covered carts, or tilt-waggons, as they are called here. Upon inquiry, I found that these contained the goods, and were, indeed the movable stores, or shops, of that much enduring class, the Yankee pedlars, just setting forth for their annual winter cruise amongst the plantations of the South: where, however their keen dealing may be held in awe, they are looked for with lively anxiety, and their arrival greeted as an advent of no little moment.
> Arranged in a half circle about the bow on the main-deck, I observed the horses of these royal pedlars: they stretched their necks out to examine us with a keenness of look worthy their knowing masters' reputation and their own education.

Apparently the transfer was soon carried out. One can imagine no shipmaster wishing to prolong such a delicate maneuver:

> Our business being completed, the hissing sound of the waste-steam pipe ceased, this force being once more applied to its right use; the paddles began to move, the lashings were cast off, and away the boats darted from each other with startling rapidity: the *Columbus,* with the gale aft, rushing down the great bay of the Chesapeake, and the *Washington* breasting its force right for Baltimore.

After a few days spent in the "Monumental City," Tyrone Power continued his southern trip, embarking on the *Columbus* or a sister ship for Petersburg via Norfolk. "We had a fine day and night whilst steering through this great bay of the Chesapeake," he wrote. "Went to bed late in consequence."[22] He got up early, however, viewed with interest the partially completed earthworks and moat of Fort Monroe, took in the sights of the Elizabeth River and, at 8 A.M., transferred at Norfolk to the *Pocahontas* for City Point while several of his fellow passengers embarked on the *Virginia* for Charleston.

Tyrone Power's century-old observations are decidedly refreshing. At a time when numerous foreigners were visiting this country and, on their return, penning derogatory remarks for their compatriots' edification, Power's "impressions" stand out as being a fair, enthusiastic, and intelligent appraisal of this young nation and show their author to have been not only an unbiased observer, but also one who managed to enjoy himself in the unfamiliar surroundings and customs he found abroad.

However, we have slighted the memory of Lieutenant The Hon. Frederick Fitzgerald De Roos, Royal Navy, whose *Personal Narrative of Travels in the United States in 1826*[23] contains the following choice description:

> The prospect, on entering the Chesapeake Bay, was striking to the greatest degree. The numerous ships, the stillness of the waters, the setting sun shedding its rays on the surrounding beacons, and the rapid course of the steamboat, the ample deck of which was covered with many well-dressed and *some beautiful passengers* [our italics!], combined to produce a most enchanting effect.

Mr. Power mentioned that on arrival at Norfolk several of his fellow passengers transferred to the *Virginia* for the outside run down the coast to Charleston. The *Virginia*, commanded first by Captain James Hart and then by Captain William Rollins, had been considerably rebuilt and newly coppered a short time previously. Included in her alterations was the stepping of three masts so that she would be well found under sail alone.[24] By this time, almost all the Bay boats had dispensed with extensive auxiliary canvas, except for a single masted rig. Evidently, the *Virginia's* ownership passed to the Atlantic Steam Company and, in 1835–6, this organization added two new vessels to their Atlantic Line, the *South Carolina* and the *Georgia*, 172 feet and 194 feet long respectively. These two vessels came back to Chesapeake Bay shortly before the Baltimore Steam Packet Company was founded.

The Maryland and Virginia Steam Boat Company was running the *Pocahontas, Columbus*, and *Norfolk* in 1834 and 1835 and in the latter year they purchased from the People's Steam Navigation Company the *Kentucky*, then the fastest boat on the Bay. The line had not enjoyed an uncontested monopoly of the Baltimore-Norfolk run, however. In the autumn of 1831, the *Sandusky* had been brought south to offer opposition and she had to be bought off since she could make the trip in only fifteen hours and offered cut rates. In 1835, the *Champion*, Captain Reese, was taken from the Potomac and placed on an opposition line and she, too, had to be vanquished. The *Kentucky* arranged that, however, for twice she made the run in a little over thirteen hours and her speed killed any permanent or serious opposition by water.

However, the closing years of the Maryland and Virginia Steam Boat Company were marked by stiff opposition from the railroads and, to meet this competition, they probably overspent themselves in the construction of two brand new boats, the *Jewess* and the *Alabama*.

Discounting a private railroad serving a stone quarry in New England, the first regular rail carrier chartered in the United States was the Baltimore and Ohio in 1827. This was designed for horse-drawn cars and it was not until half a dozen years later that steam locomotives came in the reckoning. With the advent of the steam engine, however, railroad building increased so rapidly as to become a mania. Unstable land values, defaulted bonds, and other tangible evidences of this sudden growth resulted in the panic of 1837, but this merely proved a hiatus in railroad building and, the depression weathered, the railroads continued spinning their iron webs across the countryside.

At first, the tracks merely replaced existing stagecoach lines and travelers in 1832 who journeyed from Philadelphia to Baltimore still used two lines of steamers, but crossed the neck of the Eastern Shore Peninsula on the 16-mile Frenchtown-Newcastle Railway. Later, however, the rails struck out over virgin territory. This same year, the Portsmouth and Roanoke Railroad was chartered to build a line for almost eighty miles between Portsmouth, Virginia, and Weldon, North Carolina. As was to be expected, this line became a vital feeder to the Norfolk-Baltimore steamboats from the South when, in 1836, the ten-ton engine, *Raleigh*, first hauled its cars over the newly laid rails.

The sixth railroad to receive a charter in Virginia was the Richmond, Fredericksburg and Potomac, which in 1834 began its line from Richmond northward. Within a few years the rails had been laid to Fredericksburg and a stage line connected with Potomac Creek. Meanwhile, Baltimore and Washington had been connected by rails and thus two separate lines were offered the southbound traveler between Baltimore and the Roanoke River in North Carolina. The first consisted of the already established line of Bay steamers from Baltimore to Norfolk and Portsmouth, whence the rail line extended seventy-seven-and-one-half miles farther on to Weldon. The other line, which became known as the Inland or "Upper Route," consisted of a system incorporating the railroad from Baltimore to Washington, the steamer *Augusta* to Potomac (later Aquia) Creek, horse-drawn stage to Fredericksburg, whence the R. F. & P. Railroad continued to Richmond, connecting with the Petersburg Railroad which continued South to the Roanoke River at Weldon. At this point, both systems employed the single railroad line which had been built to Wilmington, North Carolina, and Charleston.

Some idea of the keenness of competition between the Bay Line and the Inland Route may be gained from contemporary advertisements.[25] No punches were pulled. The Bay Line said:

Great Central Route between the North & South via the Chesapeake Bay steamboats and the Portsmouth & Roanoke Rail Road, Oct. 1, 1838: Through from Baltimore to Welston [sic], N. C., in twenty-one hours—being four hours in advance of any other Inland Line—without one moment's night travelling on Rail Roads, without loss of sleep, with but one single change of baggage—and at less expense than any other Inland route.

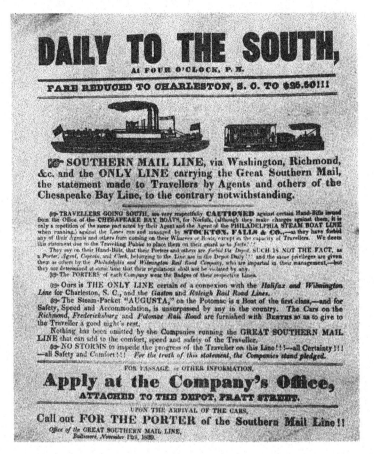

Handbill issued in 1839 by the rival Great Southern Mail Line, the "Upper Route". (Courtesy of Enoch Pratt Free Library, Baltimore)

Passengers were further assured that no "burthen" cars would be attached to their train. The disparagement of competitors was carried to an all-time high in the published statement of the Upper Route which advertised in June, 1840, that its passengers reached Charleston one day sooner than those who had taken the Bay steamers and that by their line travelers would "avoid being compelled to remain ALL NIGHT AT WELDON, on the *Roanoke*—one of the most UNHEALTHY PLACES in the Southern Country, where by the Bay Line, they are delayed SEVENTEEN HOURS."[26]

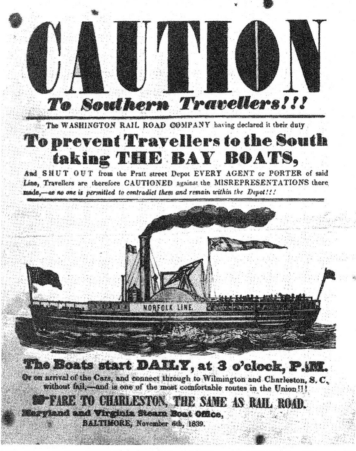

Handbill issued in 1839 by the Maryland and Virginia Steam Boat Co. (Courtesy of Enoch Pratt Free Library, Baltimore)

This endorsement is not likely to have been popular with what then passed as the Weldon Chamber of Commerce and undoubtedly Weldon citizens bent every effort to divert northbound travelers away from the Upper Route in consequence. Baltimore, however, felt the keenest competition and both lines had their agents and "runners" stationed to meet passengers arriving from Philadelphia to shower them with handbills.

Although mention of it here anticipates a strictly chronological recounting of events, it should be stated that when the Baltimore

Steam Packet Company came into being it inherited the rivalry developed by the Maryland and Virginia Steam Boat Company and the very first advertisement placed by the new company squared away with the statement: "The public are therefore cautioned to put no trust in the malicious falsehoods circulated by the Agents of the Upper Route against this Line (they keep out of view their own mishaps and deficiencies), but may rely on the Statements made by the above Line."[27]

And through the early period of its existence the company continued to seize every opportunity to remind prospective travelers of the Upper Route's peccadilloes, viz.:[28]

> For 25 years there has been a line of steamboats to Norfolk and yet there never has been an accident—therefore the croakings about "Fogs," "Rough Weather," "Storms," "Risks," "boats urged to the top of their speed," &c. are altogether the humbugs of a fruitful imagination, gotten up to impose upon the credulous. The Baltimore Steam Packet Company and the Portsmouth and Roanoke Rail Road Company hereby pledge themselves that the connection by their route is perfect.

It is amusing to note that while the Upper Route shuddered at the dangers attendant to a lengthy visit to "pestilential" Weldon, the Bay Line advertised that its passengers were privileged to enjoy a "comfortable rest" at such an attractive garden spot.

One may assume that, due to the natural skepticism and confusion which it produced, muck-raking did little good to encourage prospective travelers to use either line. In any event, there was business enough for both and the caliber of later advertising copy was noticeably toned down.

The year 1838 was an important one in the history of steam navigation. The arrival at New York on April 22 of the two British steamers, *Sirius* and *Great Western,* within a few hours of each other focused nationwide attention on the successful use of steam on oceangoing vessels. Unlike previous Atlantic crossings, these two passages had been made almost entirely under steam and the fact that sufficient fuel could be carried for an entire trip across the ocean was demonstrated.

The town of Baltimore also welcomed a transatlantic steamer in 1838. The British auxiliary bark *City of Kingston* arrived at the head of the Chesapeake from the West Indies and sailed thence for London direct on May 20. Like the famous *Savannah* of two decades past, the *City of Kingston* was essentially a sailing vessel, but Baltimoreans were nevertheless wildly excited at the prospect of establishing direct steam communication with Europe.

Disturbing to this rosy picture was the disaster to the steam packet *Pulaski.* Over a hundred lives were lost when this Baltimore-Charleston boat exploded her boiler off Cape Hatteras on June 14.

People well remembered that only the year before the New York-Charleston packet, *Home,* had fared a similar fate when her back was broken in a storm off Hatteras' raging seas. Naturally the business of the Atlantic Line from Norfolk to Charleston, in which the Maryland and Virginia Steam Boat Company was interested, suffered enormously and probably added another coffin nail to the troubles it was experiencing as a result of over-expansion plus cut-rate competition from the Upper Route.

It was mentioned that the Maryland and Virginia Steam Boat Company built two steamboats shortly before it terminated operations. The largest of these, the *Alabama,* was essentially a coastwise rather than a sound steamer and had probably been built for a run similar to that of the ill-fated *Pulaski.* This ocean route was abandoned shortly thereafter with the result that, although she was a fine vessel, the *Alabama* turned out to be too big for her times on the Bay.

When completed, she was described in a contemporary account as being "without exception the most splendid steam boat that ever floated on the waters of the Chesapeake."[29] Levin H. Dunkin, of Baltimore, was the builder and her 200 horsepower engine, installed by Messrs. Charles Reeder and Sons, gave her a cruising speed of fifteen miles an hour. Like her predecessors, the *Alabama* was a side-wheeler with wooden hull, coppered and copper-fastened, and cost $107,000 to build: exactly twice the amount of the *Virginia* that had been hailed as the epitome of the steamboat builder's art twenty years earlier.

The *Alabama's* interior accommodations (she was "carpeted throughout with the best of Brussels") consisted of: main saloon, 54 berths; ladies' cabin, 32 berths; forward cabin, 40 berths. In addition, she had four staterooms on deck. She was rigged with three masts, the custom on oceangoing steamboats, and measured 210 feet in length and 676 tons "burthen."

The second vessel built for the Maryland and Virginia Steam Boat Company during the year 1838 proved more suitable for the trade and was one of the vessels with which the Baltimore Steam Packet Company began service in 1840. This vessel was christened *Jewess* and her 173½-foot length is said to have terminated in an imposing gilded eagle figurehead. Her lever-beam engine by Wells, Miller and Clark gave her a speed of 14 miles per hour and she could carry seventy-five passengers "comfortably."

Undoubtedly some of its older boats had been sold when the *Alabama* and *Jewess* were added to the Maryland and Virginia Steam Boat Company fleet, for in the windup of affairs in 1840 these two vessels, plus only the *Pocahontas* and *Columbus,* were offered "including all their tackle, apparel and furniture" at public auction at the Merchants' Exchange in Baltimore.[30]

CHAPTER IV

The Baltimore Steam Packet Company Makes Its Bow

A T THE December session of the General Assembly of Maryland in 1839, "An Act to Incorporate the Baltimore Steam Packet Company" was passed. The preamble of Section I stated:

Be it enacted by the General Assembly of Maryland, That William McDonald, Robert A. Taylor, Joel Vickers, John S. McKim, John B. Howell, Benjamin Buck, Samuel McDonald, Thomas Kelso, Andrew F. Henderson and others, their successors and assigns, be and are hereby, created and made a corporate and body politic, by the name and title of the Baltimore Steam Packet Company,—and by that name and title shall have perpetual succession, . . . and generally [are authorized] to do all such acts as shall be proper and necessary for the purpose of employing one or more steamboats to navigate the Chesapeake Bay and its tributary streams, or to navigate the Atlantic Coast, or any of the bays or rivers emptying into the Atlantic Ocean—and to connect thereto boats, vessels, stages or other carriages, for the conveyance of passengers, towing of ships, vessels, rafts or arks, and the transportation of merchandise or other articles.

This charter then, with the exception of certain amendments added through the years, has remained the basis of the Old Bay Line's activities for more than a century, even though it has never taken advantage of its authorization to tow "arks." The "other carriages" undoubtedly referred to railroads.

Andrew F. Henderson, who became the Old Bay Line's first president, and General William McDonald had been associated with Chesapeake steamboating since its beginnings back in 1813. The new steam packet company's first general agent was John C. Moale, who had been president of the Maryland and Virginia

25

Steam Boat Company and trustee when it went into liquidation and disposed of its fleet. Thomas Sheppard was appointed treasurer and he, too, had previously been associated with steamboats, having served in the same office for the Atlantic Line.

The four boats with which the Baltimore Steam Packet Company began operations were purchased second-hand—two from the Atlantic Line and two from the Maryland and Virginia Steam Boat Company. The oldest and smallest of the quartette was the *Pocahontas*, built in 1829. She and the 1838 *Jewess* came from the former Norfolk-Baltimore Line.

From the Atlantic Line's coastwise fleet came the comparatively new steamer *South Carolina*, launched in 1835 and which, as stated, had been used on the Charleston run. The description of this vessel which appeared in the newspapers prior to her sale at auction reported that she was 172 feet long and had been recently "repaired, caulked, newly coppered, and logged; . . . has the best inventory, and is well calculated for 150 to 200 passengers; has about 150 life preservers. . . "[31]

Attention is called to the fact that her owners were quite nonchalant in advertising her capacity at 200 passengers with "about" 150 life preservers.

The *Georgia*, also built for the Atlantic Line in 1836, has been described in connection with "Mr. Smith's" voyage 120 years ago. Apparently the *Alabama* was not purchased along with the other Maryland and Virginia Steam Boat Company vessels, her acquisition by the Baltimore Steam Packet Company being noted as late as January, 1841. A story in the *American Beacon* of January 12, that year, stated that the boat had cost $107,000 when built three years before. Although mention is made in the Baltimore Steam Packet Company directors' report of the appointment of Mr. A. G. Ramsey as engineer, the *Alabama* was evidently held as a spare boat and not used in regular service. It was not long after the company commenced business that she was advertised to quit Baltimore for good, proceeding to New Orleans to be put into service as a Havana packet.

In acquiring the steamboats, the new line fell heir to their captains: James Coffey, Thomas Sutton, James Cannon, G. W. Russell, and James Holmes. Apparently Captain William Rollins, who had served as master of both the *Virginia* and the *Georgia* on the Charleston run and was alleged to have been the new company's first commander, did not remain long in its employ, for a short time afterwards he is mentioned as master of the New Orleans-Havana steam packet *Neptune* and later of the *Isabel*.

The Maryland and Virginia Steam Boat Company had inaugurated on March 10, 1840, a daily schedule leaving Baltimore in midafternoon, rotating their steamers *Alabama* (Sutton), *Georgia* (Rollins) and *Jewess* (Holmes). In its second published advertisement, the Baltimore Packet Company "informed" the public that it would maintain the same service. Shortly thereafter, the time of departure from Spears Wharf, Baltimore, was advanced to 9 A.M. with arrival at Portsmouth at 11 P.M. When winter came on, however, the schedule was abbreviated to tri-weekly and the boats again ran overnight, leaving Baltimore on Tuesdays, Thursdays and Sundays. The fare of $8.00 included meals.

However, the tri-weekly service called for sailings falling on Sundays and not long afterwards, the daily schedule was again adopted and a resolution of the Board of Directors, carried on February 23, 1841, stated that: "This board are desirous to avoid the violation of the Sabbath by causing their boats to be employed on that day. Therefore, the Agent is instructed to communicate with the President of the Portsmouth and Roanoke Rail Road, informing him that as soon as the *Jewess* can be gotten ready for this company, we will start a line of boats from each end of the line daily, Sundays excepted, until further notice."

Other manifestations of Company policy reflected by the deliberations of the board are not without elements of humor: "Whereas this board has observed the pleasure and great progress now making in the temperance cause, and believing (nay, they know) that there is too much ardent spirits consumed by persons in the employ of this Company, therefore be it resolved that the Captains, Clerks, Mates and all others. . . are hereby earnestly requested to abstain altogether in the use of intoxicating drinks. . . ."

This was all very well as far as the employees of the Line were concerned, but for the passengers it was another matter. All the boats had well-patronized bars, lucrative concessions of the captains, the profits from which were not to be ignored. At the same meeting: "Letters were read from Mr. Wilson, Clerk of the *Georgia* and Mr. Aspirl, Clerk of the *Alabama*, asking the Board to allow them to participate in the profits or losses of the Bar to be divided equally between the Captains and Clerks until further action of the Board."

As in the days of the Maryland and Virginia Steam Boat Company, excursions were always popular and the boats spent little time lying around the piers idle once they had completed their regular runs. Typical was the following "Pleasure Excursion" advertised in the Norfolk papers for the steamer *Georgia*, which, "With a fine military and cotillion band, makes the trip to Old Point and the Capes this afternoon. . . All who wish may remain at Old Point until about 8 o'clock in the evening, this giving sufficient time to enjoy the wholesome sea bath, and to partake of a fine supper of hog fish, and other delicacies of the season. . . ."[32]

Business was good for the first year of the Company's life and opposition by the steamboat *Boston* ("having the newly invented safety valves") did not last long. Captain James Holmes, who had formerly been with the Bay Line in command of the *Jewess*, transferred the *Boston* to the Norfolk-Washington run with more success.

However, the wooden steamboats of a century ago were not long-lived and on September 7, 1841, the company signed a contract for their first new ship with Baltimore builders Brown and Collyer. This specified the construction of a 180-foot steamer with a lever-beam engine and boilers of the "best Pennsylvania iron."

This vessel proved to be the ill-fated *Medora* whose boiler blew up on the trial trip. Perhaps a revengeful fate had read the advertisement which boasted that there had been no accidents on the Line for twenty-five years. However, a contemporary account of the disaster absolved the Bay Line as follows:[33]

> It should be borne in mind that the steamboat *Medora*, at the time of the accident, was yet in the hands of the builders, she having never been delivered to the Baltimore and Norfolk Steam-packet Company, for whose use she was built. No accident of the kind has ever happened to any boat while under the control of the careful agents of this Company.

Apparently this sentiment was generally accepted by the traveling public. In any event, the Line did not suffer from lack of confidence and, still having need for an additional steamer, as soon as the debris could be cleared, work went forward to reclaim what was left of the *Medora* to be applied to the construction of another vessel.

The disaster was one of the worst to have taken place on the Chesapeake, however. On the afternoon of April 14, 1842, the newly completed *Medora* was lying at the wharf of her engine builder, John Watchman, on the south side of the Basin preparatory to embarking on her trial trip. Numerous officials of the Line and invited guests were on board which, with shipyard workers and the crew, brought the total number of persons up to seventy-nine. At the second revolution of her paddles as she was backing away from the dock, the boiler exploded without warning, carrying aloft with it a considerable portion of the upper deck and those on it and blowing the smokestack high into the air. The main force of the explosion was almost exclusively towards the bow and the boiler itself, an "immense one of iron," was hurled upwards and landed crosswise on the deck. Clouds of scalding steam instantly enveloped the ill-fated craft and many persons who escaped the explosion were carried down with her as she sank.

According to Baltimore's eminent historian, Colonel J. T. Scharf: "The scene presented by the boat afforded at once a mournful evidence of the immense power of steam, and of the ruin of which it can be the instrument. Large oak beams were splintered to pieces; iron bars that would have withstood the strength of a hundred men, were broken and wrenched into many shapes; the lighter wood-work of the deck was blown almost to atoms."[34]

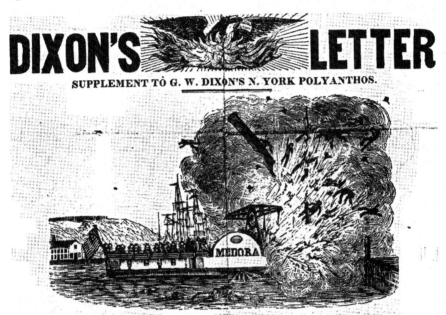

DIXON'S LETTER

SUPPLEMENT TO G. W. DIXON'S N. YORK POLYANTHOS.

Explosion of the Steam Boat Medora, April 14, 1842.

Explosion of steamboat *Medora* on her trial trip, Baltimore, April 14, 1842. (Courtesy of The Mariners Museum, Newport News, Va.)

A pall of gloom immediately settled over the town as rescue workers, answering the immediate plea of Mayor Solomon Hillen, started out on their gruesome mission of recovering the dead. At intervals during the day, a cannon was fired over the water on the assumption that the concussions would cause sunken bodies to rise to the surface.

At the final tabulation, 26 persons were dead and 38 injured, but 15 having escaped. A serious blow to the new company was suffered in the deaths of its president, Andrew F. Henderson, and its agent, John C. Moale, who was struck down along with one of his two sons. Captain Sutton, commanding the *Medora,* was thought to be fatally injured, but the hardy mariner survived to pilot many a subsequent Old Bay Line ship. Captain Coffey of the *Georgia* was slightly injured.

Contemporary newspapers made the most of the event in a ghoulish manner, one containing a hurriedly executed woodcut of the gruesome scene depicting bodies flying in all directions.[35] Others gave hair-raising accounts of various incidents which could not have made very pleasant reading for the families of those who had been lost.

Naturally an investigation was made into the cause of the explosion, but it was impossible to put the blame with certainty either on the engineers or the builders.[36] Strangely enough, although apparently trivial matters such as the bar profits were mentioned in the reports of the directors, no comment on the *Medora* disaster occurs in their annual minute books. Perhaps at the time the event seemed too bitterly recent to warrant any mention of it at all.

Robert A. Taylor succeeded Henderson as president and service with the old boats, the *Georgia*, Captain Coffey, and the *Jewess*, Captain Russell, continued without interruption. Even an excursion was advertised the next month in connection with the Volunteer Military Encampment at Baltimore on May 16, "passage and fare" for the round trip from Norfolk being set at $5.00 for those "disposed to take the trip."

Meanwhile, work on rebuilding the *Medora* continued and before the end of the year the new steamer, christened *Herald*, was added to the Line and became its first expressly constructed ship. "She is built of so stern a stuff, that we doubt whether old Neptune in all his wrath can shake her one tittle," bragged Norfolk's *American Beacon* on November 28, 1842. No mention whatsoever was made of the fact that the *Herald* had risen phoenix-like from the ashes of the ill-fated *Medora*. If the *Medora's* career was short and disastrous, rebuilt as the *Herald*, she enjoyed a remarkably long and useful life. She ran on the Chesapeake Bay until after the Civil War and was then taken to the Hudson River and used as a tug. Finally, in her forty-third year, she was dropped from the *List of Merchant Vessels* as "abandoned" on September 30, 1885.

Meanwhile, she had received at least two new boilers and had been practically rebuilt when lengthened from 184 feet to 215 feet in 1849. Captain George W. Russell was appointed master when she came out on October 21, 1842, and James Cannon, who had previously commanded Bay Line ships, was first mate.

Competition with the Upper Route continued to be keen and, when the Richmond, Fredericksburg and Potomac Railroad extended its line from Fredericksburg to Aquia Creek on the Potomac River, eliminating an uncomfortable stagecoach route, the schedule of the railroad was advanced with proportionate inducement to the traveler. When Charles Dickens visited America early in

Views of Norfolk and Portsmouth from the Marine Hospital. The steamboat *Herald* (1842) is shown leaving port in the left center of the print. Note livestock on the foredeck. Lower inset views are of Old Point Comfort and the Gosport Navy Yard. After the lithograph by E. Sachse, Baltimore, 1851. (Courtesy of the Mariners Museum)

1842, he traveled over this route on his way from Washington to Richmond and he left a memorable picture not only of his steamboat trip down the Potomac, but also of the discomforts of stage travel. The great novelist had planned to return from Richmond via the James River and the Bay Line, but he explained that, "one of the steamboats being absent from her station through some accident, and the means of conveyance being consequently rendered uncertain",[37] he elected to return to Washington by the way he had come. Thus, by this narrow margin, the Old Bay Line missed being immortalized in some form or other, probably derogatorily, in his writings.

Dickens' *American Notes* do not always speak too highly of what their author found on this side of the Atlantic, even though he did praise Barnum's Hotel in Baltimore because there he had not only curtains to his bed, but also "enough water for washing." Later in his tour, he embarked on the steamboat *Burlington* on Lake Champlain, and here, too, he penned paeans of praise in behalf of a vessel "superior . . . to any other in the world. This steamboat . . . is a perfectly exquisite achievement of neatness, elegance, and order. The decks are drawing-rooms; the cabins are boudoirs. . . ."[38]

As a result of the competing service, masters and engineers of Bay Line steamers were "strictly enjoined that they do not make their trips between Baltimore and Norfolk in less than 15 hours" even though the boats were not to be driven too hard with resultant "ware and tare" on the machinery. In 1842, with the *Herald* in operation, the regular Bay Line steamers left Baltimore on Mondays, Wednesdays, Fridays, and Saturdays at 4 P.M. The *Pocahontas* sailed once a week from Baltimore direct to Petersburg and Richmond. The former rival steamboat *Boston* was again on the route and, since her owners apparently did not possess the same pious sentiments about desecrating the Sabbath, she ran on Sundays and Thursdays.

In 1845, an affiliated steamboat company was founded expressly for navigating the James River. This, the Powhatan Line, operating ships from Baltimore to Richmond, acquired the venerable *Pocahontas* from the Bay Line, and also the old *Columbus* on which Tyrone Power had taken passage in the days of the Maryland and Virginia Steam Boat Company.

The Bay Line's difficulties in attracting through travelers increased with the abandonment of the Portsmouth and Roanoke Railroad's service south to Weldon in April of the same year when, as its President and Directors put it simply, "the cars ceased to run." This gave the Upper Route the more direct line, for now through passengers on the Bay boats had to be routed up the James and Appomattox Rivers to Petersburg. Here they caught the same railroad to Weldon that formerly had competed with the Portsmouth and Roanoke.

Naturally this increased the importance of the Baltimore Steam Packet Company's James River link and, in October of that year, the company acquired an $11/32$ interest in the side-wheeler *Alice*, running her from Norfolk to City Point. Soon afterward, the Richmond and Petersburg Railroad organized their own line of boats on the James and the Bay Line retaliated by purchasing another vessel, the iron-hulled *Mount Vernon*, to place on the Appomattox. This disorganized condition was alleviated in 1851 when a reorganized Seaboard and Roanoke Railroad took over the abandoned tracks between Portsmouth and Weldon and replaced the old wooden rails with the latest iron "T" rails. The Baltimore Steam Packet Company, for whom this southern feeder had been so vital, immediately bought a majority of the stock of the new railroad company, presumably to ensure its continuance.[39]

Meanwhile, however, the Richmond, Fredericksburg and Potomac succeeded in purchasing a controlling interest in the Bay Line—Seaboard and Roanoke combine, and the two systems, bitter rivals since the days of the Maryland and Virginia Steam Boat Company, fell under one control for the time.

In this year, 1851, Virginia had 74 steamboats in commission, an increase of 700 per cent over the number licensed in the Commonwealth twenty years before.[40] Travel by boat had been slowly and surely gaining in popularity and, during the period prior to the Civil War, many important steamboat lines were established. Perhaps the most important of these was the celebrated Fall River Line of Long Island Sound, which began in 1847 and whose lamented termination occurred in 1936 in its ninety-first year. The famous Fall River was destined to become the standard sound transportation line in the world and the record of its long existence is studded with interest and glamour.[41]

In 1852, another famous old line came into being, the Merchants and Miners Transportation Company. This line expanded its initial service from Baltimore to Providence to cover numerous routes along the Atlantic coast.[42] Regrettably, it closed for good in 1948.

Things went along fairly smoothly during the first decade of the Baltimore Steam Packet Company's history. The service averaged tri-weekly in winter and daily in summer, at which time extra boats of the line were employed, whenever possible, running excursions. Usually the latter proved to be well ordered affairs, but on one occasion events took place that proved considerably embarrassing to the steamship owners. Colonel J. T. Scharf mentions a dilly in his *Chronicles of Baltimore:*[43]

On the 5th of July [1847] an alarming riot took place between the citizens of Annapolis and a portion of the passengers of the steamer *Jewess*. The steamer left Baltimore on an excursion to St. Michael's; when about twenty miles down the river it was found that in consequence of the crowded state of the boat, it would be dangerous to cross the bay to the Eastern Shore, and accordingly, after consultation, it was determined to run into Annapolis. After a short time a fight was started on the wharf between some citizens of the town and some of the young men who were on the boat. In a few minutes the fight became general, and for the time assumed a fearful character. Stones, bricks, and missils in abundance were thrown indiscriminately upon the boat, striking ladies and children as well as others.

Shortly thereafter, some of the passengers secured rifles and began to blaze away on the Annapolis crowd, injuring five people. The citizens retaliated by procuring two small cannons which they dragged over to the common by the wharf and were preparing to fire on the *Jewess* when she shoved off for the return to Baltimore.

A vivid account appeared in the *American Beacon* of July 7, 1847, under the heading "Battle of Annapolis."

More decorous was an excursion reported by the same newspaper on August 17, 1850:

That gallant steamer *Jewess*, Capt. Sutton, from Baltimore, on a pleasure excursion, arrived here on Thursday night, filled with passengers. Many of our citizens were pleasantly awakened soon after her arrival, by a serenade by Prof. Volande's celebrated band, which accompanied the expedition.

Another event of its early years is recorded in an extract from a company resolution, dated December 21, 1846, and preserved in the annual volumes of minutes of the directors. It stated:

RESOLVED, That the brave and meritorious conduct of Mr. Geo. S. Moore, Second Mate of the Steamer *Georgia*, Capt. Russell, on her trip from Baltimore to Norfolk, and those worthy men who accompanied him in the arduous and dangerous exploit by venturing in the small boat of the *Georgia* while crossing the Horse Shoe in that dreadful gale and snow storm of the morning of the 17 December, 1846, the sea running mountains high, to save a fellow mortal, one of the crew of said steamboat who was knocked overboard by the Chain Roc [?] giving way, from a watery grave, and with great exertion saved the unfortunate man. For this humane act, the Board express their warmest praise and for the injury received by Mr. Moore in having his hand much lacerated and mashed, in order that he may apply the proper advice and remedies for restoring the same to a healthy condition, they make him a present of twenty dollars.

The Committee also in order to alleviate the suffering of the poor colored man, Westley Banks, who was extricated from this awful death in being knocked overboard on 17 December, 1846, in that dreadful snow storm and gale from which he received some injury, present him with five dollars.

In 1848, Moor N. Falls succeeded Robert A. Taylor as president of the Line. Although it had only been going for eight years and had had one brand new boat added in 1842, the need for expansion was again felt. It was mentioned that the *Herald* had been lengthened in 1849. During a waterfront fire, all too common in those days, the *Jewess*, together with the Baltimore steamer *Governor Walcott* and two schooners, had been badly burned at their wharves on January 11, 1848. The *Jewess* was about to start south when the accident occurred and, although the "Great Southern Mail" was saved, most of the boat's upper works and the cargo were destroyed. "The worthy commander, Capt. Sutton, lost all his clothes and a sum of money," reported the *Southern Argus*. She was rebuilt by Flannegan and Trimble and lengthened from 173½ feet to 199 feet in the process. In addition, she was given a new saloon on deck "capable of dining 80 persons."

This gave the Line, in the year 1851, the *Georgia* and *Herald* for overnight winter service, and the *Jewess* joined them in the daily schedule of the summer months when the boats were making their runs in daylight. As the railroad was again in operation from Portsmouth, the importance of the James River service was diminished and the company had disposed of their little river steamers *Alice* and *Mount Vernon*. The former was taken to New London, Connecticut, but the latter continued to run on the James and the regular Bay Line ships connected with the Powhatan Line which was operating the *Mount Vernon* and the *Curtis Peck* for Richmond and Petersburg, and a separate line which ran the *Star* to Suffolk. By this time, the little *Pocahontas* probably was completely worn out and had been left to fall to pieces.

It was obvious to the company officials, with the various advances made in the development of steamboats in the decade during which they had been going, that their boats had been rendered obsolete. In order to remain in business, therefore, they realized they would have to supply an increasingly more discriminating public with new and larger vessels.

On Long Island Sound, the Norwich Line steamer *Atlantic* had come out in 1846, the first sound steamboat to use gaslight. Although until the advent of electricity in the 1880's, the danger of fire on this account was ever-present, piped illuminating gas on shipboard was a considerable improvement over the feeble kerosene lamps, spitting candles, and whale-oil tapers that it replaced.

Engines and boilers had seen remarkable changes both in increased power and safety, too. Passengers were no longer satisfied with the more or less public dormitories which characterized the accommodations on early steamboats, and demanded private cabins. When the *Herald* was rebuilt and lengthened in 1848, she was, said the *American Beacon* of January 18, "fitted up in a style of superior elegance and comfort" and also performed the journey down the Bay "in the unprecedented time" of eleven and a half hours. When reboilered four years later, her "furnaces were altered so as to burn coal."

CHAPTER V

A Pair of "Superb and Commodious" Steamboats

TAKING technological advances into consideration, a building committee was appointed which reported to the Bay Line directors on June 17, 1851, that it had received estimates from five shipbuilding firms in Baltimore and Philadelphia for the construction of a 235-foot steamboat of 31½ feet in beam and 11-foot hold. It is interesting to note that in those days, the owners themselves seem to have selected the various sub-contractors for the construction of machinery, joiner work, painting, and furnishings. Today the shipyard usually estimates on the whole job and does not merely expect to furnish a bare hull.

For comparison with present-day prices, here are some of the estimates of the various successful bidders, broken down for the wooden side-wheel steamer under consideration. This vessel entered the Bay Line the following year as the *North Carolina:*

To Cooper & Butler, $20,000 for the hull of the boat at $25. per ton.

To Murray & Hazelhurst, $29,200 for a vertical beam engine, 56 inches in diameter by 11-foot stroke and two tubular boilers, "suited to the use of wood or coal," plus installation.

To Charles & Geo. W. Morris, $10,000 for joiner work, "including the gilding."

To Walter Ball, $2,500 for painting.

To S. Beacham, 7½ cents per pound for iron work.

The committee concluded its report with the statement that the "probable cost of the new steamboat may be, including suitable and appropriate furniture, somewhat upwards of $70,000."

It was upwards. On the books, the value of the *North Carolina* stood at $111,272.03. However, in the end they got a better equipped and slightly larger ship, for, as completed, their new steamboat measured 239.3 x 33.5 x 11.2 and had an engine of 60-inch cylinder diameter.

The *North Carolina* was warmly received at both ends of the Chesapeake and the *American Beacon* of July 1, 1852, cited her as "a model boat in every respect and reflects infinite credit upon her proprietors and the various artisans employed in her construction." Her maiden voyage to Norfolk took place on June 30 and was thirteen hours long. "She will do better when she becomes accustomed 'to harness,'" the paper prophesied.

"She would attract attention even among the splendid palaces that float upon the North River," the *Beacon* writer continued and then quoted the following detailed description of the boat, as given in the Baltimore *Patriot:*

> The main saloon is 80 feet long, 20 feet wide, and fitted up with an elegance of taste and liberality which will compare favorably with any of the steamers in the country—Brussells carpets, elegantly carved and velvet-cushioned chairs and *tête-a-tête* sofas, marble topped tables. Gothic mirrors and decorated lamps are the prevailing features of the furniture, which correspond well with the polished white panellings and gilded and carved mouldings which ornament the sides of the saloon.

Officers for the *North Carolina* were listed as Captain George W. Russell, "Clerk" David T. April, Chief Engineer Thomas Roberts, Pilot Solomon Pearson, and Mate W. C. Diggs.

Despite the increased cost of her construction, the *North Carolina* proved so satisfactory from the first that the company decided to sell the *Jewess* and build a new running mate. The various proposals for the construction of this second new steamer were carried out in similar manner, Cooper & Butler again furnishing the hull, but Charles Reeder & Sons, the engine. On May 1, 1854, the building committee mentioned their ". . . regret to conclude this report by announcing their great disappointment in not having it in their power to inform you of the boat having been launched, which has been through no fault of theirs."

A week later they stated: "The *Louisiana* is doubtless one of the most substantial, commodious, and elegant boats of the day, but exceeding in expenditure of money the sum which our former views indicated."

From the contemporary views of her that have survived, we can agree that the *Louisiana* did represent about the best that American shipbuilders could then produce. Her hull was of tough white oak and cedar, copper and iron fastened and painted white above the waterline as was customary. She carried the characteristic "hog frame" typical of all wooden hulled sound steamers.

This consisted of a pair of heavy timber bridge trusses which ran parallel to each other for the greater part of the length of the boat. These gave rigidity and stiffness to a shallow draft hull which might otherwise sag at the ends or become "hogged" when the weight of cargo did not evenly balance the concentrated weight of the machinery amidships.

The *Louisiana* measured 266 feet, 2½ inches in length, and she was not only one of the longest boats on the Chesapeake Bay, but also she remained the largest wooden-hulled craft ever operated by the Old Bay Line. Her maiden voyage, commanded by Capt. Russell, took place on November 9, 1854, and on an excursion to Old Point Comfort and the Virginia Capes, which took place on the following day, the captain's Norfolk and Portsmouth friends presented him with a "magnificent silver speaking trumpet."[44]

The *Louisiana*, built by Cooper & Butler in 1854. Largest of Old Bay Line's wooden sidewheelers. An interesting feature is the "hog frame." (Contemporary lithograph in Eldredge Collection of The Mariners Museum)

Although by this time a system of bells had been evolved to communicate signals from pilothouse to engine room, captains still gave most of their orders orally and one can well image that feminine hearts palpitated at the sight of this fine seaman brandishing his gleaming trumpet from his lofty command station on top of one of the sunburst decorated paddle boxes.

The acquisition of its two splendid new and modern steamboats raised the Old Bay Line to a class second to none, and inspired the Norfolk historian, William S. Forrest, to write that "this line is so well and ably conducted, that accidents seldom or never happen. The boats are very superior, kept in the finest order, and are in charge of officers of long experience, and well-tried skill and judgment."[45]

With the *Louisiana* joining the *North Carolina* on the run, it was possible to maintain an eleven-hour schedule. Thus, two boats leaving port simultaneously were sufficient for daily service.

Meanwhile, travelers' written opinions of the line varied between highest praise and severest condemnation. Suffice it to say, the passenger business picked up so much that even the large new boats were often crowded. One choleric passenger en route to the Baltimore Fair in 1855 was forced to seek repose on the deck of the main cabin, where he complained that "the heat was fearful, but odours of tobacco juice and liquors were worse." On arrival in port, however, he confessed that the steamer had made "great progress."[46]

Still another voyager on Chesapeake Bay steamboats described them[47] as "elegantly carpeted and furnished; frequently with most profuse gilding, mirrors, ottomans, etc." He mentioned that the dining saloon was below the main deck and although smoking was not allowed in the "grand saloons," passengers might employ the weed on the "piazza." Shower and "plunge" baths were advertised.

The year 1855 has been described as one "that will never be forgotten in Norfolk."[48] During the summer a case of yellow fever was discovered on board the ocean steamer *Benjamin Franklin* anchored in the Elizabeth River and almost overnight the disease spread rapidly throughout Portsmouth and then Norfolk. Events of those critical times when people were dropping "like withered leaves shaken by the winds" are graphically described in contemporary accounts which read like Defoe's *Journal of the Plague Year in London* [1666]. Suffice to say, the Old Bay Line rendered invaluable assistance in evacuating refugees and carrying "the necessaries of life for the relief of the sufferers" freight free. And a nice tradition has been perpetuated even to today by providing free passage on board its vessels to the Catholic Daughters of Charity of St. Vincent de Paul as a continuing testimonial to the heroism of eight nuns who remained in the plague-stricken area as volunteer nurses. These dedicated Sisters performed acts of mercy "like ministering angels."[49]

On January 2, 1856, the Maryland General Assembly extended the charter of the Baltimore Steam Packet Company to run another twenty years and later also passed an amendatory act authorizing the company "to make contracts for breaking tracks through the ice." Apparently the winter of this year was a very severe one and for several weeks all shipping was frozen in, unable to move. At this time the *Georgia* was said to have been "much damaged" but no particulars have survived.[50] The same

THE SOUTH!

Direct from NEW YORK, PHILADELPHIA and BALTIMORE, via the

"BAY LINE,"

To Norfolk, Welden, Raleigh, Wilmington, Charleston, Augusta, Atlanta, Montgomery and New Orleans.

SPRING AND SUMMER ARRANGEMENT

DAILY, Except Sundays, Via

BAY LINE

AND

SEA-BOARD and ROANOKE R. R.

TO THE ABOVE MENTIONED PLACES.

The SCHEDULE being so arranged that the Traveler is subject to No NIGHT TRAVEL on the RAIL ROAD from

NEW YORK TO WILMINGTON, N. C.

THROUGH TICKETS from NEW YORK to NORFOLK and PORTSMOUTH, Va.........$8 50
     FARE from PORTSMOUTH to WELDON,.........................4 00
     Making $12.50 from NEW YORK to WELDON.

do.   do.   PHILADELPHIA to NORFOLK and PORTSMOUTH, Va......... 6 50
     FARE from PORTSMOUTH to WELDON,.........................4 00
     Making $10.50 from PHILADELPHIA to WELDON.

do.   do.   BALTIMORE to WILMINGTON, N. C.......................14 50
do.   do.   do.   WELDON, N. C.............................. 9 00
do.   do.   do.   NORFOLK and PORTSMOUTH, Va......... 5 00

PASSENGERS and their BAGGAGE conveyed FREE of CHARGE between the Depots on the route
☞ PASSENGERS by this Line enjoy a comfortable NIGHT'S REST on the Bay Steamers, and are privileged to LAY OVER AT NIGHT at any POINT, and resume their Trip by DAYLIGHT.
☞ Particular Notice.—Passengers from NEW YORK and PHILADELPHIA, by this Line, will have their BAGGAGE checked from those Cities to BAY BOATS, from whence it will be checked to different points South.
☞ For Further Information and THROUGH TICKETS, (which are good by the Bay or Mail Line, apply

In NEW YORK, at the Company's Office, No. 299 Broadway, corner Barclay st., above the Astor House; or at the NEW JERSEY Rail Road Office, Foot of Courtland street.
In PHILADELPHIA, at the Company's Office, N. W. Corner of Sixth and Chesnut streets, or at the Depot, Broad and Prime streets.
In BALTIMORE, at the Office Baltimore Steam Packet Company, Foot of Union Dock, or on Board of the Bay Steamers.

THE NEW AND BEAUTIFUL STEAMERS,

LOUISIANA and NORTH CAROLINA, of 1,120 Tons Burthen Each,

Replete with EVERY COMFORT and CONVENIENCE, has been added to the line.

The Line being now Composed of the Splendid Steamers

LOUISIANA, Capt. George W. Russell, and NORTH CAROLINA, Capt. James Cannon,

Having Unsurpassed STATE ROOMS and BERTH Accommodations.

The NORFOLK or BAY LINE STEAMERS will leave the

Company's Wharf; UNION DOCK, Foot of Concord Street,

DAILY, SUNDAYS EXCEPTED,

☞ AT 5 O'CLOCK, P. M. ☜

Or immediately after the arrival of the EXPRESS TRAIN, which leaves NEW YORK at 8 A. M. and PHILADELPHIA at 12½ P M. The following is the SCHEDULE:

Leave NEW YORK at.........8 o'clock, A. M.	Leave PORTSMOUTH at...7½ o'clock, A. M.	
Leave PHILADELPHIA at 1 " P. M.	Leave WELDON at............12 " M.	
Leave BALTIMORE at.......5 " P. M.	Leave WILMINGTON at....9½ " P. M.	

For AUGUSTA, CHARLESTON and the SOUTH, via the Manchester Rail Road, now finished

---

PASSENGERS FOR RICHMOND AND PETERSBURG,

Or any other POINTS on the JAMES RIVER, connect with the JAMES RIVER BOATS early next morning after leaving BALTIMORE.

PASSENGERS for EDENTON, PLYMOUTH, NEWBERN, WASHINGTON, WELDON,
Goldsboro', Beaufort, Warsaw, Raleigh and Wilmington, N. C. will find it a most pleasant, direct, and agreeable route.

Baltimore, Sept. 1858.   M. N. FALLS, President.

THE ADAMS EXPRESS COMPANY FOR THE SOUTH!

FORWARD

Via the BAY LINE to Norfolk, Portsmouth, Weldon, Halifax, Goldsboro', Rocky Mount, and Wilmington, N. C. and Charleston, S. C., and to all points on the Sea-board and Roanoke and Weldon and Wilmington Rail Roads. A SPECIAL Messenger in charge of the GREAT SOUTHERN EXPRESS, leaves BALTIMORE DAILY, Sundays excepted, at 5 P. M

ADAMS & CO. 164 Baltimore street, BALTIMORE.
Do.   116 Chesnut street, PHILADELPHIA.
Do.   59 Broadway, NEW YORK.

year employees of the company purchased "a set of silver as a present to M. N. Falls, Esq., the popular president."[51]

By this time the rebuilt railroad lines running south from Portsmouth were in good order and agreements with this and other rail lines made it possible for the Baltimore Steam Packet Company to offer through tickets from New York to Wilmington, North Carolina. With the faster steamers ("replete with every comfort and convenience") in operation, departure from Baltimore was put off from four until five P.M. Tickets, Baltimore to Norfolk, had been reduced to $5.00.

In 1859, the line suffered its second major catastrophe in the destruction by fire of the *North Carolina,* then less than five and a half years old. Fortunately only 26 passengers were on board the boat when, early in the morning of January 30, a fire started in one of the upper staterooms and almost instantaneously ignited the whole vessel. Two persons were lost, a passenger, the Rev. Dr. Thomas Curtis, and a colored steward, Isaac Watters.

"Harry Scratch," the Norfolk newspaperman, mentioned[52] that "seven ladies barely escaped in their night clothes," and one wonders if this should not be taken literally as well as figuratively. Apparently the heroes of the occasion were Captain Cannon, master of the ship, and a passenger, Captain Henry Fitzgerald, who jumped out of his lifeboat several times to rescue women and children in the water. William Denby, Jr., was also "highly complimented for his coolness and presence of mind in that trying time" and Purser Lloyd B. Parks "did all in his power to save the lives of the passengers and inspire them with the courage he himself possessed."

When passengers and crew were safely in the lifeboats, they rowed over to the lightship at Smith's Point, where they remained until the steamer *Locust Point* could come and pick them up to carry them down to Old Point Comfort. Ship and cargo were a total loss and most of the passengers escaped with only their lives.

Occasions like this call for an almost superhuman display of seamanship and the prompt action of Captain Cannon and his crew undoubtedly prevented the disaster to the North Carolina from becoming an appalling tragedy.

Although obviously the *North Carolina* was badly burned before sinking put out the fires, it was considered possible to salvage some of her gear and machinery and, accordingly, the company gave notice that it would entertain sealed proposals to raise the wreck. The successful bidder, Richard W. Crosset, proposed to employ four large canal barges and was to receive seventy percent of what he could realize from the operations.

The contract was awarded within a week of the disaster and Crosset immediately went to work. However, after struggling along through the rest of the spring and summer with scant success, the unfortunate diver was forced to give up and wrote the following pathetic letter to the owners:

M. N. Falls, Esq.

Dear Sir:—Above you will find Bill of Lading for all the articles I have been able to get out of the *North Carolina*. I wish you to pay the freight, and charge it to my account.

It is with feelings of the deepest regret that I am compelled to let you know that I have given up all hopes of raising the *North Carolina*. I have striven almost against hope for some time, and I find that the longer I stay the worse it is for me—for I am afraid that this unfortunate affair will be the means of leaving my family houseless, as I see no other way now left for me than to sell my house to raise money to pay what I yet owe on this affair. Five thousand dollars will not leave me in as good circumstances as I was on the 4th day of March last. But if I can get a little time, I hope I shall be able to work through yet. This is the first job I have ever undertaken in my life which I did not finish with credit to myself and satisfaction to my employers; but the fault is not mine, for I cannot fight against the frown of God. The oldest settlers here say they have never seen such a Summer for wind as this has been; the wreck lies in such a bleak place, and so far from land, that the least wind which blows makes such a heavy sea that it is impossible for me to work more than one day out at a time. My barges are very badly strained, and the worms are getting into their bottoms so badly that I am compelled to go home with them.

I will be in Baltimore as soon as I can get my business fixed a little at home. I have to raise some money to settle with my men, &c. Till then, I remain,

Yours respectfully,

R. W. Crosset

P. S. Excuse this, as I am scarcely able to hold the pen. I have a severe attack of the fever. God knows how it may end.

R.W.C.

Despite poor Crosset's hard luck, another diver, Isaiah Gifford, made a further attempt to disconnect the machinery later on in the fall, but he, too, had no success, the water being "as thick as tar, and the tide running as much as five knots." Thus the whole project was abandoned.

The Bay Line's services were much crippled with the loss of the *North Carolina*. In the interim, the company chartered the 447-ton paddle steamer *George Weems*, but immediately set about looking for a permanent replacement. Their selection fell on a comparatively new wooden side-wheeler, the *Adelaide*, which had been operated by the Calais, Maine, Steamboat Company on the ocean run between Boston and St. John, New Brunswick. It is interesting to note that this steamer had been designed for a truly "deep water" route, for W. W. Vanderbilt, who ordered her from the Greenpoint, Long Island, builders of Lupton and McDermott, intended to send her out to California, via Magellan Straits, under her own power.

It will be remembered that as a result of the Gold Rush, shallow draft steamers were in enormous demand for use on the Sacramento and other river services in California. The first to arrive, an ex-Long Island Sound steamboat named the *Senator*, which made the perilous voyage out in '49, proved a bonanza boat for her owners and could command from $40 to $80 a ton for freight, with passenger rates proportionate, and not infrequently gathered in as much as $50,000 on a single trip![53] However, the *Adelaide* was deprived of enjoying a similarly glamorous career by being purchased on the stocks for the coast of Maine service.

In size, she was an almost identical steamer to the *North Carolina*, and on her arrival at Baltimore, the crew of the ill-fated ship was assigned to her, bringing her in to Norfolk on her first voyage exactly one month after the former steamer's career was terminated.

The *Georgeanna*, 1859. Built 1850 in Wilmington. Harlan & Hollingsworth drawing. (Courtesy of Bethlehem Steel Co.)

Further additions to the Old Bay Line fleet were made the following year when the *Georgeanna* was acquired in March, the *Philadelphia* in July, and the *William Selden* in November, 1860. The *Georgeanna* had been built the year before by the Harlan and Hollingsworth Company for G. R. H. Leffler. Excepting the little river boat *Mount Vernon,* the 199-foot *Georgeanna* was the first iron-hulled steamer to be employed on the regular run and dispensed with the "hog frame" characteristic of the wooden steamers. It is interesting to note that her employment on the Bay antedated the use of iron-hulled passenger vessels on Long Island Sound by several years. The *City of Lawrence* of the Norwich Line appeared there in 1867.

Fortress Monroe, Old Point Comfort and Hygeia Hotel, Va. The Old Bay liner *Adelaide* (1859-1881) appears in the right foreground. Meteorologists will be amused to note that although the topsail schooner (center foreground) is sailing close-hauled on the starboard tack to a northwest wind, the *Adelaide's* smoke shows that she actually has a southeast wind. (After the lithograph by E. Sachse, Baltimore, 1861, in the collection of The Mariners Museum)

The *William Selden,* a slightly smaller wooden steamboat, had been used on the Potomac since her launching in 1851, and had been lately employed by the Maryland and Virginia Steam Packet Company (a new organization, not connected, of course, with the Old Bay Line's precursor, the Maryland and Virginia Steam Boat Company) running on the Rappahannock River. In 1853, she had been chartered by the Old Bay Line to run while the *Herald* was undergoing repairs. H. W. Burton remarks that on January 25 of that year she established the record between Baltimore and Norfolk of 10 hours and 45 minutes which, he wrote in 1877, "we don't believe has ever been beaten."[54]

The *Philadelphia* had been built by Reanie, Neafie and Company for the Old Bay Line's affiliated organization, the Seaboard and Roanoke Railroad, which had established a line of boats running between Norfolk and Seaford, Delaware, on the Nanticoke River in connection with the Wilmington and Baltimore Railroad's Delmarva Peninsula branch. The *Philadelphia* was taken off this run shortly after the Old Bay Line acquired her and they, in turn, chartered her to the Potomac Steamboat Company on October 2, 1860. Some time thereafter, they took her off the Old Bay Line's hands entirely. These additions and replacements still left the *Louisiana* the "most commodious" vessel of the fleet which, however, now numbered several excellent modern steamers.

Occasional mention has been made of the excursion business in which the Old Bay Line and other steamboat companies participated. In the Summer of 1860, the Bay Line staged a coup which completely outdistanced all competitors. During July of that year, the mammoth iron steamship *Great Eastern* came across from England. This 692-foot vessel, born before her time and considered as nothing short of an eighth wonder of the world, was visited by thousands daily as she lay in New York harbor and, accordingly, her agents decided to send her out on "barnstorming" cruises to various other Atlantic ports.

The first of these trips brought the liner to Cape May, New Jersey, and turned out a thorough fiasco owing to mismanagement all along the line. However, crowds thronged aboard despite a stiff admission charge, and so, even though few passengers signed on for the trip, a second voyage was planned which took the giant ship down to Chesapeake Bay. In the meantime, officials of the Old Bay Line had not been idle and, in return for the inducement of a thousand tons of coal, the *Great Eastern's* agents granted to the Bay Line the exclusive privilege of placing passengers aboard the liner for the daylight trip from Virginia Capes to Annapolis Roads.[55]

On August 5, weighted down with a full load of excursionists, the *Louisiana,* under Captain Russell, met the *Great Eastern,* then at anchor in Hampton Roads off Old Point Comfort, and transferred her passengers to the steamer by small boat. The liner then proceeded to Annapolis while the *Louisiana* and practically everything that floated in Chesapeake Bay followed. On arrival, the Bay Line passengers reembarked on the *Louisiana* and were returned to Baltimore. Thus, although thousands visited the *Great Eastern*, only the Bay Line passengers got a ride on her. This triumph was extensively advertised in the daily papers under the heading, "Ho! for the *Great Eastern*." The round trip, all included, cost only $6.00.[56]

One who made the voyage, "J. W.," special correspondent of the New Orleans *Daily Picayune*, reported enthusiastically in a dispatch from Baltimore dated August 4, 1860, that "a ride down the Chesapeake in one of the Bay Line steamers is perfectly luxurious and healthful. . . . Col. M. N. Falls, president of the company, is a perfect Napoleon in steamboating. . . ." Much awed by the famous British leviathan, he remarked that "the waters parted before her as if cleft by an omnipotent power. I watched her until from a huge monster, she diminished to the size of a small pungy."[57]

Burton estimated that 10,000 people came to Old Point Comfort for the express purpose of seeing the great ship.[58] She was unquestionably the talk of the day and many who viewed her still believed that an iron steamship of that size could not be real.

During the twenty years it had been in operation, the Baltimore Steam Packet Company had been successful in establishing itself in a strong position and had played from the first a major role in the history of communications on the Chesapeake Bay. The end of the period found the company managing a splendid fleet of up-to-date steamboats which included the *Louisiana, Adelaide, Georgeanna, William Selden, Herald* and *Georgia*. Of a total of some fifteen steamboats which they had owned up to this time, only one, the *Georgia*, remained of their original vessels.

Meanwhile many changes in the towns and settlements around the route of the Bay Line had occurred. Populations of both Baltimore and Norfolk had materially increased; Old Point Comfort with its famous Hygeia Hotel had grown to be the most fashionable resort of the South; travel was no longer restricted to the wealthy alone; and the ever-expanding railroad lines brought an increasing number of passengers and tons of freight to the steamboat wharves.

All was not well, however. Differences between North and South were daily increasing and ominous storm clouds gathered on the horizon. It was not to be long before the rifts would widen into bridgeless chasms and hot words would give way to hotter flames and powder. Eighteen-sixty-one dawned and events drew on to an inevitable climax. Abraham Lincoln came to the White House in March and, a month later, word was brought to Norfolk that South Carolinians had opened fire on Fort Sumter in Charleston harbor. Officials of the Bay Line, gateway between North and South, anxiously wondered how it would all turn out.

CHAPTER VI

The Civil War and Its Aftermath

HERE is no place for a comprehensive history of the naval operations in Chesapeake Bay during the Civil War, but, insofar as possible, mention will be made of those events which directly concerned the Old Bay Line. It might be remembered that when the war broke out, the Bay Line's terminal ports were decidedly pro-Confederacy. Norfolk was a Southern city and Baltimore was Southern in sentiment even though Maryland remained in the Union. As the Federal Navy gained control of the Chesapeake and blockades were established of Southern harbors, the Bay Line's operations were curtailed and made to conform to United States direction. Nevertheless, the Line managed to maintain daily service between Baltimore and Old Point Comfort for the duration of the war and, although passenger travel dropped off, there was a large amount of freight to move which, according to Burton,[59] "paid the line very handsomely." However, no longer we're there northbound shipments of cotton, which previously had made up a large percentage of the cargo.

The situation of the Federal navy yard at Gosport, now a part of Portsmouth, Virginia, surrounded as it was by increasingly hostile country, gave concern to the Union government. The Gosport Yard was unquestionably the most important in the United States but, with Virginia proposing to secede, Commodore McCauley felt that it would be better to abandon the post rather than attempt to hold it in the face of eventual and certain hostilities.

Virginia formally withdrew from the Union on April 17, 1861. The United States Navy intended to send down a large company of naval recruits to put on the warships at Gosport in the attempt either to defend or to withdraw them immediately to safer waters. It was intended to ship these men down via the Old Bay Line, but President Falls wrote Captain W. W. Hunter on the 19th, saying that the company "declined to take them."[60] Since war had not yet

48

been declared between Virginia and the Union, this was a reasonable decision, as the shipment of troops to Portsmouth would have been an overt act capable of but one interpretation.

The very next day, however, those in charge of the Gosport Yard decided to evacuate the facility and warships which could not readily be moved to Northern waters were slated to be burned. Included in the systematic destruction of the Yard was an attempt to blow up the dry dock and the sinking of several fine vessels including the auxiliary steam frigate *Merrimack*. It will be recalled that later on the Confederates raised the hulk of the *Merrimack* and, in spite of appalling odds, contrived to rebuild her as an ironclad. Rechristened *Virginia*, she fought the Union *Monitor* on March 9, 1862, in the epic battle of Hampton Roads—the first contest between ironclads.

The populace of Norfolk and Portsmouth rejoiced at the Federal evacuation of the Yard and an immediate survey clearly showed that the destruction had by no means been complete. It was apparent that a large part of the guns and stores could be reclaimed for the Confederacy. Meanwhile, the Old Bay Line continued its services from Baltimore to Norfolk with the *Louisiana* and *Adelaide*, but on May 7, the latter steamboat, under the command of Captain Cannon, was detained at Fort Monroe and required to disembark all passengers and mails. With most of Chesapeake Bay under their control, the Federal naval authorities advised the company that thereafter the boats' regular voyages would terminate at Old Point Comfort. If they wished, however, they might put on a small steamer to run between Old Point and Norfolk. The *William Selden* was sent down for this purpose, but as Norfolk was now declared by the Union to be in a state of blockade, the Confederates retaliated by seizing the *William Selden* when she came into port.[61] The vessel remained tied up at Portsmouth for as long as the South was able to hold the Elizabeth River.

Shortly thereafter, the Union Navy chartered the *Adelaide* to be used as a transport attached to the Joint Atlantic Blockading Squadron. The most important engagement in which she participated consisted in the bombardment of Forts Hatteras and Clark on August 28 and 29, 1861. Captained by Commander Henry S. Stellwagen, the *Adelaide* together with another former Chesapeake Bay passenger steamboat, the *George Peabody*, carried large numbers of Federal troops in support of an operation against strong points on the Carolina Outer Banks. This succeeded in routing the Confederate defenders and brought all of Albemarle and Pamlico Sounds under eventual Federal control.

The *Louisiana* and *Georgeanna* maintained the regular service down to Old Point through the remainder of the year, but being in need of an additional vessel, the company decided to purchase, on

February 15, the steamboat *Thomas A. Morgan* from the Delaware River Steam Boat Company. This iron side-wheeler had been built in 1854 by Harlan and Hollingsworth of Wilmington, Delaware, and measured 192 feet in length. However, on her arrival from the Delaware River, the *Thomas A. Morgan* was immediately secured by the War Department and used as official mail boat between Fort Monroe and Yorktown. Commanded by Captain Thomas Edgar, she was at Old Point on March 9, and witnessed the famous *Monitor-Virginia* (ex-*Merrimack*) battle.

As the Federal blockade tightened, apparently there was no further need for the *Adelaide,* and she was returned to the Company. The next year, she was back on the regular run with the

Bombardment of Forts Hatteras and Clark by the U. S. Fleet, Aug. 28-29, 1861; *Adelaide* in center foreground as transport. (Litho. by Bufford, Boston, 1862, courtesy of The Mariners Museum)

Georgeanna, for the Navy was carrying out experiments on the machinery and boilers of both these boats while they maintained their usual services in 1862 and 1863. The *Georgia* and *Thomas A. Morgan* were the only Old Bay Line ships appearing on a list of vessels employed by the War Department in *Virginia* as of March 11, 1863.[62]

To all intents and purposes the *Monitor-Virginia* fight was to a draw with neither ship able to destroy the other. As long as they had their powerful ironclad, the South was morally in the ascendency, but the turn of events elsewhere made it doubtful that the Confederates could retain Norfolk. The *Virginia* drew too much water to be taken up the James to Richmond and, with so many powerful vessels out to destroy her and the mouth of Hampton Roads blockaded by Federal warships and sealed by the heavy guns of Fort Monroe, it was obvious that her days were numbered.

When the concentration on Norfolk began, the Union forces crossing Hampton Roads from Fort Monroe and coming in to Norfolk from the east found no opposition. But before retiring up the west bank of the James, the Confederates, like the Federals the year before, systematically set about destroying the Gosport Yard. As the troops entered Norfolk on May 10, 1862, they saw most of Portsmouth in flames and the *Virginia* herself was expressly blown up off Craney Island on the following day. Along with all other

Iron sidewheeler *Thomas A. Morgan*, built in 1854 by Harlan and Hollingsworth. (From an 1855 watercolor, courtesy of The Mariners Museum)

vessels that they were unable to take with them up the James, the Old Bay Line steamer *William Selden*, which had been tied up in the Elizabeth River for a year, was burned by the evacuating Confederate forces.

With Norfolk recaptured, the blockade of the south side of Hampton Roads came to an end, but the Bay Line steamers were still not permitted to run over the whole of their customary route until the end of the war. Later on in the autumn, though, the company obtained permission from the Union Navy to send a tug to Portsmouth in an attempt to recover the machinery of the *William Selden*.[63]

Meanwhile, the theatres of the war were shifting elsewhere and, as far as can be determined, the Bay Line was no longer directly associated with the South's now desperate struggle. Events of minor significance which related to the Line consisted in the attachment of the *Thomas A. Morgan* to the Ware River Expedition on April 10, 1863 and the collision, on April 12, 1864, between the *Georgeanna* and the U.S.S. *Iroquois*. This was caused, according to official Navy reports, because "the pilot put the helm starboard against regulations."[64]

It is interesting to note that the Old Bay Line claims against the United States Government for use of the *Georgia* and the *Thomas A. Morgan* during the war not settled until 1896.

On April 9, 1865, the end came at last. General Lee surrendered at Appomattox and peace came to the North and Reconstruction to the war-torn South. The termination of the war found the Old Bay Line, like all other organizations serving the South, in a demoralized state. Passenger traffic had dropped off, resorts were closed, and excursionists nonexistent. The steamers themselves were out of condition, but, worst of all was the complete destruction of Southern railways on which the line depended for freight. With remarkable energy, the South attacked the almost hopeless problem of rebuilding railroads.

After peace had been declared, the Bay Line boats again crossed over Hampton Roads to Norfolk and the government mail contract was extended to cover the whole route once more. With characteristic energy, the Baltimore Steam Packet Company set about regaining its feet. Anticipating their certain need for new equipment, the company had contracted with the shipbuilding firm of Reaney, Son and Company, Chester, Pennsylvania, for a new iron paddle steamer, 236 feet 9 inches long, to be delivered in five months' time. This vessel was christened *Thomas Kelso* after one of the Line's original directors, a prominent citizen of Baltimore then in his eighties.

The Line also acquired, in 1865, a little wooden paddler, the *Eolus*, built the year before by Thomas Marvel, at Newburg, New York. This 144-foot steamboat, commanded by Captain P. McCarrick, was placed on a newly established feeder day-line from Norfolk to Yorktown, Gloucester, and Mathews County, Virginia, via Old Point Comfort, three times weekly. On the alternate days, she ran across to Cherrystone, on the Eastern Shore of Virginia, near Cape Charles.

During the war, all commercial traffic on the James River ceased, but in the fall of 1865, the Powhatan Steamboat Company was revived by Jacob Brandt, Jr., and operated three steamboats from Baltimore to Richmond. These included the *State of Virginia, State Of Maryland,* and *Petersburg.* Subsequently all of them were taken over by the Baltimore Steam Packet Company. A newly established People's Line covered the same route with the *Agnes* and *Ellie Knight* and the latter vessel was also added later to the Old Bay Line. Steamship services, both day and night, were also revived between Norfolk and Richmond.

Following the war, when Southern commerce and industry was prostrate, a large number of Northern concerns found the South a ripe field for their endeavor and, in the post-bellum period, a number of Northern enterprises gained footholds through the South. It was only natural, therefore, when the Bay Line was at a low ebb, that a competitor should appear on the scene. The Leary Brothers of New York brought down three steamers which they placed on the Baltimore-Norfolk run with connecting boats for Richmond.

Wooden paddle steamer *Eolus*, owned by Old Bay Line, 1864-1869. (Photo by William King Covell)

As might be expected, a rate war immediately ensued and the traveling public prospered with fares reduced to $3.00 one way and $5.00 round trip.

As stated in the introduction, the Baltimore Steam Packet Company in the maturity of its years has earned the name of "Old Bay Line." Apparently the first time this name appeared in print occurred on July 24, 1865, when the company's advertisement in the Baltimore *Sun* announced that "The *Old* Established Bay Line" was operating daily the steamers *Louisiana, Georgeanna, Adelaide,* and *Thomas Kelso* from Baltimore to Norfolk with connection at Old Point Comfort made by the *Thomas Collyer* and *Milton Martin* for James River Landings and Richmond. And the Norfolk *Journal* of December 5, 1866, cited "the Old and Enterprising Baltimore Steam Packet Company."

The Leary Line's vessels included the *George Leary*, Captain Blackeman; the *James T. Brady*, Captain Landis; and the *Dictator*, Captain Mulligan. In addition to lowering their fares in the attempt to gather in the patronage which formerly had gone uncontested to the Old Bay Line, the Leary Line offered all sorts of inducements including "bands of musick" to woo travelers and shippers. Naturally, unofficial but highly contested races took place between the rival steamboats and, as a result, several accidents occurred which probably contributed to the withdrawal of the Leary Line. The *George Leary* rammed and sank a schooner whose entire crew was lost; four days later the *Dictator* ran into a tug in Norfolk harbor and was badly damaged; and a final straw was added when the *George Leary* collided with the *Louisiana*, causing the deaths of one passenger and three of the crew.

The *George Leary*, built for Leary in 1864. Lithograph by Endicott & Co. (Eldredge Collection of The Mariners Museum)

The Old Bay Line, likewise, experienced its share of bad luck when the *Thomas Kelso*, Captain Cralle, exploded her steam drum off Wolf Trap Lightboat on the early morning of December 8, 1866, badly scalding her firemen and engineers, five of whom died, and injuring several passengers.

However, in January, 1867, the Old Bay Line was successful in buying off its competitor, the steamer *George Leary* being added to its fleet at a cost in excess of a quarter of a million dollars, the highest price paid for any one of their steamers up to that time. The other Leary Line vessels were returned to New York and, happily, things soon returned to normalcy.

In 1867, John Moncure Robinson succeeded Mr. Falls as fourth president of the Baltimore Steam Packet Company. Mr. Robinson was the son of Moncure Robinson, first chief engineer of the Richmond, Fredericksburg and Potomac Railroad, and, like most of the Bay Line's officials at this time, was a former officer in the Confederate Army. Of the twelve presidents which the Line has had since it began, Mr. Robinson's 26-year tenure of office was the longest. Under his regime the Line was to witness many important changes bringing its ships and services to the state of perfection and efficiency associated with the heyday of steamboating. The ships gradually changed from wooden side-wheelers to iron-hulled craft. The screw propeller replaced the cumbersome paddle wheel and, at the last, iron hulls gave way to ships of steel. Steam steering gear replaced the cranky, manually-operated wheels; gas light was abandoned for electricity; pot-bellied stoves gave way to steam-heated radiators. Likewise, the high silk hats and frock coats of captains and pursers were discarded for uniforms, first resplendent and gaudy, later more utilitarian and conservative.

These changes did not come overnight, but slowly and inevitably as their efficiency was demonstrated, the Old Bay Line adopted those improvements which kept its fleet ever at the forefront of American steamboat lines.

CHAPTER VII

The Mosquito Fleet

A T THE end of the Civil War, the Federal Government had left on its hands a considerable number of small steamboats which had been used as gunboats and transports. With the exception of blockade running and the spectacular cruises of such Confederate commerce raiders as the *Sumter, Alabama, Florida* and *Shenandoah,* naval actions of the war became confined to sounds and rivers as the big Union warships succeeded in establishing their effective blockades which bottled up the South. In order to prosecute the conflict, the Union forces had acquired a flotilla of boats that were sufficiently small to be effective in narrow waterways and, having no further use for them when the war was over, they were sold to private steamship operators at comparatively low prices.

The three steamboats with which the Powhatan Line resumed service on the James River were all war veterans of this character. Most of the ex-gunboats and transports were converted to freighters and, since the Old Bay Line steamers were primarily passenger boats sailing on scheduled service, it was obvious that small roving freighters might be successful in cornering a lion's share of the cargo transportation business since they could readily go where freight offered.

For at least a decade after the end of the war, freighting on the Chesapeake amounted to more than the passenger business, anyway, and it was undoubtedly this factor which determined at this time the acquisition by the Bay Line of their first boats designed to handle cargo only.

The Old Bay Line's first freighter and also its first steamboat to be propelled by a screw instead of paddle wheels was the 305-ton *New Jersey,* built in Baltimore in 1862. She was obtained in 1867 by trading the *Thomas A. Morgan.* Two years later the company acquired a similar wooden-hulled propeller steamer, the *Transit,* which had been built during the war for the Montauk, Long Island,

Steam Navigation Company. A few months before, the company had sold the *Georgeanna* and *Eolus*, together with their almost new steamer, *Thomas Kelso*, leaving the passenger business to be handled by the *George Leary, Louisiana,* and *Adelaide.*

The career of the *New Jersey* was short. On February 26, 1870, she took fire off Sharps Island and was totally destroyed. The company had found that operation of their small freighters was extremely profitable, however, and it was decided to replace the *New Jersey* with a similar screw freighter built of iron. An agreement was made in June of the same year with the shipbuilding firm of Harlan and Hollingsworth, of Wilmington, Delaware, for the construction of a vessel of this type to measure 167.7 feet in length.

Iron freight boat *Roanoke*, built for the Old Bay Line in 1871 by Harlan and Hollingsworth. (Drawing courtesy of Bethlehem Steel Co.)

Harlan and Hollingsworth specialized in iron shipbuilding and they had built both the *Georgeanna* and the *Thomas A. Morgan*. The new freighter, named the *Roanoke* when she came out in 1871, was the first of many iron steamers expressly built for the Old Bay Line by the Wilmington concern.

The black painted *Roanoke* and the little freighters that followed it were not beautiful, but they were well built and economical to operate. As in modern tankers, the machinery and boilers were placed well aft, and since the crew's quarters, galley, and other accommodations were confined to a narrow deckhouse, practically the entire main deck could be devoted to cargo, in addition to the lower hold.

Though ocean steamers continued to carry auxiliary sails almost until the twentieth century, sound and river passenger boats gave up canvas well before the Civil War. However, the Bay Line's new freighters carried three masts and fore-and-aft sails which could help them along in favorable winds and kept them from rolling in a cross swell.

In 1873–74, two more new iron freighters were built for the Line. These were the sister ships, *Westover* and *Shirley*, named for the famous James River plantations. A slightly larger freighter, called *Seaboard*, was also built in 1874. The same year a little 102-foot side-wheeler, the *Vesta*, was acquired. She was probably used both as a tug and a transfer steamer in Norfolk harbor. Later on, a half-interest in her was secured by the Wilmington, Weldon and Seaboard Railroad.

Although the cargo boats could be dispatched entirely as freight offered, the Old Bay Line operated them on fairly definitely established routes. The *Transit, Roanoke,* and *Seaboard* plied between Norfolk and Baltimore with freight from Philadelphia connecting with the Philadelphia, Baltimore, and Washington Railroad at Canton, Maryland. This route became known as the Canton Inside Line. The *Shirley* and *Westover* ran between Baltimore, Petersburg, and Richmond, via Norfolk. The Powhatan Line was then operating on the James, but as the Old Bay Line was successful in purchasing control of the stock of the Powhatan Line, they took over this route and later the three steamers with which the Powhatan Line had inaugurated service in 1865.

Back in 1854, a railroad had been projected to connect Richmond with West Point, Virginia, then little more than a hamlet at the head of the York River. Just as the line was completed, the war came along and, during its course, the line was completely wiped out. At the close of hostilities work went forward to rebuild the railroad and, in 1870, the Powhatan Line alternated tri-weekly service on both the James and the York Rivers. Owing to the expense connected with its rebuilding, the railroad found itself in bad financial straits and so hopelessly in debt that it was sold under a decree of the Chancery Court to R. S. Burress and Thomas Clyde, of Philadelphia. The latter, a prosperous shipowner, set up a new steamship line between Baltimore and West Point, absorbing the Powhatan Line's York River business.

It would be virtually impossible to trace all the moves and countermoves which took place during the early 1870's by which the control of the various steamboat lines of the York and James Rivers became established. It is plain that the Baltimore Steam Packet's interest in the Powhatan Line was secured merely to protect itself from the competition which threatened if the York River Line became sufficiently well entrenched to take away their Richmond freight business. This move proved but a temporary stopgap, however, for, although the Bay Line acquired the Powhatan Line steamers, when the Richmond and York River Railroad changed hands and the Clyde interests took charge, they established a line with new ships that the Old Bay Line could not disturb.

This new line was incorporated by the Maryland Legislature in 1874 as the Baltimore, Chesapeake and Richmond Steamboat Company and became the parent of the Chesapeake Steamship Company which survived until 1940. The boats that were brought to the York River were the *Louise, Sue, Havana,* and *Empire.*

Before it disbanded, the interests of the Powhatan Line personnel were sharply divided between the Old Bay Line and the York River Line. Those favoring the latter naturally came into the Baltimore, Chesapeake and Richmond Steamboat Company, but before doing so, this faction in the Powhatan Line instigated a lawsuit against the Bay Line, charging that,

> Influential shareholders in the Baltimore Steam Packet Company bought a controlling amount of stock in the Powhatan Company and so managed that the Powhatan Company became more and more embarrassed and sold to the Baltimore Steam Packet Company the steamers *State Of Virginia, State Of Maryland, Ellie Knight,* and *Fannie Lehr.* The bill of complaint is filed to recover damages for the loss in consequence of the alleged breaking up of the business of the Powhatan Company and the subsequent loss of its stock.[65]

The case was tried at the October term of the Circuit Court in 1875, and satisfactory adjustments were made. It was, of course, only natural for the Old Bay Line to make every effort to hang on to the freight business which was threatened by the new line via the York River. The effort proved both abortive and costly, for in 1875 the Bay Line found itself owner of thirteen vessels—many more than could be used profitably. These boats were the *Adelaide* and *George Leary,* which maintained the regular passenger service; the *Roanoke, Vesta, Shirley, Westover, Seaboard,* and *Transit,* practically all new freighters; and the *State of Virginia, State Of Maryland, Ellie Knight, Cockade City* (ex-*Fannie Lehr*), and *Petersburg,* all former Powhatan Line ships.

It will be noted that the name of the *Louisiana* does not appear on the roster. This crack steamboat had been rammed and sunk by the Baltimore-Charleston steamer *Falcon* the year before. This was extremely bad luck for the company for, although it owned a veritable navy, only two of the thirteen boats were equipped to handle the regular passenger service adequately.

Although launched back in 1854, in 1871 the *Louisiana* had been completely rebuilt and modernized by the shipbuilding firm of William Skinner and Company at a cost of $50,000, and this made her still one of the finest steamboats on Chesapeake Bay.

Disaster to the *Louisiana* came about on the night of November 14, 1874. Since the vessel remained afloat for almost forty-five minutes after the collision, there was plenty of time for all passengers, together with their baggage and the mails, to be safely trans-

ferred to the only slightly damaged *Falcon*. Captain Wyndham R.
Mayo, who had joined the line only shortly before, was highly
praised by the passengers who prepared a glowing testimonial in
his behalf.

With the York River Line established and backed by strong
financial interests, competition between it and the Old Bay Line
attained startling proportions. One of the first moves of the new
company was the invasion of the Norfolk passenger field. Excepting for the brief period of existence of the Leary Line, the Old Bay
Line had had no competition on this run from its beginning. The
rival company put two boats on a "People's Line" which paralleled
the Bay Line route. The fare was set at $3.00 one way and, as
before when direct competition threatened, the Old Bay Line was
forced to reduce its tariffs accordingly.

Finally a compromise was reached and, by an agreement signed
by both Thomas Clyde and John M. Robinson on January 11, 1877,
the People's Line was discontinued. For their part, the Old Bay
Line contracted to sell the *Shirley* to the York River Line for three
quarters of her initial cost and they also agreed to give up any
business they might have on the York River together with their interests in a freight line between Baltimore and Philadelphia. The
year before they had managed the Seaboard Railroad's steamer
Astoria on this route for the express purpose of opposing the Clyde
interests in the Ericsson Line. Finally, the Old Bay Line agreed to
abandon direct service from Baltimore to Richmond and to give up
any competition with the outside Clyde Line.

In turn, the Baltimore, Chesapeake and Richmond Steamboat
Company agreed not only to keep out of Norfolk but also the James
River below the Appomattox and to abandon to the Old Bay Line
their feeder interests on the Roanoke, Chowan, and Black Water
Rivers in Carolina. The agreement was to be in effect for five years
and carried a $75,000 penalty for infringement by either party.

These moves and countermoves will give some idea of the far-
flung interests with which the various lines had surrounded themselves during this critical period of establishing the permanent
trade agreements and feeder routes which characterize modern
transportation systems.

When "peace" returned, the Old Bay Line set about to reorganize
its fleet of cargo vessels for more efficient service. Although one
freighter, the *Raleigh*, was added to the Line in 1877, the old
boats were either sold or broken up so that in this year its freight
fleet had been cut down to five boats as opposed to the eleven it had
owned two years before. Meanwhile, the Canton Inside Line continued to be profitable and there was other work for Bay Line
freighters on the James.

In 1881, Harlan and Hollingsworth provided the Line with another new iron freighter christened *Gaston*. This screw steamer measured 212 feet in length and was driven by a two-cylinder compound steam engine, the first of this type with which a Bay Line boat had been equipped. In contrast to the earlier freighters, the *Gaston* was a beautiful little craft, well modeled and of pleasing proportions. President Robinson jokingly called her his "flagship."

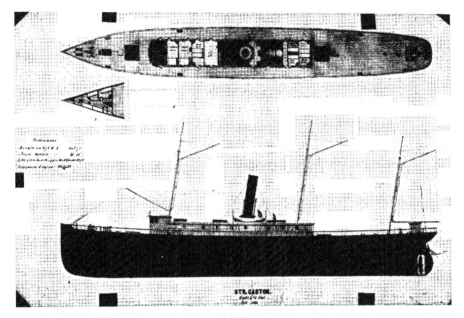

Deck plans and outboard profile of the *Gaston*. From original drawings of the builders, Harlan and Hollingsworth, 1881. (Courtesy of Mariners Museum)

In 1884, the New York, Philadelphia, and Norfolk Railroad (later designated the Delmarva branch of the Pennsylvania) completed its line down the Eastern Shore peninsula to Cape Charles whence a freight car barge connection was established across the lower Chesapeake direct to Hampton Roads and Norfolk. Since the majority of freights became diverted to the new route, the Canton Inside Line was no longer profitable and was forced to suspend operations the following year.

Meanwhile, three new passenger steamers with increased cargo space had been built for the Old Bay Line and a fourth came out in 1887. Since the work of the tramp freighter had been absorbed by the railroads on one hand and regular steamship lines on the other, the "mosquito fleet" came to an end, the Bay Line retaining only the *Seaboard* and *Gaston* as auxiliaries to its regular service.

CHAPTER VIII

Through the Turn of the Century

WARS inevitably stimulate advances in all fields of science and invention. Although ships had been built of metal well before the year 1860, nevertheless the famous duel between the ironclads, *Monitor* and *Virginia*, gave considerable impetus to iron shipbuilding and the development of naval architecture for commercial craft as well as warships. These advances came to bear fruit in the comparatively prosperous and expansive period enjoyed by this country following the Civil War. The South had a very hard time of it, it is true, and its effort to rebuild itself, coupled with over-optimistic post-war prosperity in the North, was largely responsible for the financial panic of 1873. However, by far the greatest single advance the country had known followed the reunification of the Nation.

With iron replacing wood for a considerable part of all new ship construction, it was possible not only to have larger vessels, but also far stronger and more seaworthy ones. In 1869, steam steering engines first appeared on the transatlantic steamship, *City Of Brussels,* and a single quartermaster could direct the movements of a large ship. Previously, it had taken as many as four men to struggle with a fighting double steering wheel in heavy weather. In 1878, nine years later, another transatlantic liner, the *City Of Berlin,* put to sea with a small generator and six electric lights. Underwriters were skeptical at first, considering this an unpredictable fire hazard. Safety features were soon demonstrated, however, and it was not so many years afterwards that people might be reluctant to travel on any boat not equipped with electricity.

Not all the pioneering in shipbuilding was reserved for ocean-going vessels and the Fall River Line steamboat *Pilgrim,* launched in 1883, was not only the first vessel built that was designed to have electricity as the sole means of illumination, but she also furnished an early example of the double bottom and watertight compartment construction.

It was immediately following the war that the Fall River Line, under the direction of notorious "Admiral" Jim Fiske, Jr., entered into its. own, and true *de luxe* travel was born. At the time when the Old Bay Line was trying valiantly to suppress competition and regain its feet following the trials of operation in a combat area, the Fall River established itself at the forefront of all sound steamboat lines. Its two new spotlessly white steamers, *Bristol* and *Providence,* coming out in 1869 and costing a million and a quarter each, made the vessels of other lines seem poor and insignificant by comparison. Two Scotch travelers visiting America in the autumn of the same year came up from Fort Monroe to Baltimore and cryptically remarked that on the Bay Line "the accommodation on board was not of the best."[66] Later on, they proceeded to New York and, having "dined at the famed Delmonico's, and paid three prices for the privilege," they "embarked on board the steamboat *Bristol* at 5 P.M., en route for Boston, via Fall River."

Describing this vessel in glowing terms, they said:[67]

Seven officers in uniform, gold lace and dress boots, receive the passengers as they arrive to embark, porters in white gloves being in waiting to open the carriage doors. Punctually to the time of starting the paddles went round, the splendid band of music struck up, and we were off with the speed of a railway train. Till the shades of evening drew in we enjoyed immensely the lovely scenery on either hand, and then one by one the hundreds of passengers retired to their respective chambers, to be lulled to sleep by the almost noiseless sweep of the vessel on the water, and the sweet low strains of the distant orchestra.

True to form, these good Scots concluded their description with the remark, "All this luxury only costs three cents per mile."

The particular mention of uniformed officers in the American merchant service is interesting to note in view of the fact that the Fall River Line apparently was a pioneer in the innovation of uniforming its crews. At this time, captains and pursers of the Old Bay and other lines were still wearing their tall hats and frock coats. Jim Fiske did not stop with dressing up his officers, however. Declaring that if Vanderbilt could be a commodore, he would be an admiral, Fiske had a uniform made for himself that would have made a regular fleet commander appear in *mufti* by comparison! With his actress friend, Josie Mansfield, similarly attired, for a time he made it a daily practice to be on hand, strutting about before the boats sailed and, to the "ohs!" and "ahs!" of impressionable lady passengers, he "piloted" the steamers around the southern end of Manhattan into the East River, whence a tug came alongside and took Josie and him ashore again.

To compete with the luxurious appointments of the Fall River boats, all American lines went in heavily for rococo plaster decoration, gingerbread, and gold leaf and, in 1875, another foreign visitor remarked: "Boats navigating the rivers and bays of the United States are constructed on a scale of magnificence quite unknown to European waters. . . . The grand saloon is not unlike a hall in a palace."[68]

A woodcut accompanying the above description in a British periodical showed that the main saloon extended two decks high with a dome ceiling. It was lit by clerestory windows by day and fancy gaslights by night. An enclosed well containing the machinery divided this saloon from the slightly smaller forward saloon and cabins led off from both decks. Below, in the after hold, was situated the "elaborately provided" dining room which could be converted to a dormitory after meals, if traffic demanded. Here, we are told, "crowds of civil negroes, in spotless white jackets, wait at the tables which are ornamented with artificial flowers."[69]

It is interesting to note that it has been only during the present century that the dining rooms on sound steamers have been lifted out of the hold and given outside portholes and fresh air.

But even though the Fall River boats were certainly stupendous, the Old Bay liners came in for their share of compliments as well despite their comparatively inferior size. The *Louisiana* was cited in the Norfolk *Journal* of February 28, 1867, as being quite plush. "Money seems to have been forgotten in the disposition to rival the steamers of the North and East Rivers," the paper commented.

However, the *Journal* went completely overboard in its account, given in the issue of August 2, 1869, of the steamer *George Leary* which by this time had been purchased from the temporary rival Leary Line and added to the Bay Line fleet. As this description of the interior fittings of a typical American steamboat is so vividly complete, it is printed here in its entirety:

> Upon entering the main cabin from the deck below, by a flight of stairs shining like burnished gold, the first thing that strikes the vision is the gorgeous style of furniture and the elegant fittings. The saloon is attractively painted with pure lily white, while upon the panel work the painter's pencil has drawn some very beautiful and chaste devices, pleasing to the eye and appreciative to the refined mind for the ideals of the beautiful and pure.
>
> At the head of the stairway is a large and richly carved mirror, of the finest French plate glass, encased in a black walnut frame. On either side of the stairway is a bronze statue of a knight in full armor holding a lance, which is used as a staff to support a magnificent bronze lamp.
>
> The ladies' cabin, situated on the lower deck, is magnificently furnished with upholstered sofas and lounges of rich red vel-

vet, and fine damask curtains of like hue. In the after part of the cabin is a special boudoir and wash room, which to every lady must be an agreeable convenience.

Proceeding down a short flight of stairs, we were conducted to the supper room. Two rows of tables run longitudinally along the sides, so constructed as, when occasion requires, they can be joined into one. The seats are richly upholstered with "reps," while on the deck is an elegant oil cloth of chaste design. The tables are magnificently adorned with the very best vases, containing elegant flowers, both natural and of the finest French artificial wax-work. The saloon is lighted by elegantly adorned bronze lamps. The light is subdued, but amply sufficient to view the boundless repast spread before the hungry traveler.

Currier & Ives lithograph of the *Florida*, after painting by C. R. Parsons, 1878. (Eldredge Collection of The Mariners Museum)

It has been observed that, as a result of the Civil War, passenger traffic on the Bay fell off heavily and that the various moves made by lines plying the Chesapeake were towards consolidation of freight business. Even though their boats were kept in condition and periodically overhauled, when passenger travel in the South revived, the Old Bay Line was still operating boats of *ante-bellum* construction. With the unfortunate loss of the *Louisiana* coming in 1874, the necessity of embarking on a thorough building program was obvious, despite the financial depression.

The *Florida*, the first of the new passenger steamers, was constructed by the Baltimore shipbuilding firm of William Skinner and Son. In size, she was approximately the same as the boat she was to replace and, being built of wood and equipped with the customary hog bracing, she closely resembled the *Louisiana* in outward appearance, as well. In these times, a good engine would often survive the wooden hull for which it had been built originally. One of the ships acquired by the Old Bay Line from the Powhatan Line was the *State Of Virginia,* constructed in 1849 for use on Lake Ontario as the *Northerner.* The old beam engine was apparently still in good condition, for when the *State Of Virginia* was scrapped in 1875, her machinery was put into the new boat.

Iron sidewheeler *Carolina,* 1877-1894. Sister ship of *Virginia,* built in 1879. After a contemporary oil painting formerly owned by President John R. Sherwood. (Courtesy of the late Watson E. Sherwood)

As it turned out, the "magnificent" *Florida* was to be the last wooden hull boat of the Line. She began service in the spring of 1876, arriving at Norfolk on her maiden voyage on May 2, in command of Captain Darius J. Hill, "one of the most popular gentlemen ever known to the traveling public."[70]

In the sumptuous quality of her interior fittings, the *Florida* was probably never equalled on the Chesapeake Bay and for a decade she floated nightly several thousand square inches of gold leaf through the waters of the States of Maryland and Virginia. Although fast, she was a crank boat and hard to steer and she vibrated so badly that some additional bracing had to be installed, the beams for which cut through several staterooms to the annoyance of those passengers who were later assigned to them.

The *Florida* came out at the time that the new People's Line was competing on the Norfolk run with the steamer *Sue* and the Old Bay Line was fortunate in having at this moment a brand new boat as an attraction for passenger travel. The *Louise* was the name of one of the other boats of the Baltimore, Chesapeake and Richmond Steamboat Company and she was used also for excursions out of Norfolk. An account of one of these, printed in 1877, shows that times have not much changed, for we learn that on this occasion, "the trip was greatly enjoyed, and the party returned— nearly all sober."[71]

The *Florida* was followed by the iron side-wheeler, *Carolina*, a Harlan and Hollingsworth product, launched in 1877. This new boat likewise made use of a second-hand engine, hers being salvaged from the wreck of the *Louisiana* three years previously. A sister ship, the *Virginia*, came two years later, having been built "upon the guarantee that she would outstrip the *Carolina* in a fair race upon the Bay."[72]

Iron sidewheeler *Virginia*, 1879, Last Old Bay Line paddle boat. Oil painting formerly owned by Chief Engineer T. J. Brownley. (Courtesy of his granddaughter)

Both *Carolina* and *Virginia* were a little smaller than the *Florida*, but being built of iron, they did not require a hog frame and the passenger accommodations and deck space were not cluttered as a result of it. Both boats regularly made eighteen miles an hour, described at the time as being "almost the speed of a railroad train." Although they still resorted to hand steering, an innovation of "necessary 'speaking pipes' from pilothouse to engine room" was included. Even though not originally built with electric lights, they had them installed during the first part of the 1880's and thus were equipped with electricity some half a dozen years before incandescent lights came to the White House.

With these three brand new boats in operation, the Line had no further need of the *George Leary* and the *Adelaide*. The former was sold in 1879 for use on the Potomac River, while the latter was taken over by Harlan and Hollingsworth in part payment for the new *Virginia*. The *Adelaide* appears as a Long Branch, New Jersey, steamer the next year when, on June 19, 1880, she was rammed and sunk in New York Harbor by the excursion boat, *Grand Republic*. Fortunately there were no casualties, but the summer of 1880 proved a disastrous one in the annals of New York shipping. The ghastly *Narragansett-Stonington* collision and fire claimed an appalling toll.

With the disagreements between the York River Line settled amicably and new boats in its fleet, the Old Bay Line settled down again to a prosperous period. On March 15, 1882, the company charter was further extended for a forty-year span. Although the work of the tramp freighter had waned, freight movements over the regular line were increasing and the line had plenty of work for the two cargo boats that it had retained in the windup of the "mosquito fleet." A stronger bond was being forged daily between the Bay Line and the Seaboard and Roanoke Railroad which delivered its freights from the South, and as early as 1868, it had been announced that both were operated under identical management. President Robinson served in the same capacity for both organizations, as have many succeeding presidents of the Line.

In this respect the Bay Line's position was further strengthened when, in 1889, an association of southern railroads was formed which later became the complex system of the present Seaboard Air Line. The roads which thus banded together were the Seaboard and Roanoke, Raleigh and Gaston, Raleigh and Augusta Air Line, and the Wilmington, Charlotte and Rutherford Railroad.

A memorable vessel was built for the company in the year 1887. This was the iron hull screw steamer, *Georgia*, the first boat to be assigned the same name as an earlier member of the Bay Line's fleet which, incidentally, had then totaled some thirty-seven steamers since 1840. The new *Georgia* was the largest boat that the company had owned up to this time, measuring 280 feet in length, and she was also the first screw-propelled passenger steamer. Other noteworthy items of her construction consisted of steam steering gear, steam-heated cabins, and electric lights throughout.

All the elegance of the "Elegant Eighties" went into this vessel's interior accommodations. Deep pile red carpets; gleaming brass spittoons; brass handrails, hardware, and grapevine chandeliers; heavy armchairs and ottomans covered in crimson mohair plush; cherry bedsteads with carved panels and ornamental tops; dressers surmounted by polished marble slabs; and mirrors in gilded frames. Present dictates of good taste would undoubtedly condemn the ornate *Georgia*, but for her era the lavishness of her appointments could not have been surpassed and her luxurious bridal suite was the talk of the town. The career of this proud steamboat was a long one. After serving the Bay Line faithfully for twenty years, and Long Island owners for twenty more, plus an interlude as a floating night club in New Haven, she was only at length brought back to her first home port to be scrapped.

With the new *Georgia* added to the Line, the cranky *Florida* was withdrawn and held as a spare boat. The company's advertisement, issued in 1887, stated that service with the new iron steamers, *Georgia*, *Virginia*, and *Carolina*, was unexcelled, the cuisine unequaled, and that the boats were equipped "with every appointment assuring Luxury, Comfort, and Reliability."[73]

Steamer *Georgia*, built 1887. First Old Bay Line screw passenger ship. (Photo courtesy of Elwin M. Eldredge)

The improvements brought to the service by the addition of the *Georgia* again gave the Line an unbalanced fleet. Accordingly, it was decided to build a similar running mate at an early opportunity. This plan was carried out in 1892 with the construction of the *Alabama* at the yard of the Maryland Steel Company. If the *Georgia* had been considered to epitomize the arts of the shipwright on the Chesapeake Bay, the new *Alabama* carried the standard to new heights. She was not only larger and faster but also had a steel hull, an improvement over iron construction. Propelled by a single screw, the *Alabama* was equipped with a four-cylinder triple-expansion engine of the same type and size as in the present Bay Liners. Her licensed capacity was 400 passengers and she had 110 staterooms "tastefully decorated in white and gold."

The *Alabama*, christened by Miss Champe Robinson, daughter of the Line's president, slid down the ways into the Patapsco on October 1, 1892. She made nineteen and one half miles an hour on

her trials early the next year and joined the line on April 17.
Samuel Ward Stanton, then editor of *Seaboard Magazine* (now *The
Nautical Gazette*) and an authority on American steamers of all
types, called her not only a "peerless addition to the Chesapeake
Bay fleet" but also the "finest passenger boat ever turned out for
service" on that body of water.[74]

The addition of the *Alabama* gave the company two fine new
screw steamers leaving the terminal ports of Baltimore and Nor-
folk nightly every day in the week except Sunday. The side-wheel
Virginia was retained as the extra boat of the Line and both the
Carolina and *Florida* were sold. The former was purchased by the
Richelieu and Ontario Navigation Company and operated on the
St. Lawrence River in Canada, first under her old name and later
as the *Murray Bay* and the *Cape Diamond* until 1932. The *Florida*,
cantankerous to the last, was sold to James H. Gregory, of New
York, for $3,500 to be broken up. On the way north, however, she
sank at the end of the towline off Atlantic City on the stormy afternoon of April 28, 1892, and even what little scrap value she had
was thus lost.[75]

Steamer *Alabama*, built 1893, from a Company advertising lithograph. It
is amusing to note that in order to make the boat seem larger, the people on
deck are drawn the size of dwarfs. A. Hoen & Co. Lithograph. (Courtesy of
The Mariners Museum)

The same year that the *Alabama* came out, the company ordered
a small steam tug, the *Elsie*, built in Baltimore for use in Baltimore
harbor in docking the passenger ships, moving barges, and other
work. This gave a total of six vessels owned by the line in 1893.

It is no discredit to the present management to point out that the
1890's, for the Bay Line as well as for other American steamboat

lines, undoubtedly witnessed its heyday. Florida was yet to be "discovered" and the hotels and resorts around Hampton Roads attracted scores of winter vacationists. Automobile travel had not been born and the proud steamboats of the era captured the cream of fashionable travelers. Naval architects had evolved splendid, safe and seaworthy vessels, sufficiently fast to satisfy a nation not yet too drunk with a mania for speed.

It was at this time that the Old Bay Line, long famous for its meals, was offering its celebrated $1.00 à la carte dinner. This feast began with Mobjack Bay oysters and included such delicacies of the season as diamondback terrapin, canvasback duck, quail, Norfolk spot, turkey, beefsteak, and all of the best of seafood and game which could be obtained in the epicurean paradise surrounding the waters of the Chesapeake. One old gentleman who had been traveling on the Old Bay Line since 1868 wrote that his favorite portion was a dish of oyster fritters cut into small pieces and fried in butter. "My, how good they did taste!" he concluded nostalgically. Even though the meals furnished on board Bay Line boats are good today, canvasback and terrapin have vanished from the scene forever.

The late Mr. Watson Sherwood, a son of a former general manager of the Line, was kind enough, in 1940, to furnish the following word-picture of early times as he remembered them:

In its heyday, about fifty years ago, the Old Bay Line was, if I recall correctly, the only quick connection between the North and the South. The traveler from New York was brought in to Baltimore by the Pennsylvania Railroad to a junction on the eastern outskirts of the city where his car was detached from the train and brought into the Bay Line wharf at Canton.

The purser whom I most clearly recall was Mr. Charles Spotswood of Norfolk, a typical Virginia Cavalier. When he sold a passenger his ticket and selected his stateroom it was like a court ceremony. Captain Bohannon of the *Alabama* was a magnificent figure of a man from Mathews County, Virginia, who always stationed himself in the social hall both to welcome his passengers coming aboard and, the next morning, to bid them goodbye.

The bartender on the *Alabama* was John Page Harris, dead these many years, but whose son, Willie Harris, is still a waiter on the *President Warfield*. I think that John Harris, a colored man, must have come from Ethiopian stock because he had the bearing and dignity of royalty.

In those days life was leisurely and we have lost forever a way of living and a mental attitude which the people of today will never know.

The serenity of this picture was shattered when, in 1896, the Southern Railway, which had by this time absorbed the management of the Baltimore, Chesapeake and Richmond Steamboat Company, transferred its terminal from West Point on the York River to Pinner's Point on the Elizabeth River, directly opposite Norfolk, in the outskirts of Portsmouth.

Claiming that the agreement with the Baltimore Steam Packet Company, by which they had abandoned their People's Line to Norfolk, had expired in 1881, the York River Line with the backing of the Southern Railway, diverted two of its passenger steamers, the *Charlotte* and the *Atlanta,* to the Baltimore-Norfolk run in direct opposition to the Old Bay Line. The latter naturally protested, claiming that at least a gentleman's agreement was still in force. The opening guns of a major rate war were thus sounded as competition waxed hotter at every contact.

One of the first of the Old Bay Line's countermoves was an attempt to re-enter the Richmond trade, on the theory that if their rivals had broken their part of the agreement, their own promises to keep off the York River territory were thereby made invalid. At the time, the *Georgia* and the *Alabama* were on the regular service and the side-wheel *Virginia* was being held as alternate boat for excursions and charters and to replace the regulars when they underwent periodic overhauls. Accordingly, the *Virginia* was immediately prepared to undertake direct service from Baltimore up the James to Richmond, thrice weekly. This all-water route would undoubtedly capture some of the York River Line's transshipped freight at West Point.

The first trip of the *Virginia* on the "New James River Route" of the Old Bay Line was scheduled to leave Baltimore on July 17, 1896, with arrival at Richmond after an eighteen-hour run. In flowery terms, company circulars advertised the scenic beauties of the mighty James and the close bonds of fellowship that would be cemented between Baltimore and the capital city of Virginia. These fooled nobody, however, and Richmond newspapers unabashedly announced that a "lively" rate war was promised.[76] This became a reality when the Bay Line announced that its fare would only be $2.00 one way between Baltimore and Richmond and $3.00 round trip. Meanwhile, of course, the York River Line was forced to follow suit, just as the Bay Line was compelled to meet the rate cut with the rival line on its regular Norfolk-Baltimore run.

Commanded by Captain William Porter and laden with notables, the *Virginia* left Baltimore on schedule and churned its paddles furiously in order to arrive within the allotted time. Richmond was pleased to welcome the new line and the *Virginia* was described in glowing terms as being a superior boat, very fast, with accommodations for three hundred passengers and safeguarded at night by a 10,000 candlepower searchlight.

She arrived safely on the morning of July 18, but was delayed slightly by grounding below Richmond. This omen presaged worse luck to come. The same afternoon, sometime after the speeches of welcome had been delivered by the reception committee, she left her dock for the return trip to Baltimore. Only a few miles down the James, she grounded again and then drove on a rock below Dutch Gap and stuck fast. It was obvious that she would not come off in a hurry this time and one can well imagine the chagrin of the officials as their first northbound load of passengers was returned to Richmond on board a tug.

The newspapers of July 21 announced that "the rate war goes merrily on, another fierce cut was made yesterday." Meanwhile, the *Virginia* still defied all efforts to dislodge her and the same article observed that she was "wedged in between two rocks that would not hold her better had they been made for the purpose."[77]

Having inaugurated the new line with such fanfare, it was imperative that an immediate successor be found for the *Virginia*. As their other passenger boats were fully occupied, the Old Bay Line was forced to look elsewhere for a suitable charter. They first obtained the old side-wheeler, *Enoch Pratt*, and she was immediately dispatched to Richmond, but arrived so hopelessly behind schedule that it was obvious she could not begin to fill the bill. The company next secured the screw steamer, *Tred Avon*, a somewhat larger and faster boat used on the Choptank River. But she took twenty-six hours to come down and this was eight hours over the schedule the Old Bay Line had hoped to maintain. Temporarily giving up the passenger business as a bad job, they put on their own freighter, the *Gaston*, to handle cargo only until such time as the *Virginia* could be restored to service.

In the meantime, the Merritt Wrecking Company succeeded in getting the *Virginia* off and she was immediately towed down the river to Newport News and put in the big dry dock operated by the new shipbuilding firm. The damage was considerable, but fortunately not serious. Forty feet of keel plates were torn off, leaving six ribs entirely exposed, but the watertight hull was still intact and unstrained. A repair crew was put on the job right away and the success of their efforts is evidenced by the following article that appeared in a trade journal shortly afterwards:[78]

The Newport News Shipbuilding and Dry Dock Company, as is well known, has one of the largest and most complete shipyards in this country. It is specially equipped for rapid repair work and demonstrated this fact recently when the steamer *Virginia*, of the Old Bay Line, was placed in its dock for repairs. The *Virginia's* bow was badly damaged by striking a rock in the James River. As soon as placed in the dry dock, a force of men was put to work on her, and operations were carried on night and day, electric lights being used after dark. As a result, she was completely repaired in a remarkably short time considering the extent of the damages, and again placed in commission as good as new. It is claimed that this is one of the quickest pieces of repair work which has ever been accomplished by any company in this country. In fact, the work was done sooner even than the superintendent of the shipyard estimated, by several days.

On July 31, having been off the line for only two weeks, the *Virginia* resumed her tri-weekly service on the James with tariffs reaching an all-time low, the fare between Richmond and Baltimore, normally costing about $8.00, being reduced to a single dollar. Meanwhile, on the regular run, the *Georgia* and *Alabama* continued to offer stiff opposition to the smaller Chesapeake Line boats, *Charlotte* and *Atlanta*, and for the third time since 1840, the names "Old Bay Line" and "New Bay Line" accompanied published advertisements.

At the time, it looked as if the Old Bay Line, despite its initial setback, would be permanently committed to the James River "new" line. Although navigation as far up as City Point was comparatively simple, above the confluence of the Appomattox and the James, the channel thence to Rocketts Landing below Richmond was so narrow and tortuous that a repetition of the *Virginia's* first misadventure seemed inevitable. Accordingly, the company contracted with Harlan & Hollingsworth, in 1897, for a new steel steamer, only 245 feet in length, and equipped with twin screws which would render her capable of maneuvering quickly in the narrow, curling waterway.

It was obvious this time that rivalry on the Chesapeake was there to stay and equally obvious, with tariffs cut to the bone, that neither organization could hope to keep solvent much longer. Recognizing this, the companies finally got together and agreements were reached whereby normal rates were restored. But the Chesapeake Steamship Company, which was reorganized from the Baltimore, Chesapeake and Richmond Steamboat Company in 1900, continued for forty years to maintain a service down the Chesapeake Bay which exactly paralleled that of the Old Bay Line, even though the latter gave up its James River service. The last Old Bay Line trip on the James took place on December 31, 1897, and three years later the old side-wheeler *Virginia* was sold. After passing through several hands, she joined her sister, the *Carolina*, in Canadian waters.

The new twin-screw steamer, named *Tennessee*, was completed after the Old Bay Line had come to an understanding with its rival and so was never given an opportunity to put to the test in the upper James the maneuvering ability for which she had been expressly designed. However, since she was so much smaller than the boats assigned to the regular run, when, in 1906, opportunity provided to dispose of her to advantage, she was quickly sold to the Long Island Sound Joy Line. In this service, she was described as "one of the best little sea boats Point Judith ever tackled."[79]

The *Tennessee* sported an elegant, golden eagle on top of her pilothouse and, as was customary in an age not completely given over to utilitarian considerations, her stem was decorated with gilded, carved arabesques, a survival of the day when sailing ships had their figureheads and trailboards. Her career was terminated in Boston Harbor on September 9, 1936, when, as an excursion steamer renamed *Romance,* she was rammed and sunk by the Eastern Steamship Line's *New York.*

The *Tennessee*, a twin screw vessel owned by Old Bay Line, 1898-1906. (Courtesy of Elwin M. Eldredge)

It was obvious to Bay Line officials that the activities of the Chesapeake Line would seriously diminish the volume of business which they had previously handled uncontested and that their fleet would have to be proportionately reduced. The first move after peace had been declared was to sell the iron freighter, *Seaboard,* then almost twenty-five years old. This venerable craft joined the fleet of the Hartford and New York Transportation Company and regularly carried freight and passengers from New York to Bridgeport, Connecticut, until 1930. For three years thereafter she lay in an abandoned slip until a new purchaser came along and rebuilt her as a coastwise tanker. Her original iron hull was covered with quarter-inch soft steel plates, arc-welded into place. A large percentage of frames and beams were renewed, but essentially she was still the same old boat. A steeple compound steam engine, that had replaced her original simple cylinder at some intermediate period of her career, was removed and a modern Worthington Diesel installed. In 1940, the *Seaboard* was owned and operated out of Providence, Rhode Island, and her sixty-six odd years' service then made her one of the oldest steamers afloat under American registry.

On the night of May 17, 1898, a fire of undetermined cause swept through and completely destroyed the Baltimore Steam Packet Company's establishment on Union Dock at the foot of Concord Street, Baltimore. The buildings were horseshoe-shaped with berthing facilities for several steamers. Sixteen hundred bales of cotton, over fifty hogsheads of tobacco, and other freights awaiting shipment were destroyed, as well as a large percentage of the early records of the Line. The schedule followed at that time called for departure from Union Dock at 6:30 P.M., southbound, with a brief call at Canton to pick up through passengers arriving by train. The incoming *Alabama* was diverted to dock the next morning at Pier No. 10, Light Street, and service went on from there, without interruption, for many years.

Shortly thereafter, the company permanently acquired the Light Street property with a 274-foot frontage and erected the buildings surmounted by the tower which became familiar to countless travelers. These quarters were badly damaged in the famous Baltimore Fire of February 7, 1904, and again by similar cause in 1911, but, on each occasion, the buildings were rebuilt to conform to their original design, a clock with four faces being added to the tower after 1911.

Prior to the fire of 1904, that destroyed an enormous section of downtown Baltimore, Light Street was narrow and crowded. When the company's new buildings were completed just before the turn of the century, an overpass was constructed, and it was stated that, "by means of this bridge, passengers are not compelled to cross the bed of Light Street, thereby avoiding the risk of being knocked down by the many teams that surge through the thoroughfare."[80]

Congestion had become a major problem and, when the waterfront properties were rebuilt in 1905, the city authorities wisely decided to widen Light Street by condemning real estate on the west side. In the process, the Old Bay Line's overpass was torn down, but though its life had been short, undoubtedly it had justified its existence and probably prevented numerous accidents.

Old Bay Line terminal, Pier 10 Light Street, Baltimore. From a photograph to widening of Light Street after 1904 fire. (Courtesy of

President Robinson's long term in office was terminated by his death in 1893. Richard Curzon Hoffman succeeded to this post and continued in command during the critical period of adjustment with the Southern Railroad and the Chesapeake Line until his resignation in 1899. John Skelton Williams was then elected president, holding office for five years. At the turn of the century, despite the permanent rivalry of the Chesapeake Line, the Old Bay Line was in good condition and was operating the passenger steamers *Alabama, Georgia,* and *Tennessee;* the freighter *Gaston;* and the tug *Elsie.* The new docks, warehouses, and offices were an enormous improvement over the old and the outlook for the new century was bright.

CHAPTER IX

The Dawn of Modern Times

S HORTLY after the advent of the twentieth century, the Seaboard Air Line Railroad acquired the entire capital stock of the Baltimore Steam Packet Company. Although the Bay Line preserved its individuality in operation and management, it thus became a unit in a large transportation system. A large number of American steamboat lines, operating coastwise and on sounds and inland waterways, were similarly secured by railroads. Although this was advantageous in a great many respects, later, in 1916, upon the passage of the Panama Canal Act, it could be instrumental in bringing real hardship to the boat lines for, under that law, rail-owned steamboats could not immediately vary their charges to meet outside competition, as could non-rail-owned lines. The Panama Canal Act further prohibited parallel rail and boat lines under the same ownership. The Interstate Commerce Commission did approve, however, rail-owned steamboat lines where there was no parallelism. This sanctioned the operation of both the Old Bay and Chesapeake Lines under railroad ownership.[81]

Since the Old Bay Line was a necessary northern link of the Seaboard system and there were no independent boat lines paralleling it, this trouble was not experienced and reciprocally profitable and pleasant relations existed between the Bay Line and the Seaboard Railroad.

The same railroad ownership applied to the Chesapeake Line, as later both the Southern and the Atlantic Coast Line held the capital stock in its corporation. This meant that, although competition between the Chesapeake and the Old Bay Lines was keen, particularly with respect to local passenger traffic, the competing railroad systems provided each of their lines with through freight.

With the transfer of its terminals from West Point to Portsmouth, the importance of the Chesapeake Line's York River service diminished in direct proportion to the increase in their Norfolk business. Their *Charlotte* and *Atlanta* had inaugurated the new line and, in 1900, they added a new steamer, the *Augusta*, to the Baltimore-Norfolk run. The *Augusta* was larger than their old boats and, being a "two-piper", she was a distinctive looking craft and well appointed inside. It is said that she introduced to the Chesapeake Bay brass double beds in the better cabins.

Although the Old Bay Line was operating larger boats, a brand new vessel was always a heavy drawing card with passengers and the *Augusta* proved a popular ship. The Old Bay Line's *Tennessee*, especially built for the James River, was their latest vessel but, being considerably smaller than the *Georgia* and *Alabama*, she was unsuited to a balanced fleet. In 1905, the company decided to build a new steamer somewhat larger than the *Alabama*. This vessel, their second to be named *Virginia*, was constructed by Harlan & Hollingsworth and carried the name of their iron side-wheeler sold in 1900. On completion, this 296-foot steamer joined the *Alabama* on the regular run, the *Georgia* became the spare boat, and the *Tennessee* was sold.

Freight was picking up and, since the Bay Line then had only one cargo boat, the *Gaston*, they chartered the *City Of Philadelphia* to help her out in 1904, and two years later built the *Raleigh*, a fine little modern steel freighter. Meanwhile, the Chesapeake Line decided that they could use a new boat and their new *Columbia*, coming out early in 1907, was a worthy rival of the *Virginia* to the title, "Queen of the Chesapeake."

The Jamestown Tercentennial Exposition, held during 1907 at specially prepared grounds near Seawell's Point, Norfolk, brought an unprecedented increase in passenger traffic to both lines. The old rivalry between them flared and manifested itself in numerous unofficial races between the *Virginia* and the *Columbia*. One of the more exciting of these took place on September 11, 1907. Though technically "unofficial," the outcome was anxiously awaited in both camps. Both ships were carrying full passenger lists of Exposition tourists. The *Columbia* got away from Baltimore first and maintained her lead almost to Old Point Comfort, when the *Virginia*, carrying less cargo, was able to take a short cut across the "Horse-shoe" Bar and arrived at Norfolk with a ten-minute lead over her rival. As the *Columbia* had actually left Baltimore ten minutes before the *Virginia*, this still left the winner open to question, and this point was heatedly argued on both sides.[82]

It is interesting to note that in the year of the Exposition, the Old Bay Line carried some 107,217 passengers, a staggering gain of over 48,000 previously transported. Further statistics are not without interest; in 1906, the steamers of the Bay Line traveled a total of 163,999 miles—a distance equal to approximately six and a half times around the world.

The new *Virginia* was followed in 1907 by a new *Florida,* built by the Maryland Steel Company, builders of the *Alabama.* She was completed too late to take part in the Jamestown Exposition traffic, but her speed of twenty-one miles an hour automatically gave her the title of "Queen of the Chesapeake" without the necessity of a race to prove it.[83]

The *Virginia,* built in 1905. (Photo from Robert T. Little Collection, courtesy The Mariners Museum)

Both the new *Florida* and *Virginia* had reciprocating steam plants similar to the *Alabama,* and although turbines were considered in the case of the *Florida,* it was decided to install the old type up-and-down engine so that the "black gangs" could be transferred from one ship to another without any lost motion because of lack of familiarity with the newer type. The new boats were beautifully finished in Elizabethan style. The main saloons and galleries were cream and gold with mahogany trimmings, while the dining rooms and social halls had quartered oak and interlocking rubber tiling floors.

The *Florida* was slightly larger than the *Virginia,* having 136 staterooms, as opposed to 110. In 1909, both *Alabama* and *Virginia* had additional after galleries added and their staterooms were increased to the same number as the *Florida.* In both cases this entailed extensive alterations and the hurricane decks were extended to the extreme stern. With these improvements made, for the first time in its career, the Old Bay Line had three up-to-date screw steamers which were, to all intents and purposes, identical in size, speed, and passenger and freight accommodation.

One additional feature of the *Florida* was the illumination of the main saloons by handsome domes piercing the gallery deck and glazed with cathedral glass. The company had every reason to be proud of its modern steamers and rightfully advertised them as the "finest and fastest south of New York." In 1912, President John R. Sherwood wrote to H. S. Meldrum, then chairman of the board, that "our steamer *Florida* is looking just beautiful!"

Steel screw steamer *Florida*, built by Maryland Steel Company in 1907. From a contemporary advertising lithograph by A. Hoen & Co., Baltimore. (Courtesy of Mariners Museum)

The same year these improvements were made in its fleet, the Old Bay Line sold the *Georgia*, since the two regular steamers with their one alternate were sufficient to handle the passenger service. The old *Georgia* had been very useful to the company as a day excursion steamer during the summer of the Jamestown Exposition and many old friends felt a sense of loss when she joined the *Tennessee* on Long Island Sound.

The year 1909 was another busy one for the Old Bay Line, a noteworthy drawing card being the arrival at Hampton Roads of the United States Fleet after its memorable round-the-world cruise. During the summer of this year, the Old Bay Line fitted out all three of its passenger steamers with "the Marconi Wireless." This was installed by the United Wireless Telegraph Company and made the boats the first to be so equipped on the Chesapeake Bay. A contemporary account stated that wireless communication between ship and shore would be highly favored by traveling business men, but that it would hardly prove popular with young couples attempting to elope secretly on the Old Bay Line.[84]

Although both the Old Bay and Chesapeake Lines had come to an agreement with respect to tariffs, competition held the rates to a minimum and the prices charged in 1909 were $3.00, one way from Baltimore to Norfolk, and $5.00, round trip. To Richmond, via Bay steamboats and boats of the Virginia Navigation Company operating on the James, tickets cost $3.50, and there was also a "second class" fare of $2.00 from Baltimore to Norfolk.

In 1907, John R. Sherwood, who had served almost forty years with the Line, was elected President and General Manager, breaking the precedent which had given the presidency of the Bay Line to the president of the Seaboard. "Captain" Sherwood was a popular choice for this post and, in his former capacity of vice-president in charge of operations, he had been largely responsible for the new steamers that had added to the popularity of the Line.

During the summer of 1910, due to the pressure of an extraordinary volume of perishable food movements, it was decided to schedule Sunday trips in addition to the weekday ones. The trucking business in season amounted to a large part of freight shipped via Old Bay Line and the scruples against "desecrating" the Sabbath, in vogue in 1840, found no place in these, the dawn of modern times. Both lines then regularly ran Sunday boats, although the service was suspended through the winter on the Old Bay Line until as late as 1931.

Having had ample opportunity to observe the efficiency in operating almost identical boats, the Chesapeake Line, under the presidency of Key Compton, former traffic manager of the Old Bay Line, decided to build two new steamers for the Norfolk run in 1911. Passenger traffic is a fickle miss to woo and the new boats of the rival line proved a big attraction. In the new *City of Baltimore* and *City Of Norfolk*, costing a total of well over a million and a half dollars, the Old Bay Line was faced with one of the most serious situations in its career. The Chesapeake Liners, one of which survived to join the Old Bay Line in 1941, were considerably larger and were one deck higher, too. This placed their pilothouses three decks above the main deck, on sound class steamers the one above the waterline.

A fire on their premises in Baltimore on February 2, 1911, forced the Old Bay Line to return to Union Dock while necessary repairs were being made to their new buildings. Fortunately, this fire was covered by adequate insurance.

Though temporarily outclassed by the taller Chesapeake Line steamers, during 1911 the Old Bay Line was given two opportunities to demonstrate that it could not be surpassed in seamanship. On the night of May 11, the watch on board the *Florida* observed a fire in the vicinity of Poplar Island. Several other steamers had seen the blaze but had gone their ways, judging it to be a brush fire ashore. Captain W. C. Almy, however, decided to investigate and, after steering four miles off course, he came upon four men clinging to a sea-swept raft while their schooner, the *Nellie Ruark*, blazed to her water line. A boat was lowered and the miserable survivors were brought aboard the *Florida*, "more dead than alive."

A similar rescue of five men from the waterlogged launch, *Smiles*, occurred on November 13, 1911. The men were waving a red lantern to signal their distress but were not observed until the *Florida* came along. A forty-five mile gale was blowing at the time and it proved a ticklish procedure to back the *Florida* around to make a lee so that a line could be sent to the launch to tow her alongside. In the process, the *Florida* got into shallow water and grounded, but came off without too much difficulty after the rescue had been effected.

Naturally, these events were given official recognition. President Sherwood concluded his annual report to the stockholders on March 31, 1912, with the statement that, "In both of these instances other vessels had passed them, which I think makes it more commendable to Captain Almy and his crew in keeping a sharp lookout."

Further recognition took place on August 5, 1912, when William B. Hurst, a director of the company, made a presentation of medals to Captain Almy; First Officer R. S. Foster; Second Officer George U. McGrath; Lookout Floyd Miles; Watchman E. Johnson; and Ernest Seldon and Albert White, waiter and deckhand.[85]

To balance the score, the *Virginia* performed her good deed and a resolution of thanks appears in the minutes of the company of December 18:

> . . . tendered to Captain W. G. Lane, his officers and others instrumental in prompt relief afforded the passengers of the steamer *Atlantic* of the Eastern Shore Development and Steamship Company on the morning of December 8, 1912, when sixteen passengers, three of whom were women, were taken from the disabled steamer which was lying near Bloody Point, and transferred to the steamer *Virginia* and brought to Baltimore.

Due to a succession of extremely severe winters, Old Bay Line mariners were given other opportunities to demonstrate their seamanship. In the winter of 1905, ice in the Bay caused the loss of ten round trips in the month of February, alone. Jagged floes were piled up like icebergs in the winter of 1909, causing the Bay to appear an unbroken ice field in some places. The noise of the steamers' steel hulls grinding laboriously through the ice was not conducive to the good night's sleep promised in advertising copy.

Probably due to excessive straining, the steering gear of the *Florida* ceased to function on one occasion, and she ran amok in the Elizabeth River until she could be gotten under control. These derelictions of duty were sufficiently rare, however, that they may be mentioned without embarrassment. Three years later, another slight mishap occurred when the *Florida* grounded while looking for a place to anchor in a snowstorm. At the time the ice in the Bay was five and six feet thick in some places.

Even though the Chesapeake Line was operating fine new boats, the Old Bay Line kept its three steamers in good condition and they were periodically overhauled and modernized. Jarman refrigeration plants were installed on the *Virginia* and *Florida* in 1912 and the number of lifeboats carried per steamer was increased from six to twelve. Passenger travel was light in 1912, probably due to the memorable *Titanic* disaster on April 14, an event which affected water lines all over the world. As a result, stiffer government inspection laws were passed, but it is worthy of mention that in increasing its safety appliances, the Old Bay Line acted long before laws were passed to make this obligatory.

Between the years 1910 and 1918, the company published a monthly periodical, entitled *The Old Bay Line Magazine*, edited by Alfred I. Hart, of Baltimore. Topical articles of all kinds were carried and there was a department entitled "Briny Breezes" in which stock jokes of the day were printed. Some of these jocose items were pretty sad, it is true, but the little magazine was a pleasant one and furnished passengers some free entertainment. It was a good advertisement for the Line, too, even though it did print such obvious extravagances as "the menu has defied the criticism of the most fastidious epicureans."[86]

The volume of business enjoyed by American transportation lines doubled as a result of war in Europe and, when the United States joined the Allies later, the Old Bay Line ships ran capacity loads of passengers and freight. Of the four wars in which this country had been engaged since the Old Bay Line began, two of them, the Mexican in 1846 and the Spanish in 1898, had little effect on the operations of the Bay Line. However, like the Civil War, World War I, though far removed from the Chesapeake Bay, made a decided mark on the management of the Line. The port of Hampton Roads, always an important entrepot of trade, increased its activities enormously as whole communities mushroomed into being on its shores. Despite an exceptionally bad winter in 1917, when the Bay was frozen solid for six weeks, the Old Bay Line transported 107,664 people during the year. A large proportion of the passengers were servicemen.

As a war measure, on January 1, 1918, the United States Government took over the management of all American railroad and steamboat lines and, for convenience in operation, the Federal transportation authorities decided to combine the New and the Old Bay Lines. Under the consolidation, Key Compton, president of the Chesapeake Line, was appointed Federal Director, President Sherwood, in his fiftieth year of service with the Old Bay Line, having declined this appointment in favor of a younger man. "Captain" Sherwood resigned on October 23, and although S. Davies Warfield was elected president, he did not exercise that office until the war was over and the government returned the railroads and ship lines to their owners.

It will be recalled that the menace of German submarines caused inhabitants of the Atlantic seaboard to develop a good case of jitters. The War Department was especially concerned with the numerous strategic points of military and naval significance surrounding the Hampton Roads area. In March, 1918, a submarine net was strung between Forts Monroe and Wool to block the chance entrance into the Roads of an enemy undersea boat. A second net was placed off Thimble Shoal a few months later. These were opened only for brief periods during the day to let ships in and out. Naturally, the Bay steamers' schedules had to be adjusted so that their movements would conform. The majority of Chesapeake mariners felt that the nets served only as an unmitigated nuisance and that their defense value was nil. Fortunately, this was never put to the test.

It is no secret that all American transportation systems suffered tremendous depreciation under Federal operation. The scrub brush was used sparingly on the Old Bay Line's steamers and they were never painted.

During this demoralized period, disaster came to one of the steamers that the Government was operating. On the night of May 24, 1919, the *Virginia* caught fire and was a total loss. The ship was crowded with passengers bound for Newport News to welcome returning troop transports from overseas. Many of them did not even have time to grab their clothes before abandoning the steamer. The *Florida, City Of Norfolk,* and *City Of Annapolis* hastened to the scene of the accident and picked up the survivors. Of the disaster, Mr. Compton the Federal Director, said: "Too much praise cannot be given Captain Walter G. Lane of the *Virginia*. He stayed by his ship till every soul was off despite the fact that his hands were burned and he was suffering great pain."[87]

Although the skipper was in no way personally responsible for the unfortunate event and had handled the situation with rare judgment and skill, it is said that Captain Lane never completely recovered from the disaster and retired from the sea the following year, a disheartened man.

Though the National Railroad Administration was in charge, the Old Bay Line inherited a black eye from this occurrence. It is true that the same Bay Line officers commanded the ships for the Federal Authorities, but the war period was characterized by labor troubles all over the country and it was impossible to maintain the willing and well-disciplined crews for which the Chesapeake had long been famous.

It was some time after the Armistice before the government returned their property to the railroads and not until March 1, 1920, did the occupation officially terminate and the Old Bay Line resume its own management.

CHAPTER X

The Bay Line's History
Between World Wars

THERE is consolation in numbers and the Old Bay Line was not alone in facing critical times at the end of World War I. Not only was its equipment almost hopelessly out of condition, but the general nationwide slump was not conducive to an immediate rehabilitation of the shipping business. Having been spared the loss of one of its most important units, the Chesapeake Line was in far better condition, even though its status, too, was far from enviable. In 1920, the Old Bay Line's fleet numbered the following venerable craft: passenger steamers *Alabama*, twenty-seven years old, and *Florida*, thirteen years old; freighters *Gaston*, thirty-nine years old, and *Raleigh*, fourteen years old; and the tug *Elsie*, twenty-seven years old.

In the operation of daily overnight service, the ownership of at least three passenger steamers is to be desired, for a third vessel is needed to replace the regulars on the line, in case of accident or periodic overhaul. The Old Bay Line not only lacked that necessary third vessel, but the condition of the *Alabama* was critical since she required immediate boiler replacement. Suitable vessels to fill in an established service are not located easily and the Old Bay Line had to make out as best it could through the winter of 1920-1921 with the *Benjamin B. Odell*, chartered from the Central Hudson Steamboat Company. Had it been a heavy winter, the *Odell* could not have been used at all for she was of the excursion boat type, suitable only for her designed service—operating on the Hudson River in the summertime.

A further review of equipment determined the sale in October, 1920, of their old freighter *Gaston* to the Gulfport (Mississippi) Fruit and Steamship Company. The *Gaston* needed considerable repairs and, since their other cargo boat, the *Raleigh*, seemed sufficient for handling the limited amount of freight, the move was a logical one. The *Gaston* served various owners in the Gulf of Mexico area until dropped from the Register in 1935 in her fifty-fourth year.

In order to recapture former high standards of service and efficiency in its passenger department, the Old Bay Line appointed a "Director of Service" on January 1, 1921. The announcement of this appointment frankly stated that, due to the "demoralization of service incident to Federal Control . . . the accommodations offered to the traveling public on Bay steamers became unattractive and untrustworthy."[88]

The biggest move was still to come, however. In 1922, President Warfield announced an extensive rejuvenation program for both the Seaboard Railroad and the Old Bay Line. To effect this replacement, a new corporation, the Seaboard-Bay Line Company, was organized *pro tem* to enable procurement of rolling stock for the railway and new vessels for the Line. The outlook was considerably brightened when the means for acquiring modern ships was in sight. This was coupled with a further extension of the Baltimore Steam Packet Company's 1840 charter by the Maryland General Assembly, giving the right of perpetual succession.

During this period, contracts were awarded to the Pusey and Jones Corporation, of Wilmington, Delaware, for the construction of two identical ships, the *State Of Maryland* and the *State Of Virginia*. Like the Chesapeake Line boats of 1911, these Old Bay liners would have three passenger decks but would be considerably larger, designed to carry seven hundred tons of freight and a maximum of six hundred passengers. It may be recalled that when the Line began in 1840, its little *Jewess* could carry only seventy-five passengers "comfortably" and that the side-wheel *Virginia*, coming out in 1879, had room for three hundred.

In the new steamers, dining rooms seating one hundred people were transferred from the hold to the after end of the main deck where passengers were afforded a fine view of Chesapeake Bay while dining. The saloons were fitted out in Colonial style and gave a cool and comfortable appearance. Glass-enclosed music rooms were on the gallery decks.

It is significant to note that in size and power, the engines of the new boats, although of improved balance, duplicated the machinery installed thirty years previously in the *Alabama*. This may seem strange, but a review of the history of the steamboat on the Chesapeake Bay reveals that the need for increased speed disappeared when the successors of the little *Virginia*, which took 24 hours to make the trip in 1819, had perfected their machinery to the point where the time was cut in half. The evening meal was a great attraction on the Old Bay Line and this would be lost if departures were postponed until late at night. To apply a reduction on the other end would be equally profitless, for to arrive in the very early morning hours would be of no conceivable advantage since the debarkation of freight and passengers would have to wait for daylight, anyway. Although capable of covering the run in considerably less time, the Old Bay Line continued to operate on a twelve-hour schedule. Reserves of speed would be of use only in case of delays before starting or en route, and a further reserve would be unnecessary and expensive.

The *State of Maryland* on trial trip, December 1922. (Photo courtesy of the Pusey & Jones Corp.)

The keel of the first of the new steamers, the *State Of Maryland*, was laid on March 4, 1922, and she was launched with appropriate ceremonies on July 25, making her maiden voyage to Norfolk on January 8, 1923, commanded by Captain W. C. Almy and with J. L. Marshall as first mate. The *State Of Virginia* followed closely, being launched on September 6, 1922. She joined the Line under the command of Captain R. S. Foster in February of the next year, less than a month after the *State Of Maryland* began service.

As on previous occasions, when new ships were put in commission, the Old Bay Line disposed of its old ones. The 1893-*Alabama*, although considerably older than the *Florida*, was retained as the spare boat of the Line and the latter was sold in January, 1924, to the Monticello Steamship Company. This organization operated a line of boats on San Francisco Bay.

The *Florida* was boxed in and prepared for the long voyage to the West Coast via the Panama Canal under her own steam. Renamed *Calistoga,* she entered service on October 11, 1924, and subsequently had her bow squared off with a ramp so that she could load automobiles fore and aft like a double-ended ferry. Later on, a merger of the various San Francisco Bay ferry lines took place and the *Calistoga* was acquired by the Southern Pacific Golden Gate Ferries, Limited, and operated until the new San Francisco Bay bridges put her out of business. Recalled from idleness, she was commissioned in the United States Navy in World War II and was stationed at Mare Island. The scrap heap claimed her in 1948.[89]

The *State of Virginia.* Delivered to the Old Bay Line, February 1923. (Photo by John L. Lochhead)

The same month the *Florida* was sold, a purchaser for the *Raleigh* appeared. With the enormous increase in freight space afforded by the new steamers, the Old Bay Line, for the first time in many years, had no need of vessels designed to handle cargo only and the *Raleigh* was sold to the Saginaw and Bay City (Michigan) Steamship Company and taken to the Great Lakes. She came back to the Atlantic Seaboard in 1929 as the *Marion,* owned by the Colonial Navigation Company, operating on Long Island Sound. In 1938, she was acquired by Philippine interests and taken out across the Pacific, but returned to Panamanian Registry before World War II.

Other changes in the fleet occurred with the exchange of the tug *Elsie* for an older but better conditioned vessel, the iron-hull *Mary O'Riorden*, that had been built in Buffalo during the Civil War. Despite her age, the new tug was larger and more powerful than the *Elsie*. The Bay Line did not keep her long, however, deciding in 1927 to give up the ownership of tugs entirely and to charter them when needed. The Diesel tug *Hustler*, of the H. T. Corporation, was one vessel so used for undocking the steamers at Baltimore, shunting barges, and performing other duties before World War II.

The *President Warfield*, built in 1928, shown at her Norfolk pier in 1939. (Courtesy of the late P. S. Gornto)

When the new steamers had been conceived, it was decided to build three of them to identical plans. On August 22, 1927, the third contract was awarded to the Pusey and Jones Corporation and the new vessel, tentatively named the *Florida*, began to take form. Less than two months later, President S. Davies Warfield died. Since he had worked diligently and successfully to put the Old Bay Line back on its feet after the war, it was decided to name the new boat *President Warfield* in his memory.

Legh R. Powell, Jr. succeeded to the presidency of the Bay Line and Seaboard Railway and wisely guided the policies of the Line from 1927 to 1941.

Although identical in plan to her sister ships, the *President Warfield*, flagship of the Line, was given a few minor alterations and additions suggested in the operation of the other steamers. For this reason, her gross tonnage was computed at 1,814 tons, as opposed to 1,783 for the two other boats. All three were built of steel, the shell plating carried up one deck higher than the main deck. This made the ships stronger than other steamers in operation on the Chesapeake. Although all three were originally coal burners, the *President Warfield* and *State Of Maryland* were converted to the use of oil fuel in 1933, when Todd oil burners were installed by the Maryland Dry Dock Company. The *State Of Virginia* received a similar installation in 1939.

The addition of the *President Warfield* to the Line marked the termination of the *Alabama's* useful thirty-five-year career on the Chesapeake. Like the *Florida*, the *Alabama* found a purchaser on the West Coast and, in the summer of 1928, she made the long trip out via the Panama Canal. On arrival, she was converted to a car ferry by her new owners, the Progress Improvement Company, of Seattle, Washington. As the *City Of Victoria*, she operated between Everett, Washington, and Victoria, British Columbia, and in 1939, was purchased by the Puget Sound Bridge and Dredging Company, contractor for Alaska's $3,000,000 naval air base construction. Her new owners towed her to Sitka, where she was used as a floating hotel to house construction workers. During World War II, she was taken into the United States Navy as U.S.S. *YHB–24*. In naval abbreviation, *YHB* stands for Yard House Boat. Returning from this barracks-ship duty, the old *Alabama* was towed back and put in mothballs in Puget Sound. In the summer of 1948, she was purchased by the Victoria Salvage Company and was burned on the beach near Everett, Washington, for her metal.[90]

In 1928, Captain Almy was given command of the *President Warfield*, Captain Foster took over the *State Of Maryland*, and the *State Of Virginia* became the spare boat of the Line. Alternating, the *Virginia* and the *Warfield* were chartered for the summers of 1929, 1930 and 1931 and ran on Long Island Sound with the Colonial Line and the Eastern Steamship Company's Boston to New York service. Later, however, it was decided to keep all three boats in the Chesapeake, since the spare vessel could earn its keep by running local excursions.

On August 3, 1932, the *State Of Maryland* ran down and sank the watermelon schooner *Milton S. Lankford* off the mouth of the Potomac River. Since the schooner apparently was carrying no lights visible to the steamer, the accident seems unavoidable. Another collision occurred on July 14, 1936, when, for no accountable reason, the steamer *Golden Harvest* rammed the *State Of Virginia* as the latter was returning from an excursion with Governor Harry W. Nice and 263 passengers aboard. Although shipyard workers had to use acetylene torches to burn off the bow of the *Golden Harvest* to separate the vessels, no one was injured in the mishap and the *State Of Virginia* was easily repaired.

In addition to the many troubles inherited by the Old Bay Line from the National Railroad Administration, Prohibition presented additional ones. No longer were appetites of Bay Line passengers whetted by tall mint juleps and what meal is not improved by a gentle libation beforehand! More serious, however, was the smuggling and transportation of liquor on Old Bay Line steamers. Although the company made every effort to comply with the unpopular law, occasional bootleg shipments secreted on board from foreign ships at Hampton Roads made up Old Bay Line cargoes not appearing on the manifests.

Since the company diligently cooperated with the United States Coast Guard in endeavoring to prevent liquor from getting on board, Bay Line officials were highly incensed when a Coast Guard cutter, suspecting a bootleg shipment, fired a shot across the *President Warfield's* bow one March night in 1929 and ordered her to heave-to for examination. President Powell justly expressed his indignation and Coast Guard officials were not in sympathy with the action of the commanding officer of this particular cutter. Captain P. H. Scott, USCG, commandant of the Norfolk Coast Guard base, stated that it was "unthinkable that a passenger steamer should be stopped . . . as if she were trying to escape,"[91] and criticized his subordinate for not postponing examination until the steamer docked. However, it was no wild goose chase, for an automobile well loaded with whisky was making the trip. Not a soul on board stepped forward to claim ownership of the car the next morning when the steamer docked.[92] Although the Bay Line's years had spanned four wars, this marked the first occasion when one of their ships was fired upon.

The winter of 1934 was a repetition of the severe ice conditions of 1917 and both Bay lines were forced to suspend service occasionally. The Chesapeake Line's *City Of Norfolk* was forced to go in dry dock at Newport News to secure shell plates damaged by ice floes. The previous August, both lines experienced varying amounts of damage when a hurricane struck the Chesapeake area. The *State Of Maryland* managed to come through with the loss of only a few lifeboat covers and some broken crockery. The storm was so unusual, however, that it is recounted in more detail in Chapter XI.

During the summer of 1935, the *State Of Virginia* was again chartered to the Colonial Navigation Company, but the following year, the management decided to employ her regularly during the warm months in "houseboat" cruises. In this capacity, she operated from Baltimore to Ocean View, a popular Virginia bayside resort, and to Yorktown, to afford passengers an opportunity to visit Colonial Williamsburg, Jamestown, The Mariners Museum, and other Peninsula attractions. Numerous American ship lines used their vessels for cruises when occasion offered and the Old Bay Line found its new venture well patronized. The schedule of these cruises called for sailings of the *State Of Virginia* from Baltimore on Friday evenings, arriving off Ocean View the next morning, where she remained at anchor for a day and a night. Passengers, meanwhile, used the steamer as their hotel. A 25-foot launch, the *Marguerite*, was acquired in May, 1936, to be used as a ship-to-shore tender.

A year-round business developed by the Line after World War II consisted in attracting Florida-bound motorists and others to use the steamers instead of hotels. Their driving time was shortened by the elimination of 230 miles of crowded roads and they were placed in the heart of Virginia's many historic shrines. When automobiles first began to be considered as competition to the steamboat, lines all over the country were scornful and attempted to ignore them. Motorists were not wanted. They had to pay heavy freight charges and were subjected to annoyances imposed by underwriters, such as draining gasoline from the tanks and seldom returning it.[93] The 1929 depression and resultant unfilled cargo space brought shipowners to their senses and, realizing the automobile tourist was here to stay, they endeavored to do all that was possible to attract his patronage. The Old Bay Line was a pioneer in recognizing this trend and they have been successful in luring the motorist off the road and giving him a good night's sleep on board a Bay Line steamer.

Another vessel was added to the Line in 1936 when the company acquired the *Alcyone,* once an elegant Lawley-built auxiliary steam yacht, since converted to a cargo boat. The *Alcyone* was purchased at rock bottom price and after spending some money in fixing her up, the Old Bay Line had at its disposal a substantial Diesel-electric freighter available for charter or to use in transporting special freight shipments. She was so used until sold in 1941.

In order to present a comparison in prices, it is interesting to observe that a steel barge built for the Company by the Old Dominion Railroad Corporation in 1936 cost $8,000, precisely the same cost of their passenger steamer *Pocahontas* in 1840. The length of the contract covering the construction of this barge is further evidence of how life has become increasingly complicated during the past century, for a memorandum scratched on the back of an envelope would have sufficed for a fleet of barges in 1840.

The period spanned by this chapter saw the termination of two famous old steamboat lines, brought about by a variety of economic causes happily not affecting the Old Bay Line. In 1932, the Champlain Transportation Company, then the oldest steamboat line in the world, abandoned its night-boat service running the length of

Lake Champlain, and a ferryboat concern operating a summer ten-mile automobile ferry across the lake acquired the property in 1937. With more nostalgia than accuracy, the ferry advertised itself as the oldest steamboat line in the country but, as the Champlain Transportation Company's name was no longer included in current issues of the *Official Guide of the Railways and Steam Navigation Lines of the United States,* it is an unfortunate but accepted fact that its end had come.

Only seven years younger than the Old Bay Line, the famous Fall River Line wound up its affairs on July 27, 1937, in its ninety-first year, and the big side-wheelers *Priscilla, Commonwealth, Plymouth,* and *Providence* were converted to scrap shortly thereafter. The Fall River Line might have survived as an independent organization, but in the attempt to get the New York, New Haven, and Hartford Railroad back on its feet, the famous old line received shock after shock until a sit-down strike proved more than it could carry and its doom was sealed.

However, the Old Bay Line, well grounded from the first, had survived previous depressions and began its second century of operation under optimistic auspices in 1940. Its fleet of steamers had been kept in good shape and was constantly modernized by the addition of the latest improvements affecting comfort and seaworthiness. In 1938, Grinnell sprinkler systems were installed throughout and, during the summer of 1939, the steamers were given radio direction-finders and ship-to-shore radio telephones, again scoring a first for steamboat lines on the Chesapeake Bay. All three boats carried a social directress and passengers enjoyed the usual deck sports. In its centennial year, Captain R. S. Foster was master of the *President Warfield* and Captain J. L. Marshall of the *State Of Maryland.* Captain P. L. Parker commanded the *State Of Virginia* on excursions and Captain J. W. Gresham, the *Alcyone.* The Diesel tug *Hustler* was chartered at Baltimore and large fleets of covered barges owned by the company were located at both terminal ports.

CHAPTER XI

Storm on the Bay

IMPASSIONED writers describing the great Bay of the Chesapeake dwell at length on its calm, pellucid waters and its balmy, sun-drenched shores. Although the Chesapeake has a fair share of clement weather, when howling winter Nor' easters sweep down the Bay and growling ice-packs choke its rivers, it is decidedly more comfortable in a chair by the fire at home than in the pilot-house of a steamer feeling her way cautiously through the murk.

Two steamers of the Old Bay Line nightly leave their terminal ports of Baltimore and Norfolk in fair weather or foul. Their captains learn to expect fogs and snow squalls in winter. Increased vigilance is necessary, but Chesapeake shipmasters seldom fail to make scheduled time. Today radar probes into the unknown and lays a safe course.

Not all bad weather is reserved for winter, though. Tropical hurricanes are dreaded by mariners. These violent disturbances that skirt our southern seaboard states usually swing out offshore below Cape Hatteras, following the path of the Gulf Stream to dissipate themselves in mid-Atlantic. Occasionally they do not, however, and New England will long remember what happened in 1938 when one of these freak West India hurricanes played havoc along its shores. Fortunately, this storm passed by the Chesapeake area, but in 1933, the Bay had not been so fortunate. Old residents called that "August storm" the worst that ever wracked its normally hospitable coast.

As is well known, the general form of a hurricane is circular with winds sweeping around and converging on a calm spot of abnormally low pressure in the very center, or axis, of the storm—like a giant whirlpool of air. In the West Indies variety, this center itself is in motion traveling northward in a great arc at a relatively slow speed. Not so the raging blasts which surround it: meteorologists have measured speeds well over a hundred and fifty miles an

97

hour. Since the winds are circling the center low pressure area that
is in motion itself, both the direction of the wind and its force will
vary in relation to one's position to the storm track. In the regions
frequented by hurricanes, it is possible for the experienced mariner
to plot in advance the path the storm will take and, if he is offshore
with plenty of sea-room, he may be able to get out of its track entirely. It is the center of a hurricane that is most dreaded.

It was dark and blustery on the evening of August 22, 1933, when
the *State Of Maryland*, Captain John L. Marshall commanding,
sailed from Baltimore for the southbound trip to Norfolk. Northeast storm warnings were flying at the staff surmounting the
American Building. Earlier Weather Bureau reports had, of
course, noted that a hurricane was sweeping up the coast, but since
its normal path would take it out to sea, Baltimore shipping went
about its usual business considering a stiff Nor' easter the normal
corollary to disturbed conditions offshore. Promptly at six-thirty
the *State Of Maryland's* deep-throated steam whistle blared, the
tug came alongside, stretched taut the steamer's stern line and, as
she backed out of her slip, helped to swing her around in the narrow
basin. Under way and gingerly steaming along the lane of flashing
buoys that marked the channel, the *State Of Maryland* headed down
the Patapsco for the open Bay. Twilight was short, and with the
gusty wind striking the ship on her port quarter, she leaned
slightly as she encountered choppier water where the river widened
near its mouth. At a comfortably safe distance behind, gleaming
running lights marked the position of the Chesapeake Line steamer
City Of Norfolk, Captain Edward James, also Norfolk-bound and
following the same course down the Bay.

Despite the rolling of the *State Of Maryland* and the blustery
wind on deck, it was comfortable and cozy in the Old Bay liner's
saloon, and after dinner, her passengers went about the usual
business of amusing themselves until bedtime. Horse racing and
other games claimed their devotees in the palm room on the galley
deck; some passengers read, wrote, or chatted in the saloon; still
others, ensconced in the comfortable leather chairs in the social
hall below on the main deck aft, sipped their tall glasses and argued
on the evils of prohibition. Watchmen made their ceaseless rounds;
stewards and pantrymen put away the dishes and straightened the
dining saloon against the morrow's breakfast; down below engineers and watertenders hovered over their pulsing machines; and
in the pilothouse the second mate on watch peered intently out
through the "middle window" and gave muted instructions to his
quartermaster. The lookout, collar turned up, had wedged himself
by the rail at the bow and occasionally ducked to dodge a dose of
spray sweeping across the foredeck. Four bells rang, ten P. M.,
twenty-two-hundred Navy time. All snug and running smoothly,

the ship settled down to her normal nightly routine as Captain
Marshall, having taken his customary last look around, closed the
door between his quarters and the pilothouse and turned in. Fate
had decreed that his night's rest would not be an unbroken one.

Rudely awakened from a sound sleep, he was almost thrown
from his bunk by a violent lurch. Jumping out and quickly dressing,
he glanced at the clock screwed to the bulkhead above his desk. Two
A. M. In another moment, he was in the pilothouse. Conditions
had radically changed.

Four hours ago, the barometer had been normal; now the pointer
was dropping rapidly, as wind and sea increased. The wind was
blowing gale force from the northeast. The steamer's stern would
rise to waves dashing up behind as the bow buried itself deep into
the smother while the ship seemed to gather herself together for a
yawing rush down the wind. Rolling and careening, she plowed on
into the night.

Anxiety could be read in every face in that darkened pilothouse.
What was the best course to follow? The safety of a hundred people
lay in the judgment of the *Maryland's* captain. Even though the
ship was laboring, rolling her guards well under in the troughs of
those sickly seas, she must and would keep on. Intermediate ports
of refuge could not be considered. To attempt to bring the ship into
a river for shelter would be inviting disaster, for the wind had
swung more to the eastward and the only possible havens lay along
a dreaded lee shore.

On such a night as this, the shipmaster has to face his fate alone.
On the following *City Of Norfolk,* an experienced captain doubted
that his ship could survive in such raging seas. He had kept her up
to the eastward hoping to break the force of the swell by getting a
lee under Maryland's Eastern Shore. Edging her in towards Poco-
moke Sound closer than he dared, the Chesapeake Line ship ran
hard aground near Watts Island. Providentially, she held together
and abandonment was unnecessary. It was some time before her
people could be gotten off and taken ashore. Despite the fact that
the ship remained aground for several days, she suffered only minor
damage and no one was hurt.

Meanwhile, the strongly built *State Of Maryland* was holding her
course. Lighthouses and buoys which normally would have guided
her were obscured in the raging night. Taking into consideration
the drift caused by that terrific wind, her captain unerringly held
her on her course by dead-reckoning, guided by that uncanny sixth
sense which is the seaman's heritage. It was too hazardous to
attempt to turn the ship around and heave to. Her salvation depended upon her being able to withstand the punishment of driving
on southward, and reaching port before the storm center engulfed

her. To delay would prolong the danger and the agony of suspense. With confidence in his ship and crew, the captain kept her throbbing engine full ahead and slowed down only in the blinding squalls.

Torrents of rain drove against the pilothouse windows, blocking vision. At times, even the flagstaff on the bow momentarily disappeared from view. Sea and sky were fused into one aqueous element that relentlessly tore at the ship, bent on her destruction. The noise of screaming wind and smashing wave was deafening. Sailors detailed to put extra lashings to secure objects on deck had their breaths beaten back when they faced the blast and, cupping their mouths and shouting, they could not be heard by their companions only a few feet away.

Below was a shambles; freight loose in the hold, crockery smashed, chairs and tables overturned and sliding around the cabins. Understandably, few passengers elected to remain in their bunks and a solemn and dejected group assembled in the saloon as the steamer cavorted, groaned and twisted beneath them. No complaints were voiced, however, for all felt that the ship was fighting a gallant fight and her company doing their best to aid her.

On she lunged through the darkness. By now the wind had increased from a roar to a shriek. Lifeboat covers were ripped off and sent scudding down to leeward. Guy wires supporting the tall funnel sang like tightened bowstrings. Ropes beat a continuous tattoo against their staffs while the short steep seas crashed and raged all around. Convulsive shivers ran through the ship as unrelenting waves smashed into her stern. She could take this punishment for a while, but what if it got worse?

Meanwhile, the barometer continued its headlong descent. Squalls of hurricane force followed each other without break. The watch in the pilothouse peered intently forward for some landmark to guide them. A momentary lull and a beacon loomed up to starboard. It was comforting to know that she was still on course. Dawn came gradually, while black night thinned out to gray morning. Thimble Shoals lay to leeward and it would not be long before the ship could turn westward towards the mouth of Hampton Roads. A lee would be found under Old Point Comfort and the captain decided to try to make the dock. Fate decreed otherwise. As the *State Of Maryland* tried to swing around, the wind caught her broadside and all the power of the engines and her rudder was not sufficient to drive her into the wind. Back she swung, bound for the Elizabeth River and a haven at last. Waves were breaking clean across the Old Point wharf.

Hearts were lighter with the goal in sight and, though the wind still raged with unabated fury, the seas were lower in the more protected water. The steamer's passengers could see the remains of small craft thrown up on land and smashed to matchwood. Trees uprooted, houses blown down, all gave mute evidence of what the night had experienced. Lambert's Point was left astern, then Pinner's Point and presently the pier itself loomed up through the flying scud.

It took almost an hour for Captain Marshall to bring the *State Of Maryland* alongside. The wharf was flooded and only the tops of the bollards were visible. Rowboats ferried ashore those passengers who had to leave immediately, but, with the lower part of Norfolk inundated, many preferred the safe haven of the vessel.

Their thankfulness took form in a resolution of gratitude to the ship and her master. It was just luck, he said, but those who know the Chesapeake and her mariners realize that to come out on top, luck must be combined with the years of training and skill that go to make up the seaman's arts.

CHAPTER XII

The Impact of World War II

A HIGH point in the long career of the Old Bay Line was reached in 1940. During this hundredth anniversary year, not only was business generally good all around, but the company's facilities were in excellent condition to handle it and morale was high. With the blessing of the Interstate Commerce Commission, negotiations were under way to double the size of the fleet by consolidating the two lines that had been rivals so long—and not always friendly ones at that—in the Norfolk-Baltimore carrying trade. Since both were owned one hundred per cent by sprawling railroad systems, the Old Bay Line by the Seaboard and the Chesapeake Line jointly by the Atlantic Coast Line and the Southern Railway, the contemplated merger proved an involved transaction which required considerable time to consummate. It was not until June 20, 1941, that all was signed and sealed and the Old Bay Line once more found itself in undisputed sway on the Chesapeake. After the consolidation, the Line was owned one-half by the Seaboard Air Line Railroad, one-third by the Southern Railway, and one-sixth by the Atlantic Coast Line.

The logic behind the move, of course, was obvious. Except during peak seasons, one line could handle passengers and freight adequately and, during the depths of the 1929 depression, it was ridiculous for two half-empty steamers to attempt to maintain parallel services successfully.

The question logically arises as to why in the merger the Old Bay Line took over the Chesapeake Line and not vice versa. Certainly there were reasons beyond the fact that the older company was in sounder financial shape at the time and owned more up-to-date vessels. Possibly these other reasons, intangible in themselves, may best be summed up in the vision and foresight of those pioneers who, a hundred years earlier, had determined to give the public a transportation system of the best possible quality—a tradition which continues to be faithfully upheld by their successors.

Meanwhile, plans were made to celebrate the centennial of the Baltimore Steam Packet Company appropriately. The climax occurred on May 23, 1940. This was a day of well-photographed fun and merry-making with costumed actors and actresses portraying their bewhiskered and hoop-skirted ancestors of 1840, riding around Baltimore in horse-drawn buggies and parading in front of the Light Street piers. Later, a splendid dinner was served on board the *President Warfield*. Here were used for the first time handsome commemorative dinner plates in blue and pink depicting a decorative map of Chesapeake Bay. The map was surrounded by pictures of five representative steamers, from the 1815 *Eagle* to the then flagship *President Warfield*. The *Warfield* had postponed her regular time of departure to permit these festivities and later in the evening she started on her overnight run down the Bay to Norfolk to the accompaniment of congratulatory salutes from many ships in the harbor.

This did not conclude the celebration, however. That evening, as the *Warfield* steamed along, a sprightly skit was presented in the social hall, highlighting the first one hundred years of Bay Line operation. Considerable mirth was evoked over the fact, undoubtedly distressing to some of our forebears, that since the first steamers on the Bay did not have private cabins and men and women occupied more or less open "births" at opposite ends of the vessels, honeymooning couples might find themselves unintentionally separated at the very outset of their matrimonial careers. Such a calamity was reenacted, accompanied by realistic displays of woe, consternation and recriminations.

Another observance of the centennial year of the Old Bay Line was the publication of the first edition of this book and its distribution to the company's many friends, stockholders, and business associates, as well as to the book trade. Published by the Dietz Press of Richmond, Virginia, under the enthusiastic supervision of the late August Dietz, Jr., the work was jointly sponsored by the Old Bay Line and The Mariners Museum, of Newport News, Virginia, where the author was then Corresponding Secretary.

As far as the general public was concerned, there was little indication on June 20, 1941 that the two long-standing rivals of the Chesapeake had become one line. In order to cushion the changeover, the boats kept their same crews and for some time continued to use their old docks and to follow the same schedules serving their respective partisans.

It may be recalled that the Chesapeake Line originally operated its ships to the York River only, connecting West Point, Virginia, at the junction of the York's tributary streams, the Pamunkey and Mattaponi, with Baltimore. They used the old *Columbia*, rival of the *Virginia* in 1907 for the Jamestown Exposition traffic, and the 1913-built sister ships, *City Of Annapolis* and *City Of Richmond*, on their York River Line until 1923, when the *Columbia* was converted to a freighter and renamed *City Of Atlanta*. A Newport News-built passenger steamer of similar appearance, named *Yorktown*, was added to this service in 1928. This was the same year the Old Bay Line launched its *President Warfield*. Both were the last passenger boats built for their respective lines. In 1940, however, attrition of the York River Line business had reached the point where one steamer twice or three times weekly was sufficient and the next year the line closed permanently.

The *Yorktown*, as delivered to the Chesapeake Steamship Co. by the Newport News Shipyard, 1928. (Photo courtesy of Newport News Shipbuilding and Dry Dock Co.)

It has been mentioned previously that the Chesapeake Steamship Company invaded the Baltimore-Norfolk field in direct competition with the Old Bay Line in 1896. Plying this route ultimately became their principal preoccupation. When the new Chesapeake Line steamers, *City Of Baltimore* and *City Of Norfolk*, came out in 1911, the "New Bay Line" boats had a decided advantage over the smaller and more venerable craft of the Baltimore Steam Packet Company. This advantage was lost a dozen years later when the older company introduced its two new ships in 1923.

Two serious setbacks to the Chesapeake Line occurred in the period between the world wars. The *City Of Richmond* ran into and sank her York River Line running mate, the *City Of Annapolis*, on the foggy night of February 24, 1927, off Smith Point in the Bay. Then, on July 29, 1937, a fire of undetermined origin broke out on the *City Of Baltimore* shortly after she had left her home port. The boat burned to the water line and three people lost their lives. The destruction of this steamer left the *City Of Norfolk* without a partner on the Norfolk run. The new *Yorktown* was diverted to join her, leaving the *City Of Richmond* to handle the York River Line business alone.

The Chesapeake Line boats remaining to consummate the merger with the Old Bay Line in 1941 were: *City Of Norfolk*, *City Of Richmond*, and *Yorktown*, plus a small wooden-hulled steam tug, the *Southern*, built in 1905. Owing to their advanced ages, the Old Bay Line planned to retire both the *City Of Norfolk*, then 29 years old, and the *City Of Richmond*, 27, as soon as all details of the merger had been ironed out. But fate decreed otherwise. On December 7, the same year, bombs fell on Pearl Harbor and the Allied cause needed anything that could float to use in defense of the Atlantic sea lanes.

All systems of transport were taxed to their utmost in the early part of World War II and the Old Bay Line had no trouble in keeping all six ships of its recently combined fleets fully occupied, though manpower became increasingly difficult to obtain. But it was soon apparent to the United States Government that there were others who had greater needs to be filled. Accordingly, in the spring and summer of 1942, the War Shipping Administration set about to requisition all available sound-class steamboats on the American eastern seaboard, among them the four youngest passenger steamers of the Old Bay Line. Many vessels so acquired were destined for transfer to the British Ministry of War Transport.

It may seem rather extraordinary that shoal draft, essentially inland water pleasure boats should ever have been considered in the light of warships, but there was a pressing need for hulls that could be converted to hospital ships, training craft or short-haul cargo carriers, particularly in the United Kingdom. Even these "skimming dishes" (as the contemporary press took pleasure in calling them) were considered suitable. Before it was all over, virtually every American coastwise steamship line was obliged to relinquish a major part of its fleet. But use of this type of vessel served to free actual naval ships for more pressing war duties. This country solved one such problem by converting two big side-wheel Great Lakes steamers, the *Seeandbee* and the *Greater Buffalo*, into practice aircraft carriers for training pilots.

The *State Of Virginia* was the first of the Old Bay Line boats to go. She was taken over by the government in Baltimore on April 1,

1942, and was followed by her sister ship, the *State Of Maryland*, the next day. The *President Warfield* and the *Yorktown* joined them on July 12 and 13, respectively, and the rosy picture of complacency the Line enjoyed in 1940 was no more. Under these new terms, the Old Bay Line was forced to continue service as best it could with what it had left—the two old coal-burner ships that had been earmarked to be scrapped. And the line was without a substitute in the event of an accident or breakdown. This represented the irreplaceable loss of sixty-seven per cent of the company's floating property and new construction was curtailed for the duration of the war.

The U.S. Army Transport *State of Maryland* at New Orleans Port of Embarkation, New Orleans, La., May 11, 1944. Formerly Old Bay Line passenger steamer; requisitioned from the Baltimore Steam Packet Co., 1942. (U.S. Army Photograph)

Both the *Northland* and the *Southland* of the Norfolk and Washington Steamboat Company were acquired in July of 1942. Only the *District Of Columbia* remained on the venerable Norfolk-Potomac River Line. It seemed odd that the government should want two river boats, both more than thirty years old, but the official statement explained emphatically (and euphemistically) that they were needed "for war purposes," and that was that![94] Another vessel lost to local waters was the *Virginia Lee*, a comparatively new steamer requisitioned from the Pennsylvania Railroad's cross-bay connecting line running from Cape Charles to Old Point Comfort and Norfolk.

To prepare these comparatively shoal draft steamers for transoceanic war duty, considerable amounts of interior fittings and passenger accommodations had to be ripped out. Foredecks were covered with turtle-back shields, mooring chocks were plugged and open spaces boxed in with heavy planking. This effectively protected the areas between main and saloon decks aft and those between saloon and gallery decks forward against boarding seas. The *State Of Maryland* and the *State Of Virginia* received even greater alterations, however. The superstructures and cabins of these boats were cut back almost as far aft as the funnels where they were squared off for the addition of navigating bridges and pilothouses. Typical ocean-going freighters' masts and cargo booms were installed to serve deck hatches giving access to cargo holds in the forepart of the ships. On deck, in the bow, gun tubs contained offensive armament. In the case of the *President Warfield*, the after deck was trimmed off and redesigned into a platform to accommodate a three-inch rifle and she also carried four twenty-millimeter guns in her armament. The other boats were similarly armed and all were painted a somber gray from stem to stern.

The *Yorktown* as converted to war service, Sept. 8, 1942. (U. S. Coast Guard Photo)

In some instances, the hulls proper were altered by applying steel sponson plating to fill up the considerable flat overhang customarily found beneath the main decks on ships of this class. They were deemed more seaworthy for offshore work for they were less apt to pound heavily in seaways with resultant strain and the danger of sprung seams. But the changes raised hob with the fine lines that had previously enabled the boats to make easy speed and their steaming abilities were cut down materially. Loaded with great quantities of barrelled fuel oil, the ships were immersed so much that, in some instances, the water lines were brought up to main deck level, even further spoiling the vessels' navigational performances.

After making the radical alterations cited, the United States Army commissioned the first two Bay Liners, the *State Of Maryland* and *State Of Virginia,* as small freight and troop transport craft and used them throughout the duration of the war in various parts of the West Indies and in South American waters. But the *Warfield* and the *Yorktown* were destined for more spectacular roles on the high seas. Only one of them returned.

Though the need for the services of a "Dishpan Fleet" on the other side of the Atlantic was increasing daily, there still was, of course, the problem of getting the boats over there. London was said to have received the news of the charter "with mixed feelings", a transport ministry official recalled.[95] Many seasoned mariners doubted that it could be done with highsided vessels designed for use by holiday-makers on protected waters. One man, however, Captain R. T. Park, superintendent of Britain's Coast Lines, Limited, of Liverpool, voiced the considered opinion that not only would the boats prove dependable and fast enough to make the trip across, but that it would not be too difficult to find volunteer crews to man them for the voyage, despite the obvious risks.

Accordingly, in July, Captain Park was appointed a committee of one to implement the matter. Crews were collected in England swiftly and efficiently. Masters and other officers came from Coast Lines, Ltd., while ratings were drawn from the Liverpool shipping pool. In all, some 550 Britishers were detailed to come over to America to man the ships. Meanwhile, preparing the vessels went on as swiftly as possible in various East Coast shipyards already overburdened with other priority work. Naturally, there were heartbreaking disappointments. One steamer destined for overseas, the *John Cadwalader,* was burned out at Philadelphia. The Chesapeake's *Virgina Lee* and the *Colonel James A. Moss,* formerly the excursion steamer *Belle Island,* developed structural troubles which could not be overcome in time if the fleet were to be assembled and dispatched to Britain before the season of equinoctial gales set in over the North Atlantic. Parenthetically, it might be stated that the difficulties on both steamers were remedied subsequently and they were sent to South America to ply the Amazon River for the war's duration.

At length, however, having proceeded up the coast independently, some eight steamboats assembled at St. John's, Newfoundland, and made ready to sail across the submarine-infested North Atlantic in convoy. A dedicated member of the Steamship Historical Society of America, who shall remain nameless, defied the security ban guarding the movements of all shipping and perched himself on the banks of the Cape Cod Canal. From this cynosure, he sneaked photographs of every one of his old favorites as they steamed through in their war paint, thus putting steamboat-lovers the world over in his debt without particularly endangering the security of the nation or affecting the outcome of the war.

Eventually all was ready, and on September 21, 1942, in company with their escorts, H. M. Destroyers *Veteran* and *Vanoc*, the following ex-pleasure boats assembled for the grim business of war: the *Boston* (Captain R. S. Young, commodore) and *New York* (Captain C. Mayers, vice commodore), came from Eastern Steamship Lines; the *Northland* (Captain James Beckett) and *Southland* (Captain John Williams), from the Norfolk and Washington Line; the *New Bedford* (Captain R. Hardy) and *Naushon* (Captain J. J. Murray), from the New Bedford, Martha's Vineyard and Nantucket Line; and the *President Warfield* (Captain J. R. Williams) and *Yorktown* (Captain W. P. Boylan), from the Old Bay Line. A macabre humorist had assigned the code name "Maniac" to the convoy, less colorfully designated RB-1.[96]

Apparently, security regulations were more strictly enforced in Newfoundland. In any event, no photographs seem to have been taken of the departure of what was probably the oddest appearing convoy ever assembled to tackle the North Atlantic in time of war. But residents of St. John's well recall the sailing of the brave little fleet. It was a clear, crisp, autumn day—a pleasant change on that normally mist-bound coast—as the ships left fiord-like St. John's and took steaming positions outside the harbor. The course was set towards Iceland and the convoy commenced its perilous eastbound voyage at fifteen knots.

The first two days were uneventful, but the disquieting news that a German surface raider was in the vicinity was received on the third morning. Nothing materialized, but the next day brought confirmation of submarines in the area. On the fifth day out, in the afternoon, in broad daylight, and without a sign of warning, two torpedoes slammed into the convoy commodore's ship, the *Boston*. She immediately heeled to starboard, but righted herself and started to settle down on an even keel. Then she slowly upended and slipped under, stern first. The *New Bedford*, previously designated rescue ship, and the *Northland* immediately went to her assistance while the rest of the convoy steamed ahead. But this was just the prelude of worse to come. The wolf packs had had their first taste of blood.

In the excitement of taking evasive courses after the *Boston* was torpedoed, the steering gear of the *Northland* jammed. Then it seemed that everything happened at once. As soon as the *Northland's* trouble was rectified, a surfaced submarine was sighted. In the meantime, the *Southland* observed a periscope to the starboard, but her fire proved so effective that the U-boat was forced to submerge after fourteen quick rounds from a twelve-pounder had been dispatched in its direction. A few minutes later, another periscope appeared on the port hand, but it could not be determined if it was the same or a different submarine. Again the *Southland's* gunners went into action, firing eighteen rounds. When it was all over, the *Southland* was credited by the Admiralty with a probable kill—not bad for a 34-year-old former river boat.

While this melee was going on, the *President Warfield* was being attacked, also. This was a far hue and cry from the single shot that a Coast Guard cutter had sent over the *Warfield's* bows back in Prohibition Days when she was suspected of harboring a cargo of illicit whisky. And this time the Old Bay Liner only narrowly escaped when a torpedo was sighted approaching abaft her port beam. Quick helm action swung the steamer on a parallel course and the torpedo passed by harmlessly only thirty feet away. Two minutes later, the *Warfield* sighted the outline of a submarine close on her port quarter and opened fire with her twelve-pounder. In response to her whistle signals, the British escort ship *Veteran* joined her in the attack with depth charges and it was the official consensus that another submarine never made it home.

Throughout the day, the desperate running battle continued with a spirited defense being carried out by the now well-scattered little fleet. But the Nazi U-boats were still not through with the convoy, signaling the various ships' positions to each other in brazen contempt. The *New York*, carrying the vice-commodore, was torpedoed at dusk on the fifth day and exploded in a sheet of flame. While searching for survivors, H.M.S. *Veteran* was struck and she, too, sank with heavy loss of life, not only from her own complement but also among those she had rescued from the two other vessels. Captain Mayers went down with his ship.

The former Chesapeake Line *Yorktown* was the final casualty. On the evening of September 26, she was hit amidships on the port side, her light superstructure collapsed, and she went down in three minutes. Fortunately, survivors, adrift on rafts, were discovered the next day by a patrol plane that managed to drop supplies to some of them.

Captain W. P. Boylan reported:[97] "My cabin was wrecked and went down to the main deck with the rest of the debris. Managing to scramble my way through, I came out at the ship's side where it was blown away. The vessel began to surge and groan and then cracked under my feet. Taking to the water and clinging to pieces of wreckage, I eventually made for a raft and was hauled on board by the chief engineer and a fireman. We then rowed here and there, wherever we heard shouting or saw any sign of life, and finished up with nineteen men on the raft. Next morning I saw a raft which had the chief and third officers on board, one raft with three men on it and also a lifeboat in the distance."

The men were obliged to remain on the rafts for some forty-six hours in rough seas and with a bitter wind blowing. At seven P.M., just as they were resigned to spending another dreadful night, H.M. Destroyer *Sardonyx* located the rafts and rescued these intrepid survivors of the Old Bay Line's contribution to the war effort.

In the meantime, proceeding independently, one by one the other five steamers reached port. The *Naushon* and the *Northland* made Londonderry, the *Southland* and the *New Bedford* came into Greenock on the Clyde, and the *President Warfield* reached Belfast, Ireland. Even Dr. Goebbels, Hitler's bombastic propaganda minister, was forced to pay unwitting tribute to the spirited action of these little three- and four-hundred-foot vessels, which, incidentally, he magnified in his Radio Berlin broadcast by gleefully claiming his U-boats sank "several ships of the *Queen Mary* class." Named as probables were the *Duchess Of Bedford* and the *Reina Del Pacifico*, both big converted liners. However, the announcer observed that "the defense was so fierce that it could not be observed whether two or more of the transports hit sank or not."

It was initially reported by the Allies that the little ships were deliberately sent out as a decoy to lure enemy submarines away from another, more vital convoy carrying thousands of troops to Britain. This was not the case, however.[98]

At the final tally, the three steamboats and one of their little destroyer escorts had gone to the bottom with a loss of 131 men. Well merited decorations and commendations were awarded by King George VI to all shipmasters and chief engineers of the fleet and many others, and there were posthumous awards for gallantry, as well. Thus Convoy Maniac came to take a well-deserved place as one of the shining episodes in the annals of British Merchant Service in World War II.

Now, reasonably safe in ports in the British Isles, the boats went on to perform their various and more prosaic military duties. The next few months of the *President Warfield's* career, for example, were spent uneventfully at moorings off the little Devon village of Instow on the Torridge River where, fast in the mud at low tide, she served as a Combined Operations training and barracks ship for commandoes and marines. She was fitted with quarters for 105 officers and 500 men who later stormed the beaches of France.[99]

Subsequently the British decided that this phase of the *Warfield's* operations had been successfully concluded and, in July of 1943, she was returned with thanks to the U. S. Navy. As U.S.S. *President Warfield* (IX-169) she then began her pre-Normandy invasion role of assault boat training base for American forces. In April, 1944, she moved on to Barry Roads and, in the comparative calm of D-plus-30 Day, she crossed the English Channel to Omaha Beach where she was to serve as a station and accommodation ship for harbor control.

At Omaha Beach, moored close in to the artificial breakwater created by sinking concrete block-ships and obsolete hulks offshore, the *Warfield*, nicknamed U.S.S. *Statler*, became a happy home for many U.S. Navy personnel attached to the port director unit which operated the busy anchorage and beachhead area with its floating piers and causeways all colorfully designated as "Mulberries." One of her more satisfied residents was a naval reserve officer, I. J.

U.S.S. *President Warfield* (IX-169), at N.O.B. Norfolk, July 27, 1945, just after she arrived home from England following World War II duty. (Official U.S. Navy Photo)

Matacia, who, curiously enough, was assigned the very same cabin that he had occupied with Mrs. Matacia on his honeymoon only a few years previously.

The *Warfield's* duties were over when the regular ports in France became available to allied shipping and the beaches could be closed. She returned to England on November 13, 1944. Then, after a stretch of temporary duty running on the Seine from Le Havre to Rouen, the former Old Bay Liner eventually came back across the

Atlantic to her original home waters of Hampton Roads. Arriving on July 25, 1945, she was berthed at the Naval Operating Base at Norfolk, decommissioned and offered for sale by the Maritime Commission on September 19 of the same year. Her former owners looked her over but decided not to take her back in the face of the major and expensive overhaul which would have been required to re-convert her to a passenger steamer.

On her next move, the *Warfield* was towed up the James River to the Maritime Commission's idle fleet anchorage off Mulberry Island, already teeming with weary surplus Liberty ships and tankers, to await a prospective purchaser. But a fate, then unforeseen and even more extraordinary than could possibly have been imagined, was in store for the old steamer, eclipsing a career already sufficiently bizarre for a vessel intended merely for leisurely cruises on the Chesapeake Bay.

Meanwhile, while the hulk of the ill-fated *Yorktown* was gathering barnacles on the bottom five hundred miles off the coast of Ireland, the *President Warfield*, laden with soldiers and marines, was performing her military duties in England and France; the *State Of Virginia* was shunting troops and cargo around the islands of the West Indies; and the *State Of Maryland* ("same name, but you would not know her")[100] was serving as a freighter in Brazil, the venerable Old Bay Liners *City Of Norfolk* and *City Of Richmond* were nobly endeavoring to keep the home fires burning. It was not an easy task.

A far greater volume of passengers and freight than ever before was crying for transportation. But virtually all young able-bodied seamen were off at war, and it was difficult to locate and hold crewmen, stevedores, maintenance men, office workers and all the other people required to keep the ships sailing. Supplies and spare parts were elusive commodities and even such simple things as coal, oil and paint were in short supply, calling for the utmost ingenuity on the part of the Line's management to materialize—in some instances, almost out of thin air. Robert E. Dunn, the company's president since the 1941 merger, squarely inherited this mess and ultimately developed an almost superhuman skill in the arts of improvisation and, when they failed, in "horse trading," to get what it took to keep the boats going. More than once, it looked as if the company would have to fold its tent and drop the whole thing in Uncle Sam's lap. Steamers are as old as their boilers and both ancient coal burners were in crying need of a good rest and replenishment of worn-out parts. But it was obvious that until the terrific demand for new construction in the nation's shipyards eased, there would be no opportunity for the major overhaul desperately needed by both Old Bay Line boats.

However, the boats were kept going and nightly carried servicemen by the scores, sleepers filling every cabin and spilling over onto the chairs and settees in the halls and lounges. Sometimes movements of military and naval personnel were so great that an entire steamer would be taken over by them. Two and three servings were required to feed them all, but somehow the necessary things were accomplished with maximum good humor and patience. One added requirement for the boats was a strict adherence to schedule since Hampton Roads was protected by submarine nets which were only opened by the net tenders at stated intervals. But again, luck was with the Old Bay Line ships and they came through those crucial times without serious accident or mishap.

The *City of Norfolk* in Baltimore Harbor. (Photo by Hans Marx, courtesy of the Baltimore Steam Packet Co.)

The pressure of shipyard work in the United States slacked off somewhat in the spring of 1944 for, by that time, vast numbers of vessels had been gathered on the other side of the Atlantic in preparation for the Normandy landings in June. Fortunately, the Old Bay Line was able to charter a replacement vessel from the War Shipping Administration at this juncture. This was the former Colonial Line steamer *Meteor*, a twin screw flyer originally named the *Chester W. Chapin* and built in 1899 for New Haven service on Long Island Sound. She, too, had been taken over by the government along with the other steamboats in 1942 and latterly had been employed as a receiving station ship at the Army Base in Brooklyn.[101]

The Old Bay Line, now in almost desperate straits, was instrumental in persuading the government to fix up the *Meteor* to put her back in operating condition. But it took some $800,000 to make the old steamer navigable again and she was used only a comparatively short time. She was laid up permanently in March of 1946 and scrapped soon afterward.

When the repairs to the *Meteor* were completed, the Old Bay Line was given the opportunity of chartering her on a bare boat basis at the rate of $36,500 per annum. She was delivered to the Line by the W.S.A. on March 4, 1944 and, with Captain P. L. Parker of the *City Of Norfolk* in temporary command, she made her first trip down the Bay to Norfolk on March 7.

The *City Of Richmond,* then almost literally held together with baling wire, was rushed off to the Bethlehem Steel Company's ship repair division for much needed major repairs. As soon as this was accomplished, the *City Of Norfolk* followed her to the shipyard and, in the end, at a cost of $400,000, both venerable Bay Liners received a new lease on life and became oil-burners in the process. The *Meteor* went back to the government on October 26, 1944, having made her last Norfolk to Baltimore trip the previous week.

The *Meteor* was not through with Chesapeake Bay for a while, though. The Norfolk and Washington Steamboat Company had a similar need to repair their lone, overworked boat, the *District Of Columbia,* and they fell heir to the *Meteor,* temporarily. But the dock at Alexandria was not large enough to accommodate her and she was unpopular. For these reasons and due to insurmountable difficulties in the labor department, the government was obliged to take over the entire line eventually and all operations between Norfolk and Washington including the running of the *District* when she was released by the shipyard.

And so the final months of war drew to their long-awaited close. First, came V-E Day and then V-J Day and from all quarters of the globe weary American servicemen began their long trek home. The Old Bay Line was busier than ever with the Hampton Roads Port of Embarkation doing a land-office business receiving them. Appropriately, the Line's vitally important contribution to the war effort did not go unappreciated. On October 17, 1946, at ceremonies held in Chicago, representatives of select American transportation agencies, including President Dunn of the Baltimore Steam Packet Company, the sole water carrier, were honored. On behalf of the Old Bay Line, Mr. Dunn received from Vice Admiral Louis Denfeld, USN, then Chief of Naval Personnel, a Certificate of Achievement from the United States Navy "in grateful recognition of outstanding services to Naval Personnel during World War II." There was no doubt that it had been well earned.

CHAPTER XIII

Exodus 1947

BEFORE returning to take up the main threads of the Old Bay Line's post-World War II history, it would perhaps afford an interesting digression to trace the final episode in the extraordinary career of the former Bay Line flagship *President Warfield*, occasionally referred to erroneously, when the newspaper rewrite men were on their toes, as the old Chesapeake ferry *President Garfield*.[102]

For an inland water steamer merely intended to ply placidly up and down the length of the Chesapeake Bay, the *Warfield* had already seen excitement aplenty by the war's end. Her sum total of violent experience prior to being taken over for naval use in 1942 had been the reception of a U. S. Coast Guardman's impetuous shot across the bow to suggest heaving to for a Prohibition Days' inspection. But in World War II she had had her brush with the Nazi Atlantic wolf packs, had heard the shrill whine of Luftwaffe bombs in England and off the invasion channel coast of France, and, having crossed the stormy North Atlantic twice, was quietly biding her time tied up in the James River Idle Fleet waiting for the beginning of the third and final act of her extraordinary drama.

For about a year the *Warfield* remained secured to the inboard end of one of the vast clusters of idle ships moored in the James River. One October afternoon in 1946, along with the *Meteor* and other inactive steamboats, she was eagerly viewed and photographed from a chartered tug by members of the Steamship Historical Society on the occasion of their annual meeting, held at The Mariners Museum nearby.[103] Shortly afterward, however, as they say in the mystery stories, the plot thickened.

On November 11, 1946, the *President Warfield* was sold on an unrestricted basis for a mere $8,028 to the Potomac Shipwrecking Company of Washington. Those who had known and loved the old ship groaned in view of the ignominious fate that apparently awaited her as she was towed away from the James River. Only two days later, however, the Potomac Company turned a singularly tidy profit by reselling the steamer for $40,000 to a concern that called itself the Weston Trading Company of New York. This outfit, not listed in the telephone directory, occupied a shabby one-room office on the fifth floor of a building in downtown Manhattan, at 24 Stone Street. In actuality, Weston was a "front" for Haganah, the Palestine underground organization busily recruiting American volunteers for the so-called *Mossad le Aliyah Bet*—Committee for Illegal Immigration. And it developed later that the ship had

The *President Warfield*, off Cape Hatteras, making her first attempt to cross the Atlantic, February 27, 1947, under the ownership of Haganah. (Official U.S.C.G. Photo by Donohue, U.S.C.G. Air Station, Elizabeth City, N. C.)

been paid for by Zionist sympathizers in Baltimore.[104] At this time, Israel had not yet become a nation and Palestine was still reluctantly governed by the British under a long-standing mandate intended to maintain the status quo of Jews and Arabs in that barren but much contested region.

In the wake of World War II, thousands of displaced Jews from all parts of Europe were desperately anxious to find new homes in the long Promised Land and the Zionist Movement had a host of ardent adherents. Haganah did its part by securing available ships and men and coordinating arrangements to run the strict blockade necessitated by international agreement under the British mandate.

Including the purchase price, it was reported that the *Warfield's* new owners spent a total of $125,000 to $130,000 to repair and overhaul the boat for her dangerous duty. Around the Baltimore waterfront where she had been taken for outfitting, the first rumors were that she was bound for China—a red herring speculation that may have been encouraged by her real owners. In any event, on February 2, 1947, a double-page pictorial spread appeared in the Baltimore *Sun's* Sunday rotogravure section carrying the intriguing title, "From Canton to Canton." The first Canton, of course, referred to the commercial section of downtown Baltimore.[105]

Finally, proudly flying the flag of Honduras in whose registry she had been conveniently enrolled and, with only crewmen embarked, the former Bay steamer left Baltimore on February 25, 1947, took her old, familiar route down Chesapeake Bay, but turned eastward towards the open ocean beyond. On passing through the Virginia Capes, the *Warfield* ran into fresh westerly winds. She first steered southeastward to try if possible to avoid the bad weather. But conditions worsened and seventy-five miles or so east of Diamond Shoals the little ship began to leak alarmingly as seams were started when the hull was buffeted about in heavy seaways. The *Warfield* radioed Coast Guard headquarters that she seemed to be in serious trouble. Intercepting the message, the tankers *E. W. Sinclair* and *Gulfhawk* headed for the apparently stricken steamer. The *Sinclair* reached her first and stood by. Meanwhile the big salvage Coast Guard Cutter *Cherokee* was dispatched out of Norfolk with orders to escort the *Warfield* back to port if possible.

Damage and flooding were restricted to the steamer's forehold, however, and when the weather moderated, she was able to navigate back to the Chesapeake Bay on her own power. She had a slight list to starboard and was down by the head, but was still able to make good speed.[106] These unexpected events served to turn an uncomfortable and unwelcomed spotlight on the particulars concerning the ex-Old Bay Liner's aborted departure for parts unknown. The mystery deepened when she was unexpectedly forced to return to port and it was discovered and publicly made known that seventy per cent of her crew were adventurous young Jews. The fact that the cargo the ship carried consisted merely of twenty-five tons of miscellaneous equipment, including a vast quantity of mess kits and life preservers, gave further confirmation to the speculation that a sub-rosa employment was intended.[107] Her commander, Captain William S. Schlegel, confessed that he knew nothing of the vessel's ultimate destiny and that by his orders he had planned to deliver the boat to designated parties at the port of Marseilles in the south of France. Disgusted, he left her at Philadelphia where she had been taken for repairs following the required survey for damages which had been held in Norfolk upon her return from the high seas.

Again patched up and with a new skipper on the bridge, the *President Warfield* slipped away two weeks later and this time made it safely across to the Mediterranean, stopping at the Azores en route. She called first at Portovenera on the Italian Riviera for refitting and refueling and then she backtracked to the little French port of Sette in the Gulf of Lyon. Here, with as much secrecy as could be achieved in a mass movement of such colossal proportions, the staggering number of 4,554 Jewish would-be immigrants to Palestine boarded the steamer which in a previous incarnation on the Chesapeake Bay had been licensed to carry no more than 540 passengers. This total was broken down to include 1,600 men, 1,282 women, 1,017 young people, and 655 children.[108]

An English tourist, H. C. Timewell, motoring to Cannes with his wife, happened to spend the night of July 12, 1947 in Sette. They were awakened at a very early hour by a continuous rumble as convoy after convoy streamed through the town heading for the old port. The trucks were crammed with thousands of singing refugees who had long been waiting and praying for this very day of escape. It seemed to the Britisher, though, on going down to witness the events on the quay the next morning, that several "well-, perhaps overdressed, swarthy men attached to a sumptuous new car, were issuing what I supposed were tickets to those going aboard. We thought then what a shocking traffic in human hopes. Evidently many were making large sums of money out of these unfortunate people's misery. . . ."[109]

It was quite obvious, in days of all but instant communications, radar, and other electronic marvels, that a 330-foot steamer like the *Warfield* could not hope to avoid notice. Apparently, then, her defiant voyage was merely intended to enlist world sympathy by focusing attention to the desperate plight of the displaced Jews who were, of course, the pathetic pawns.

A member of the *Warfield's* volunteer crew recalled the actual arrival on board of the Jewish home-seekers. "I stood at the top of the gangway as the refugees streamed onto the old ferry," Stanley Ritzer reported,[110] slipping easily into the usual disparagement that generally rated the former Old Bay Liner as then being "a tired, beaten old tramp" (Ruth Gruber);[111] "an ancient, former excursion steamer" (*Life* reporter);[112] or, for the purposes of the phenomenal best-selling novel, *Exodus*, "an overaged, obsolete steamship which . . . had never sailed the ocean" (Leon Uris).[113]

"There were old men, pregnant women, thin young men, beautiful girls, teenagers, infants," continued Ritzer. "They all looked dirty, weary, hungry. The long trek across frontiers, through woods and fields and unfriendly villages, across alpine passes and icy rivers, had doused the last flicker of fire in their hearts. I saw the Nazi tattoo of the concentration camp on many arms and the deep line of pain and hardship around many eyes. Most of them wore all their clothes on their backs and had the rest of their possessions tied in little bundles around their necks. . . .

"Haganah had forged 2,000 passports marked with visas to Columbia, South America, for the 4,500 refugees. Three French immigration officers stood atop the gangplank checking each passport as the refugees filed past. . . ."

Crewman Ritzer recalled that it was then his job to collect the passports as they were tendered and whisk them down to other refugees waiting their turns to board the ship. "The French officials would have caught on to the trick," he observed, "if Haganah had not had the foresight to provide a dozen bottles of cognac for their refreshment and half a dozen shapely Jewish girls to distract them."

The British Foreign Office knew full well what was going on, however, nor were the French officials so ridiculously naive. France was willing to let the *Warfield* sail even though her course might well prove to be in the opposite direction from South America. In the end, though, she thought it wiser to defer to last-minute pressure exerted by British Foreign Secretary Ernest Bevin and impound the ship.

At this apparent impasse, the *Warfield's* twenty-one-year-old Palestinian skipper, Captain Itzak Aronowitz, took charge of the situation and, dispensing with the usual formalities of clearance papers, tugs and pilots, he boldly conned the heavily-laden steamer out through the narrow mole, bouncing her off the concrete sides a couple of times in the process, and headed eastward for the Promised Land. Naturally, a British warship, in this case H.M.S. *Mermaid*, was quietly waiting for him to come out. Docilely the destroyer fell in the steamboat's wake, adjusting courses and speed to conform.

Soon after she left port, a radio message to the *Warfield* from Haganah authorized the captain to change the ship's name to *Exodus 1947*, so to symbolize the great movement then under way. Accordingly, a refugee artist painted the letters boldly in black paint on two canvas banners which were lashed to the bow. The new name was destined to be heard around the world.

On the second day out, the British destroyer pulled up alongside within hailing distance and inquired politely if any illegal immigrants for Palestine were on board. Since, as they knew full well, the steamer was bursting at the seams with them, the question was obviously rhetorical. But it was posed again on the next day and on the day following, but always ignored by the newly-named *Exodus'* company, who elected to answer it by playing "Pomp and Circumstance" over the public address system.[114]

By the sixth day, with the territorial waters of Palestine just under the horizon at which point she would no longer have the immunity from interference enjoyed on the high seas, the *Exodus'* unwanted escort had been augmented to consist of the powerful British cruiser *Ajax*, five destroyers and two minesweepers. A final unheeded plea from the *Ajax* cited the fallacy of resistance and begged the Jews to give up a venture which could only prove suicidal.[115]

The *Exodus 1947* (ex-*President Warfield*) arriving with 4500 illegal immigrants at Haifa, Palestine, July 20, 1947. Immigrants boarded at Sette, Southern France, July 12, 1947. (Photo courtesy of the British Admiralty)

Meanwhile, preparations for the inevitable struggle were being made on the *Exodus*, now proudly and defiantly flying the blue and white flags of Zion. Sandbags were stacked around the wheelhouse and chicken wire was strung along the upper decks to impede boarders. Small arms were issued to key personnel. It was calculated that the ship would enter Palestinian territorial waters at dawn on July 18, and the plan was to head for a narrow strip of deserted beach north of Tel Aviv where trucks would be waiting to pick up the human freight. Tension mounted as the hour of battle approached, for it was obvious that the British had no other choice but to make an attempt to prevent the boat from going in by force.

The action started prematurely at 2 A.M. and, fortunately, most of the *Exodus'* passengers were out of the way asleep below. Two of the destroyers closed not too gently on either side of the unfortunate steamer, squeezing her in a giant nutcracker movement. They dropped gangplanks on the decks and a boarding party of fifty armed and helmeted Royal Marines swarmed aboard in the face of a fusillade of sticks, tin cans and potatoes. The *Exodus* also released her life rafts from their inclined racks to let them crash

The *Exodus 1947* in Haifa Harbor. Showing damage sustained by "nutcracker" movement of British destroyers, July 1947. (Photo courtesy Haifa Port Authority, Israel)

down on the destroyers, but it wasn't long before the marines had the immediate situation in hand and the steamer's decks were cleared with tear gas and clubs. Firecrackers had served to frighten off the more timorous.

The final acts of a now bloody struggle took place to gain possession of the pilothouse. William Bernstein, 24-year-old chief mate, died with a fractured skull, one of the three Jews killed in the fruitless and defiant resistance which also brought injuries to some 217 immigrants and crewmen as well.[116]

With a gaping wound on her port side where the bow of one of the destroyers had raked outboard cabins on the *Exodus'* saloon deck, the weary ship was submissively convoyed into Haifa Harbor and moored to the main dock. The great trip was over. Bypassing the overcrowded detention camps on Cyprus, the greater number of the steamer's unfortunate passengers were transferred to three "prison ships," the *Ocean Vigor, Runnymede Park,* and *Empire Rival,* for the long and desperately tragic retracing of the fruitless journey to France. Defiantly, the Jewish passengers refused en masse to debark at Marseilles, so apparently there was nothing left for the British authorities to do but to take them back to their original point of departure. And so, on September 7, 1947, some two months after their "odyssey of frustration" had begun, this tragically abortive exodus terminated at Hamburg, Germany.

Once unloaded, the broken hull of the now-abandoned *Exodus 1947* was moored to the breakwater across the harbor at Haifa out of the way. Meanwhile, a considerable fleet of other captured blockade runners joined her there. An advertisement for the sale of vessels seized for attempted illegal entry into Palestine was placed in the British shipping journals by the Palestine Railways (Ports Authority) on December 29, 1947.[117] This described the ships offered in general terms as comprising "wooden auxiliary-engined schooners of about 150 tons, to iron and steel steamships of six to seven hundred tons gross and one iron steamship of over four thousand tons gross. The condition of the ships varies; some are reasonably good, others are of scrap value only."

But no one spoke for the old *President Warfield* which looked to New York *Herald-Tribune* correspondent Ruth Gruber "like a matchbox that had been splintered by a nutcracker."[118]

Time sped on its inexorable course. On that triumphal stroke of midnight, May 14, 1948, Israel became a new and sovereign nation and was immediately recognized by the United States as the 25-year-old British mandate expired. Thus came into being the first Jewish state to exist in the Holy Land since 70 A.D. when Nero's Roman armies had destroyed Jerusalem to crush a rebellious colony of Hebrews.

At this point, the rusting *Exodus 1947* took on a special symbolic significance as a tangible representation of the violence of Israel's pangs of birth. In those days there was talk of making a museum out of the boat to preserve and record this epic phase of the struggle to attain sovereignty. But there was too much of far greater importance to occupy the new nation, immediately embroiled in war with the surrounding Arab countries. And so the old *Warfield* quietly sat out the final period of her existence.

At length, for reasons never discovered, she caught fire on the morning of Tuesday, August 26, 1952, at her moorings inside the main breakwater of Haifa Harbor. The steamer burned all through the day and though fireboats were able to quench the flames later that afternoon, her entire superstructure was burned too badly to be repaired. Soon after, she was towed to Kishon Harbor where she was sold to the Hayama Company of Haifa for scrap.

And so halfway around the world, the career of a noble vessel ended—reliable passenger steamer beloved by countless Chesapeake travelers; valiant warship in the cause of peace; desperate blockade runner dealing in human hopes; and, finally, visible symbol of the birth of a nation.

Last of the *Exodus 1947*. Burning at Haifa Harbor, August 26, 1952. (Photo courtesy Haifa Port Authority, Israel)

The Old Bay Liner has not been completely forgotten hereabouts and some tangible mementos of her remain near her original home waters. Visitors to The Mariners Museum at Newport News have the opportunity to clang her ship's bell mounted in the Museum's Chesapeake Bay Room. Farther afield, residents of Hagerstown, Maryland, govern their movements by the silver tones of her steam whistle sounding four times daily from the roof of the New York Central Iron Works.[119]

Seldom, however, has a ship seen so much of history in a brief quarter-century span. Her home port deservedly is Valhalla.

CHAPTER XIV

Postwar to the Present

THE courses that the Old Bay Line has had to steer since World War II came to an end have by no means afforded continuously smooth sailing. Maintaining the venerable service in recent times has afforded challenges taxing the ingenuity of the management to the utmost for there have been several operational difficulties of vexing and sometimes insurmountable proportions. Ravages of the inevitable "tooth of time" made replacement of floating equipment and terminal facilities a matter of great importance; yet it has proved inexpedient to make the extensive capital outlay to cover the construction of new vessels to meet present needs despite the availability of funds. And so, even though the Line was able at length to acquire a much-needed third boat, it too, was an old, comparatively inexpensive one and the same pair of antique, but still graceful steamers of Edwardian vintage, the *City Of Norfolk* and the *City Of Richmond*, were left to tote the major load.

These trim, white vessels carry their years well. But they are old ladies and it had been planned to scrap them twenty years ago before the government requisitioned the newer ships of the Line. In actuality, however, virtually every necessary major part of their original construction has been replaced as required—new shell plates, new engine parts—so that, except for their names and the same gracious emanation of hospitality that originally came with them, they are new boats operationally.

Deterioration also affected the Old Bay Line's terminals forcing the company to give up some services—some temporarily, some entirely—even though their position in Baltimore was improved considerably by moving from Pier 10, Light Street to more modern facilities on nearby Pratt Street. Pursuant to an extensive park and urban redevelopment plan, the City of Baltimore decided to clean up a badly deteriorated waterfront area by condemning all of the rickety piers, warehouses and terminal offices along the east

125

side of Light Street. After these structures were razed—most of them had been abandoned with the closing of the myriad steamboat and ferry lines that used them, anyway—a waterfront parkway could be created to afford a fine view of the harbor.

The venerable establishment the Old Bay Line had occupied since 1898, including a modern four-story office building, was a casualty to this much-needed municipal improvement. Accordingly, in October 1950, the Line's Light Street property, once surmounted by the familiar clock tower, well-known to countless travellers, was sold to the City of Baltimore for $569,420. At the same time, the lease was made with the city for the present Pratt Street facility

Old Bay Line steamboat *City of Norfolk* at full speed in the lower Chesapeake, August 1949. (Photo by Robert H. Burgess)

located at the foot of Gay Street. This pier, Number 3, had formerly been used by the Merchants and Miners Transportation Company. At first, the Old Bay Line took over only the east side of the pier, but the following spring they elected to lease the west side as well, affording an extra berth for a stand-by steamer and spare lighters. Bay Line boats began using the pier on December 1, 1950, at which time all company offices were comfortably installed in their new quarters.[120]

In two other areas, however, the company did not fare as well. Disclaiming further responsibility in the matter, the United States

Army, custodian of the wharf at Old Point Comfort, located on Federal property, declared the facility surplus and proceeded to condemn it. And so no longer can steamers of the Old Bay Line touch the shores of the Virginia Peninsula on their daily rounds.

Deterioration of the government owned pier on Washington Channel, with no other dock available, also necessitated the abandonment of steamboat service to the Nation's capital which the Baltimore Steam Packet Company had taken over upon the closure of the old Norfolk and Washington Line in 1949.

The *City of Norfolk* maneuvering off Old Point Comfort Wharf, summer of 1959, as seen from the Hotel Chamberlin roof. (Photo by Robert H. Burgess)

Then, in addition to maintaining old ships and piers, the company was forced to combat labor troubles of singular perplexity. A new element had infiltrated the organization following the war and for long periods in the 1950's strikes and picketing of the terminals by labor unions interrupted service and disrupted schedules, harassing and even insulting passengers and shippers alike. Regrettably, a considerable amount of hard-earned business then became rerouted elsewhere and never returned.[121]

This interruption proved particularly crippling and costly to the Old Bay Line. As sole surviving carrier in the so-called break-bulk general cargo coastwise freight and passenger business, it has been required to meet, without the aid of the governmental operating subsidies which are granted foreign-going American vessels, the intense competition afforded by land transport, particularly trucks. This competition must be met by providing low freight rates to shippers despite the added handling expenses. Yet the subsidies given deep-sea lines only contrive to encourage high prices for labor and materials throughout all the maritime industries. And so, operating of necessity within a narrow range of profit, secession of service and consequent loss of business could well prove insupportably costly to the Old Bay Line.

The *City of Norfolk* at Old Point Comfort. (Photo by John L. Lochhead)

Yet, despite these many difficulties, the Baltimore Steam Packet Company has contrived to keep the ships sailing and proudly pledged every effort to continue to offer what is now a unique service maintaining a tradition of commendable antiquity. One extremely important factor remains in the company's favor and always will—despite all trials and tribulations the charm of the "noble Chesapeake" has remained constant through the years and that delightfully flowery description penned by an anonymous Bay Line traveler a century and a quarter ago, quoted in the first chapter, is still equally applicable today. Yes, as a body of water, Chesapeake Bay "has no equal, not even in that of Naples."[122] Let those in a hurry take the planes or hit the hot highroads. The cool breezes over the Chesapeake are ever there for the discriminating minority who appreciate them.

Naturally, one of the first things that the management of the Baltimore Steam Packet did when World War II was over, was to explore in all ramifications the question of securing replacement steamers. The possibility of reacquiring the *President Warfield* once she had been released by the Navy was considered but rejected at the time by reason of the disproportionately expensive repairs and remodeling which would have been required to return her to her original status of first class bay steamer. Since both the *State Of Maryland* and the *State Of Virginia* had been even more completely altered when converted to transports for the Army, their use again by the company was also not considered feasible.

Brand new ships naturally would have afforded the most desirable solution. But the time and expense involved to obtain them initially made that out of the question. At first there was still outstanding the little formality of reimbursement to the company by the government for the four steamers which had been unceremoniously whisked away in 1942. This involved a long and wearying period of negotiation and it was not until 1949, more than seven years later, that the Court of Claims got around to paying the Baltimore Steam Packet Company for the use of its best ships. The value of the individual vessels was appraised by the Court at $800,000 for the *State Of Maryland*, $815,000 for the *Yorktown*, $825,000 for the *State Of Virginia*, and $990,000 for the *President Warfield*—representing a total of $3,430,000 for the four. Payment of interest at four per cent from the date of requisition up to July 1949, swelled the figure to $4,218,500. But it was promptly whittled down to $3,276,082 by income taxes, legal fees, and other expenses.

While obviously this was not a sum to be sneezed at and was equitable in representing the initial value of the boats, when considered in the light of replacement, unfortunately it could not provide enough money to cover the cost of even one new boat as built to conform to existing United States Coast Guard safety requirements and the company's needs.[123]

In casting around for an existing ship type which, becoming surplus at the war's end, might be acquired and adapted for bay passenger and freight service, the company logically hit upon the consideration of the amphibious craft produced in quantity for the U. S. Navy and our allies. The largest of these vessels, designated LSDs or "landing ships—dock," would provide a suitable hull of comparatively shallow draft, a bay service requirement. Though over a hundred feet longer than the existing Old Bay Line steamers, they would lend themselves reasonably well to peacetime conversion. The more ubiquitous LSTs ("landing ships–tank") with their gaping bow doors and loading ramps were less desirable and of course the deep sea types such as Liberty and Victory ships were entirely unsuitable for Chesapeake Bay service.

Although the U. S. Government had no scruples about taking away the busy Old Bay Liners in 1942, the Navy was unwilling to release any of its precious LSDs in the moth-ball era following the war even though their peacetime roles were then confined to training duties. At length, however, two surplus LSD hulls did become available for purchase. These 458-foot vessels, originally named the *Highway* (LSD-10) and the *Northway* (LSD-11), had been built by the Newport News Shipbuilding and Dry Dock Company in 1943 and 1944, respectively, for lend-lease to the British. After the war they were returned to the United States, ultimately ending up as the cargo carriers *Antonio Maceo* and the *José Marti*, owned by the West Indies Fruit and Steamship Company and flying the flag of Honduras.

There would have been the difficulty of re-admission to United States registry had the Old Bay Line then elected to buy them. But the enormous cost ruled out the plan in the end. Although, complete with geared turbine power plants, the pair was for sale at the price of $550,000, estimates to rebuild them according to plans and specifications worked out for the company by officials of the shipbuilding division of the Bethlehem Steel Company, ran the total up to some eight million dollars and would have taken a year or more to carry out. Even after this vast outlay, the vessels would have been makeshifts, at best, and extremely expensive to run. Accordingly, the plans were reluctantly returned to the files for future consideration and the Old Bay Line was back where it started.[124]

And so other means had to be looked into to protect the Old Bay Line's traffic. The most important of these, of course, was modernizing the two old ships it had nursed along through the war years. As stated previously, when the work load in American shipyards lessened in the final stages of the war, both of the steamers had been extensively rebuilt and overhauled, the company spending some $400,000 on them. In the years that followed, even more work was done so that, as stated, in operational respects they are virtually new vessels today. One notable addition was the installation of radar. In March of 1946, the *City Of Richmond* received a radar set with a scope range of from one hundred yards to thirty-two miles. Actually, the instrument was intended for the passenger liner *America* then in the Newport News Shipyard for conversion to peacetime duties after a splendid naval career as the U.S.S. *West Point*. But since she was not ready to receive the radar installation and the *City Of Richmond* was, the steamboat got it. A short time later, the *City Of Norfolk* acquired her radar, too.

In equipping its vessels with this miraculous electronic seeing-eye, the Old Bay Line achieved another "first." Despite the seeming anachronism, its two old boats became the first passenger carriers in the entire United States Merchant Marine to be so equipped. Back in 1909 they had been the first inland water vessels to carry "the Marconi Wireless."

It was not quite two years after it was put on board that the radar set of an Old Bay Liner gave a spectacularly practical demonstration of its value by figuring in a dramatic lifesaving episode. Thirty-four-year-old Richard Christy, a seafood packer of Crisfield, Maryland, owed his life to a tiny point of light that appeared on the radar screen of the south-bound steamer *City Of Norfolk*. Pulled from the water at the eleventh hour, Christy feelingly wrote to the company afterwards to say that "words are inadequate to express the many acts of kindness rendered me by Captain Parker and his crew."[125]

On September 1, 1948, Christy and a companion, Clayton Evans, were on the 55-foot motorboat *C. A. Christy* carrying a cargo of slag from Baltimore to Crisfield. As often happens in that part of the Bay, a stiff Nor'easter sprang up unexpectedly and, trapped offshore without a convenient lee to run behind, their boat was swamped about 3:30 in the afternoon near James Point below the mouth of the Choptank River. Evans managed to grab a life raft and was ultimately rescued by a tug. Christy clung to the motorboat's detached wheelhouse. But the boat that found Evans failed to locate Christy before dark and gave up the search at 9:00 P.M.

Meanwhile, Captain P. L. Parker of the *City Of Norfolk* learned further of the mishap by overhearing some ships talking back and forth on the ship-to-shore telephone. He determined to keep an extra special lookout when passing through the area on his regular run down to Old Point and Norfolk. Miraculously, a pip showed up on the radar when the Old Bay Liner was about three-quarters of a mile from where Christy was still clinging to his precarious float. Changing course to head directly for him, it did not take long for the captain to give orders for a lifeboat to be lowered and its crew to haul the exhausted man on board. It was just in the nick of time, too. It was 11:45 P.M. and Christy already had been overboard for more than eight hours.

Incidentally, it was radar, or, more accurately, the possible lack of it, which was instrumental in the Old Bay Line acquiring its third ship. In 1949 the company decided to take over the assets of the recently defunct Norfolk and Washington Line and these included the steamer *District Of Columbia*. Unlike the Baltimore Steam Packet Company's ships, the *District*, sole survivor of the overnight Potomac River service, had not been equipped with radar when sets became available following the war.

One foggy October morning in 1948, on her southbound run from Washington, the *District* had already called at Old Point and was headed across Hampton Roads on the last lap to Norfolk. Captain E. H. Eaton cautiously nosed his vessel through the pea soup fog, periodically sounding the steam whistle. At anchor in the Roads' quarantine area, the Texas Company tanker *Georgia* announced her presence by clanging a bell on the forecastle head at appropriate intervals as the law required. Each vessel heard the other's signal, but fog plays unaccountable tricks with sound direction. Meanwhile a strong flood tide was sweeping the steamer along. Collision was inevitable even before the danger of it could properly be evaluated. With radar's advance warning, perhaps disaster could have been averted. In any event, the point was argued pro and con by the experts with considerable heat, but it should be recalled that radar did nothing to prevent the famous *Andrea Doria-Stockholm* collision eight years later.[126]

As the steamboat was set down broadside in the path of the anchored vessel, the *Georgia's* steel bow raked a seventy-five foot gash along the wooden superstructure on the starboard side of the *District of Columbia*, opening her passenger cabins to the outdoors. Once the vessels cleared, Captain Eaton quickly ordered the *District* to be turned and run hard aground on Hampton Bar. He did not then know the full extent of his ship's damage and naturally did not want to take the risk of her sinking in deep water.

Fortunately at this time of the morning, most of the passengers had gotten up and were in the dining saloon having breakfast. But one lady was killed in her berth and three other people were injured. The *District* remained aground until it was determined she had suffered no underwater damage. She was then floated off at noon at high tide, proceeding to her own pier at Norfolk. But the accident sounded the death-knell for the venerable Norfolk and Washington Steamboat Company.

This company had been organized in March, 1891, with the new screw steamers *Norfolk* and *Washington*. The Newport News-built *Newport News* joined the fleet four years later. In due time this line became the survivor in what once was a highly competitive field. Prosperity followed good management and new ships were progressively added as the need arose. When World War II began the Washington Line was operating the venerable *Southland* built in 1908 at Newport News, the *Northland* built in 1911 at Wilmington, Delaware, and the slightly larger *District Of Columbia* built in 1925, also at Wilmington.

As previously stated, Uncle Sam took over the two older vessels on July 10, 1942, at the same time that the Old Bay Line was losing its last pair, the *President Warfield* and the *Yorktown*. The *Northland* and *Southland* were the boats needed "for war purposes" despite their considerable age and, as we have seen, they became a part of the famous "skimming dish" convoy that braved the Nazi wolf packs on the crossing to England in September, 1942. As with the *Warfield,* the next year the British returned them to the U. S. Navy over there. Since there was already a U.S.S. *Northland* on the naval roster, this steamboat was renamed the U.S.S. *Leyden,* but the *Southland* kept her same name for the duration. Sold to Chinese interests after the war, the boats made the long trip out to the Orient via the Suez Canal and the Indian Ocean, becoming respectively the *Hung Chong* and the *Hung Yung* upon arrival in 1947. Both were reported sold in 1955 to be broken up.

Like the Old Bay Line, the Norfolk and Washington Steamboat Company carried on as best it could under the difficulties imposed during the war years. With the loan of the then Navy-owned steamer *Meteor,* it was actually operated by the government at a financial loss from June 23, 1945, to April 1, 1946. Also like the Old Bay Line, the company found it impossible to rebuild their fleet at the war's end and had to be content to use their single remaining vessel leaving each terminal port every other day. This spasmodic service was discouraging. The accident proved the last straw. Line officials took a long look at the repair cost estimates staring them in the face and an even longer look at the diminishing returns of river traffic. They decided to call it quits. Petitioning the Virginia State Corporation Commission, the then 57-year-old company elected to liquidate its assets and go out of business.

The opportunity for the Old Bay Line to acquire another steamer, even though a damaged one, was too good to miss, however. The Baltimore Steam Packet Company's bid was the highest received and accordingly was accepted and they took over the *District Of Columbia* on February 28, 1949. In addition to making the necessary repairs caused by the collision, the Old Bay Line decided to convert the *District's* boilers to oil firing as well.[127]

Two months later the boat was ready to resume service upon leaving the Bethlehem yard in Baltimore. Including purchase price, repairs, conversion, and improvements, the company had invested $287,468 in her. A $10,000 radar set was one of the additions.

From the outset, Old Bay Line officials had decided to re-establish the Norfolk to Washington service on the same alternate night sailings system used by the predecessor company. The *District* would be available to pinch-hit on the more-important Baltimore run at any time, but particularly in winter when one of the regulars went out for overhaul and Washington traffic was light anyway. This would provide greater order and the much needed flexibility to the Old Bay Line's operations.

The *District* left Washington bound for Norfolk on her inaugural trip on May 5, 1949, under new management with 125 passengers on board. The liner was immediately greeted enthusiastically by press and radio, spokesmen for the military, naval, and shipping services, and the traveling public at large. Partisans of the old service were delighted to welcome her back. By ownership of both lines, the Baltimore Steam Packet Company was soon able to offer a variety of cruise possibilities to its customers, including round trips in both the Baltimore and Washington boats. Tours sponsored by organized groups, study and historical associations, civic organizations, and particularly school children from as far away as the Mid-west had for many years accounted for an important part of the Old Bay Line's passenger business, and now it was possible for them to cover a great deal of ground at modest expense. Such a typical cruise would start at Washington with the opportunity of

Steamer *District of Columbia* making first sailing out of Washington, D. C. as an Old Bay Line ship. (Photo courtesy of Baltimore Steam Packet Co.)

viewing Alexandria and Mount Vernon from the river. The next day, on arrival at Norfolk, passengers would board sight-seeing buses and so would be able to take in the historic and scenic spots of the Lower Virginia Peninsula—Jamestown, Williamsburg, Yorktown, The Mariners Museum and Fort Monroe—before embarking on the Baltimore boat at Old Point Comfort. Understandably, the steamboat ride itself was a vital part of such an educational tour, representing an important era of American transportation.

But again the relentless "tooth of time" took charge. The old government wharf leased by the company on the Washington Channel at Seventh Street and Maine Avenue became increasingly decrepit. At first the Army Corps of Engineers condemned one side of the pier, fencing it off owing to the rotting timbers below. Then a part of the superstructure was dismantled for safety reasons. Meanwhile, the Old Bay Line's reasonable complaints about its condition went unheeded. Finally, the company felt no longer acceptable the chance of damaging irreparably a hard-earned reputation for reliability and safety by requiring passengers to use a facility marked "enter at your own risk." And so, on September 30, 1957, the Old Bay Line gave up Potomac River service and cancelled the lease on the Washington Pier as of the end of November. Signs were posted on the doors of the abandoned Maine Avenue ticket office stating "service temporarily discontinued."[128]

Since no other facilities in Washington exist that are either suitable or available for the 300-foot *District Of Columbia,* and the government has shown no disposition to rebuild the pier the Bay Line was forced to vacate, the use of the adverb "temporarily" unfortunately might no longer afford a correct statement of the case. However, the company has been investigating the reasonable possibility of resuming service on the Potomac as far as Alexandria, Virginia.

Since the discontinuance of the Potomac River service after but eight years under Old Bay Line aegis, the *District* has operated to a limited extent between Baltimore and Norfolk and today serves as a stand-by boat to relieve the *City Of Norfolk* and the *City Of Richmond.* During the winter time, when it is necessary to keep steam on her anyway to prevent pipes from freezing, the *District* has been put to the additional useful, though prosaic purpose of lending her boilers to provide heat for the company offices adjacent to her berth at the Old Bay Line's Baltimore pier.

The Old Bay Line's expulsion from the government wharf at Old Point Comfort was an even sadder event, however, though actually it did not turn out as badly as first anticipated. The Hampton Roads Bridge-Tunnel, opened in 1957, has made it relatively simple for both passengers and freight from the Peninsula to be diverted across to Norfolk to catch the boat there. And the captains of the Bay Line ships were only too happy to be relieved of the daily nerve-wracking maneuver of bringing their ships alongside an exposed wharf beset by tricky tides and currents. Occasionally, if unfavorable winds entered into the picture as well, these could cause them protracted delays before the ships could be snubbed in securely, delays which then would have to be made up by burning more fuel oil for the remainder of the voyage.

However, the Old Bay Line's ships had made Old Point an important port of call both coming and going between Baltimore and Norfolk from the very inception of service in 1840 and they did not want to give it up. In fact, up to comparatively recent times, the dock provided a vitally important exchange and transfer point where passengers and freight were transshipped for and from a variety of ports on the lower Chesapeake and its tributaries. But the fact that the United States Army was an unwilling custodian of the facility in the postwar years became increasingly apparent and the handwriting on the wall indicated they planned to eliminate it as soon as this could legitimately be accomplished.

Prior to World War II, however, the wharf was a busy place all day long. Southbound bay boats of the two Baltimore lines and the Washington Line called early in the morning, often taking considerable time jockeying for position on the outboard faces of its octagonal platform if wind and tide proved contrary. Throughout the day, steamers of the Pennsylvania Railroad's Cape Charles service came alongside on the way to and from the Eastern Shore, and in the evening the three northbound bay steamboats once more briefly tied up to receive passengers and long trainloads of packaged seafood to be trucked into their cavernous holds. But loss of the bay steamers to the government during the war and the only partial resumption of service thereafter reduced the pier's usefulness materially. And then, one by one, the lines were suspended until only the Old Bay Line remained.

Naturally the Federal Government suffered a corresponding loss in rents while maintenance costs increased. However, it seemed double-talk for the Army to explain that it had been determined the wharf now "was not needed for its operations" since the last time it did, in fact, serve a strictly military function was during the Civil War. And, as the only available deepwater landing on the Peninsula lay on government property, it was rightfully felt that the Army actually held it in trust for the populace at large. Certainly military personnel as well as civilians benefitted from the steamers' visits.

First certain threats of closure came in the autumn of 1953, however.[129] And this was in spite of the fact that the wharf's usefulness had been clearly demonstrated by a known total of 22,844 Old Bay Line passengers using it the year before.[130] Then in December of 1955 the Army informed the Old Bay Line that it did not plan to renew the company's 1950 lease after June 30 the next year. The dock, declared "in questionable status", was in fact closed for a two-week period in the autumn of 1956 while temporary repairs were made by a Fort Eustis engineer unit following severe storm damage sustained as a result of the visit of Hurricane Flossy in late September.[131] Meanwhile, attempts to induce the Old Bay Line itself, the City of Hampton, the Virginia Ports Authority, or anyone else to assume the maintenance of the pier were to no avail since the facility's location on an Army post invariably placed it under U. S. Government control regardless.

In 1959, however, the cat and mouse game had gone on long enough and final word of the closing of the pier and the plan to remove it physically was made public on November 12.[132] Last ditch efforts proved to no avail. The Old Bay Line made arrangements for transshipment of Peninsula freight to Norfolk with the boats scheduled to make their final calls on the last days of December. It was announced that as of January 1, 1960, the dock would be available on an "at your own risk" basis to servicemen, sightseers, Chamberlin guests, fishermen, and mere idlers, but no more travelers by boat.

Old Bay Liner *City of Richmond* making the last stop northbound at Old Point Comfort Wharf before the army closed it down permanently. (Time exposure from the Hotel Chamberlin roof by author, December 30, 1959)

But even this was not to last for long. In the fall of 1960, an Army Engineers platoon sent down from Fort Meade was detailed to raze the wharf as a "training project" and work began on taking down the pier house and removing the decking. Invoking an ancient stipulation made by the Commonwealth of Virginia at the time the land was deeded to the Federal Government in 1821 to the effect that Virginia citizens should have perpetual right to use Old Point wharves for fishing, the Groome Brothers of Hampton, long concessionaires of the news depot and restaurant on the pier, were able to obtain a temporary restraining order against the Army. But the injunction did not stand up in federal court and the halted demolition was soon resumed. By the end of May, 1961, a civilian contractor had pulled up the last of the pilings and not a single vestige remains of the facility which had served the Peninsula so long and faithfully.

It was the *City of Richmond* that had made the last northbound steamboat stop at the pier on the evening of December 30, 1959.[133] There was a singularly forlorn and plaintive quality to the three protracted blasts she sounded from her steam whistle as she slipped her mooring lines from the well worn bollards for the last time and headed out into the night. This was a melancholy valediction to the Old Point wharf and the ghost wharves there of yesteryear that she and her predecessors had served for well over a century.

From a detached point of vantage on the Hotel Chamberlin roof garden one could pick out the approaching steamer's masthead ranges from the maze of twinkling lights of Hampton Roads and the distant shore. Then her emerald and ruby running lights came in view as, slowly increasing in bulk, the steamer approached across the Roads. Ghosting in to the dock at length, the first sound identified with her presence was that unmistakably hollow thud as a heaving line sailed across the dark intervening water and landed on the wooden decking of the pier. Then a variety of sounds attendant to securing the boat were wafted aloft; the swishing and bubbling of the propeller wash as the old steamer backed down and then went ahead to take up the slack in her spring lines, the coughing steam winches on board winding in the taut, polished manila.

Finally snubbed close in, the next noise was the chuffing of a wharf tractor nudging the gangway aboard for the final time. It was followed by the clatter of the steel rimmed wheels of the dolly cart train bringing up the last of the freight.

A viewer on the hotel roof felt curiously detached. And, for a moment, time stood still as the picture below etched itself in memory. Then one was brought back to the exigencies of the present. Final calls between ship and shore echoed across the still water.

"All ashore, that's going ashore!"

The aerie was too far removed for one to hear the familiar tinkle of the engine telegraph signaling for full speed ahead, but one could identify the swish of swift water running under the boat's overhanging counter as she slowly gathered way. Then came the steam whistle's plaintive valedictory salute to Old Point. Only then did one notice that, in the meantime, a decided chill had come into the December air.

Mention of the several major viscissitudes that plagued the operation of the Old Bay Line from the war's end to today is not meant to convey the impression that all has been sadness and woe during this, the second century of steamboating on the Chesapeake. For one thing, partisans of this no longer common form of travel have come out even more vocally in favor of it and numerous worthy articles published in national as well as state magazines have served to introduce the Old Bay Line to people all over the world.

Then too, beginning in a small way just before the war, the enthusiastic organization that calls itself the Steamship Historical Society of America has since come into full maturity. The dedicated purpose of the society has been not only to collect records and pictures of steamboats of all types and to publish them in its quarterly journal, *Steamboat Bill of Facts,* but the now well-banded members take every opportunity individually and collectively to ride on the vessels that are still available and lustily sing their praises. Several times in the period since the war, full meetings of the society have been held at The Mariners Museum at Newport News and the membership has virtually taken over the Baltimore and Washington boats' passenger lists for the pilgrimage to Virginia.

Admittedly the bay steamers can no longer be rated as providing the swiftness of passage which in the last century had induced busy travelers to use their facilities when in a hurry. Today, those who patronize the graceful old steamers do so not so much for the strictly utilitarian purposes of being transported from one end of the bay to the other, as for the sheer enjoyment of riding the boat and enjoying the luxury and comfort of a leisurely cruise.

One enthusiastic Bostonian wrote after going up on an Old Bay Liner that he considered it a fascinating "archaeological experiment to take a steamboat" and he advised his friends that as long as the service was available "the opportunity should not be missed."[134]

But this does not mean that the boats are old-fashioned to the point of denying modern conveniences. Ship-to-shore telephone service is available just as on the ocean liners. Even those who fancy television can draw up in front of the sets located in the steamers' social halls with the same comfort as they would at home, for all the boats were equipped with big TV receivers back in 1951.

Incidentally, television was the cause of what proved to be an amusing reason for delay in the departure of the northbound Old Bay Liners for Baltimore and Washington on the evening of April 26, 1957, when the ship channel off Seawells Point at the mouth of the Elizabeth River was suddenly shut down by the Coast Guard for a two hour period. At a few minutes before six o'clock that afternoon, a crewman on a navy oiler sighted a floating object which appeared to him unmistakably like "a mine with horns."

A danger signal was immediately broadcast and all ships were excluded from the area pending an investigation. Nearby, impatient passengers on the Hampton Roads ferries wondered if they would ever get home that night with the boats imperturbably snubbed into their slips. Old Bay Line travelers wondered, too, why their ships showed no disposition to be getting under way. At seven P.M., however, the watch on a launch belonging to the Virginia Pilot's Association sighted a strange object "big and round as a basketball with a horn on it," and the Navy came and gingerly recovered the "thing" from the water.

Not long afterwards the channel was reopened and the Old Bay Line and other craft proceeded on their voyages. It was not until nine o'clock that night, though, that the Navy definitely confirmed the fact that the dread menace to navigation had been nothing more nor less than a discarded TV picture tube bobbing along in the tide.[135]

Steamer *City of Richmond* stuck in ice off Baltimore Light, February 3, 1961. (Taken from an icebreaker tug by Baltimore *News-Post* photographer)

Though this was but a scare, occasional minor mishaps beset the line. The *Norfolk* came in for some damage and had fifteen to twenty feet of railing pushed in when boarded by a "freak wave" when she encountered extraordinarily rough seas in the lower bay on the night of August 12, 1955.[136] Hurricane "Connie" was the cause of a disturbance that disrupted shipping along the coast. Some 125 passengers bound for Norfolk were thankful to get there.

Likewise, extraordinary icing conditions in the bay caused all services to close down for a few days in February of 1958 and on February 3, 1961, the northbound *City Of Richmond* became stuck fast in the ice off Baltimore Light after fighting her way up the Bay through ice floes of remarkable size. This required the services of a powerful icebreaker tug to break a channel so that the steamer could proceed on into port. Hurricane threats and dangerously rough water as a result of them also caused the loss of several trips over the years. Then, as stated, labor troubles also brought on cancellations for several protracted periods. For several years now reduction in traffic dictated the elimination of weekend sailing through the winter months and latterly no passengers at all are carried from Labor Day to March.

By and large, however, the grand old steamers have responded well to the loving care their owners have bestowed upon them over the years and night after night they continue to sail majestically up and down the bay. One wishes that it might go on forever. Perhaps it will.

Steamer *City of Norfolk* coming alongside the dock at Old Point Comfort. (Taken from bugeye yacht *Gypsy* by the author, July, 1956)

Appendix

Acknowledgments
Presidents and Incorporators
Personalities in the Bay Line's History
The Old Bay Line Fleet
Footnotes
Bibliography

Acknowledgments

Many persons contributed in a variety of ways to the preparation of *The Old Bay Line: 1840-1940*. The following names were cited in the preface and are repeated in *Steam Packets on the Chesapeake* as a token of continuing gratitude.

My initial debt was to my 1940 colleagues at The Mariners Museum: the late President Homer L. Ferguson; Miss C. W. Evans, now librarian emeritus; William T. Radcliffe, museum photographer; and the late Thomas C. Skinner, staff artist. To this group I now add my great appreciation for assistance willingly given by John L. Lochhead, librarian, and Robert H. Burgess, curator of exhibits, who are both dedicated and knowledgeable steamboat buffs.

Officials of the Old Bay Line itself were tireless in their efforts to put material at my disposal and generous in their appreciation. Legh R. Powell, Jr., former president of the Baltimore Steam Packet Company, supplied the introduction which launched the first edition on the uncharted waters ahead; Robert E. Dunn, then vice-president in charge of operation, and now president, gave unstintingly of his time and good nature; and of Raymond L. Jones, passenger traffic manager, it might be truthfully stated that but for him this book would have never cast off. Thanks go, too, to the late E. P. Hook, general agent; the late W. Andrew Miller, port engineer; the late P. S. Gornto, Norfolk general agent; and to officials of the Seaboard Air Line Railroad at Norfolk and Portsmouth.

My list likewise mentioned the kindness of the late John W. and Watson E. Sherwood, sons of Captain John R. Sherwood, president of the Line for many years, and of his daughter Mrs. Perry Fuller.

Good friends, John Philips Cranwell and James W. Foster, of Baltimore, were both of more assistance than they probably realized, the former for a careful search through Baltimore Customs House records and the latter for his great help at the Enoch Pratt Library. Robert W. Parkinson supplied useful data on the San Francisco ferry *Calistoga*, ex-Old Bay Liner *Florida*. It is a pleasure also to acknowledge the invaluable assistance afforded by Elwin M. Eldredge, who probably knows more about American steamers than any living person, and who has used this knowledge to assemble one of the best collections of ship portraits in this country.

In addition to Mr. Eldredge, the following individuals and institutions have generously aided me with pictures and permission to use them: The Mariners Museum, Newport News, Virginia; the Enoch Pratt Free Library, Baltimore; the Municipal Museum of the City of Baltimore; the U. S. National Museum, Washington, D. C.; the National Maritime Museum, Greenwich, England; and the Peabody Museum, Salem, Massachusetts.

J. B. Hunter, naval architect of Bethlehem Steel Company's Quincy shipbuilding plant, furnished copies of drawings of old vessels constructed by Harlan and Hollingsworth; F. A. Hodge sent pictures of Sparrows Point ships; Daniel J. Brown, of Pusey and Jones Shipbuilding Corporation, sent photographs of the modern Bay Line steamers. Mrs. W. G. Lane furnished a photograph of her late husband; Mrs. W. W. Morgan loaned a portrait of Capt. L. B. Eddens; Mrs. Franklin James, a miniature of her father, Chief Engineer T. J. Brownley. Miss Laura E. Hartge contributed a photograph of her grandfather, one of the Line's captains during the Civil War. Miss Audrey W. Davis gave permission to reproduce a painting of one of the early side-wheelers. Richard D. Steuart loaned an old broadside covering the wreck of the *Medora*. The late Captain R. Sidney Foster, with whom I enjoyed many delightful trips on the Bay, provided not only a fund of information about the Line, but also photographs of his kinsman, the late Captain W. J. Bohannon, and of himself. The late Captain John L. Marshall was a pleasant companion of many voyages and supplied much interesting data.

Thanks are tendered also to Dr. E. G. Swem, librarian emeritus of the College of William and Mary, in Virginia, and former editor of the William and Mary *Quarterly*, for permission to use material originally published in that magazine, and to the late August Dietz, Jr., for his invaluable assistance in the production of the first edition. I am now most grateful to Howard Gibbons for suggestions covering the present manuscript and to Edith Long for skillful typing services.

Finally, I thank my good friend Walter Lord, grandson of an Old Bay Line president and author of many splendid best sellers, of which *A Night to Remember* on the loss of the *Titanic* is a classic, for casting off this book from the dock with a warm foreword to wish it *bon voyage*.

In research material I have drawn extensively on files of Baltimore's newspapers, the *American* and the *Sun*, made available at both the Pratt Library and the Maryland Historical Society. Edgar Ellis, librarian of the *Sun*, kindly placed references in my hands taken from his index. Books by Fred E. Dayton, John H. K. Shannahan, and Roger W. McAdam have shed interesting light on the history of American steamboating. Dimensions and particulars of vessels mentioned here are taken largely from the *U. S. List of Merchant Vessels*, inaugurated in 1868 and published annually by the Department of Commerce, Washington, D. C. For early vessels, records made available by the National Archives, Washington, D. C., and the Baltimore Customs House were followed.

The roman numerals in brackets which appear after the names of several of the steamers in the roster are to differentiate them from others in the Old Bay Line which were built later on and given an identical name. They do not mean that the registered names of the particular ships included such numerals. They should help to prevent confusion in the identities of the various boats, however.

Many other people have contributed in one way or another to the preparation of this story, but the place of honor is reserved for that great host of sailors, shipwrights, officials, passengers, engineers, and shippers who, without realizing it, have been making the history of the Old Bay Line for these long years. I have endeavored to record some of it before it is forgotten.

A. C. B.

PRESIDENTS OF THE
BALTIMORE STEAM PACKET COMPANY

		Years
1840-1842	ANDREW FISHER HENDERSON	2
1842-1848	ROBERT A. TAYLOR	6
1848-1867	MOOR N. FALLS	19
1867-1893	JOHN MONCURE ROBINSON	26
1893-1899	RICHARD CURZON HOFFMAN	6
1899-1904	JOHN SKELTON WILLIAMS	5
1904-1906	J. M. BARR	2
1906-1907	ALFRED WALTER	1
1907-1918	JOHN ROBERTS SHERWOOD	11
(1918-1920	Federal Control, KEY COMPTON, Director	2)
1918-1927	S. DAVIES WARFIELD	9
1927-1941	LEGH R. POWELL, JR.	14
1941-	ROBERT E. DUNN	

INCORPORATORS OF THE
BALTIMORE STEAM PACKET COMPANY, 1839-40

WM. McDONALD
ROBERT A. TAYLOR
JOEL VICKERS
JOHN S. McKIM
JOHN B. HOWELL

BENJAMIN BUCK
SAMUEL McDONALD
THOMAS KELSO
ANDREW F. HENDERSON
And Others

ORIGINAL DIRECTORS

A. F. HENDERSON, President
J. S. McKIM
BENJAMIN BUCK
JOEL VICKERS

J. B. HOWELL
R. A. TAYLOR
THOMAS KELSO
GEN'L WM. McDONALD

ORIGINAL SUBSCRIBERS

C. D. BLANEY
JOHN C. MOALE
JOSEPH TODHUNTER
HUGH W. EVANS

JOHN BROWN HOWELL
CALEB GOODWIN & CO.
LYNCH & CRAFT

Personalities in the Bay Line's History

In the endeavor to cover adequately events in the history of the Old Bay Line since 1840, we appreciate the fact that not a great deal has been said of the men who ran the ships or of the people who sailed on them. Particularly for the early years of operation of the Line did it prove difficult to obtain authentic information about ships' personnel. A few names have been handed down in contemporary documents, but essentially these are merely just so many letters strung together. Attempts to locate portraits of some of the more prominent men in the organization, as for example Andrew F. Henderson, the first president, were to no avail.

In the matter of passengers who traveled via Old Bay Line, source materials are even more elusive. We can be sure, however, that a cross section of American life was always represented on the Bay Line ships. This would run the gamut from Presidents of the United States to the lowliest citizens.

Rarely have travelers committed memoirs of their experiences on the Bay Line to writing, however, and then, with foreign visitors, it was as equally often to blame as to praise. Tyrone Power mentioned the Yankee peddlers; Lieutenant DeRoos, the well-dressed and "beautiful" passengers. That socially prominent and otherwise important people took the Bay Line is evidenced by the constant improvements made to the boats and a progressive elevating of the standards of travel.

Men, women, and children; old and young; rich and poor; happy and care-worn; in love and disillusioned; well and ill; traveling for business and pleasure; going on vacations and to war—these are the people who have trod the Bay Line's gangplanks for more than a century.

Captain Edward Trippe was Chesapeake Bay's first steamboat master. In 1813, in conjunction with two men who were later to feature prominently in the beginnings of the Baltimore Steam Packet Company, he was instrumental in having built the first successful steamboat on the body of water from which she took her name—*Chesapeake.* Captain Trippe later commanded the *Philadelphia* and the *United States,* all of which were used in the upper Bay between Baltimore and Frenchtown.

The Ferguson family also contributed several members to the steamboat fraternity. Having gained his training in sailing packets on the Norfolk run, Captain John Ferguson commanded the steamer *Virginia* when she came out in 1817. Benjamin Ferguson owned both the *Virginia* and the *Norfolk* until they were sold by his estate in 1828 to mark the beginning of the Maryland and Virginia Steam Boat Company. James Ferguson was agent for this organization in 1835 and held this post for the Old Bay Line in Norfolk as late as 1851.

Officers of the Baltimore Steam Packet Co. in the Baltimore Pier waiting room. Left to Right: Robert E. Dunn, President; C. E. Clubb, Secretary-Treasurer; Raymond L. Jones, Passenger Traffic Manager; C. M. Smyrk, Freight Traffic Manager. Model is of the former flagship *President Warfield*. (Photo by Hans Marx)

Captain Moses Rogers made the very first ocean passage in a steam vessel when he took the *Phoenix* from New York to the Delaware in 1807. He brought the little *Eagle* down to the Chesapeake in 1815 and blazed the route by steam from Norfolk to Baltimore. The following year he "imported" the *New Jersey* in the same manner, but it is in his capacity as master of the famous transatlantic auxiliary *Savannah* in 1819 that he will be long remembered as a pioneer in the arts of steam navigation.

Only the names of other early Chesapeake steamboat masters have survived: Captain John Campbell of the *Norfolk* in 1819; Captain Daniel W. Crocker of the "swift and elegant" *Petersburg;* Captain William Coffin of the *Powhatan;* Captain Joseph Middleton of the *Roanoke;* all saw service prior to 1820.

In the second decade of steamboat operation on the Chesapeake, the names of the following mariners appear: Captain Brown, relief captain of the *Virginia* and *Norfolk;* Captain William Owen of the latter vessel; Captain Chapman of the *Petersburg* and, later, *Patrick Henry* on the James; and Captain George Weems, who owned the *Eagle* and introduced steam navigation to the Patuxent.

Captain William Rollins, a redoubtable mariner, first appears as master of the *Governor Walcott* on the upper Bay in 1830, but shortly thereafter he commanded the *Virginia,* then running between Baltimore, Norfolk and Charleston, and the *Georgia,* whose construction he superintended for the Atlantic Line. Captain Rollins went farther south when the Old Bay Line took over in 1840 and, during the Mexican War, he commanded the United States steamship *Neptune* and, later, the "magnificent" *Isabel.* At the time of his death in 1877 in his seventy-second year, Captain Rollins was mentioned as the oldest commander of steam vessels, counting years of service, in the United States, and he had long been recognized as one of the best pilots on the Eastern Seaboard.

The names of the incorporators of the Old Bay Line when it made its bow in 1840 are listed on page 148. The following served the company as its first shipmasters: James Cannon, James Coffey, George W. Russell, and Thomas Sutton.

Captain Cannon commanded the little *Pocahontas* in 1836, was first mate of the *Herald* when she came out in 1842, commanded the *Georgia* in 1849, and later was master of the *North Carolina.* He was on board the *North Carolina* on her ill-fated voyage in 1859 and transferred to the *Adelaide* until his resignation in 1868. He was with the Old Bay Line for its first 28 years.

Captain Coffey was with the Atlantic Line as master of the *South Carolina* in 1836, and then took the *Georgia* for the Bay Line from 1840 until he was succeeded by Captain Cannon. He died five years later in Baltimore at the comparatively young age of forty-five, the *American Beacon* of August 1, 1845, citing him as having been "long known to our community as commander of the *Georgia.*"

Captain Russell is first heard of as master of the Talbot Line *Paul Jones* in 1838, where he earned the "reputation for care and ability." He took over the *Jewess* when the Old Bay Line started and served on all of the first boats of the company until, in 1854, he was assigned to the new *Louisiana* and received the gift of a silver speaking trumpet from his many friends at the southern end of the Bay. He was still in command of the *Louisiana* at the time of the *Great Eastern's* visit in 1860, and was given the new iron steamer *Thomas Kelso* when she came out in 1866.

Captain Sutton, another doughty mariner, took command of the *Alabama* in 1838 and joined the Bay Line as master of the *South Carolina*. He was badly injured when the *Medora* exploded on her trial trip, but on his recovery the company gave him command of the *Jewess*. He was also master of the *Herald* for a period and the last mention of his name in connection with the Old Bay Line occurred in 1851 when he was again in charge of the *Jewess*.

Other early Bay Line captains whose names appear briefly on the record are Captain James Holmes of the *Jewess* in 1840, Captain George Hardie ("thoroughbred sailor and gentleman") of the *Herald* in 1852, and Captain Pearson of the *Georgia* in 1859. All had previously been connected with the old Maryland and Virginia Steam Boat Company, the former on the *Kentucky* and the latter on the *Norfolk*. A Captain Parrish commanded the *Virginia* prior to the Old Bay Line's inception when she was trading along the Eastern Shore.

In early times it was customary to include the names of ships and their captains in all advertisements. Following the Civil War, this practice appears to have been gradually abandoned. With the standardization of steamship lines and the operation of virtually identical ships, personalities of individual boats naturally became submerged. Many Old Bay Line passengers have made the overnight trip unaware of the name of the ship or her commander.

When steamers first made their appearance on the waters of the Chesapeake, the role of shipmaster was slightly different from today. Captains were hosts and the passengers their guests, a custom proved by the fact that on the *Surprise* in the 1820's, Captain George Stiles provided his passengers with a solid silver service in the dining saloon. Hulbert Footner put it even stronger. "It was an unwritten law," he wrote, "that the captain should be of good family: in other words, a gentleman as well as a navigator. . . . It was a point of pride with them, as with a good bishop, to remember everybody who used the Line."[137]

In the postwar period, Captain Darius J. Hill, termed "one of the most popular gentlemen ever known to the traveling public", first appears as master of the *Georgeanna* in 1866. He commanded the *Louisiana* for a short time and, when the new *Florida* came out ten years later, he was stationed at the "middle window" of her pilothouse. Later he served the Old Bay Line in the capacity of superintendent, being mentioned as holding this position as late as 1892, when his long and useful career terminated.

Additional postwar Old Bay Line shipmasters included Captain A. K. Cralle of the *Thomas Kelso*, the *New Jersey*, and, as late as 1877, of the freighter *Seaboard*. At this time Captain P. McCarrick commanded the *Eolus* and, during and after the war Captain Thomas Edgar, first of three generations of Bay Line employees, the *Thomas A. Morgan*. An invitation to join the Line was extended to Captain Robert Carter in 1868.

The operation of the "mosquito fleet" in the period following the war greatly enlarged the number of captains in the Old Bay Line's employ. The following men commanded the freighters and, in many instances, they were transferred to the passenger vessels later. Captain W. C. Whittle took over the *Transit* in 1869 and later served successively on the *Adelaide* and *Carolina* in 1877, then the *Virginia* when she came out in 1879, and finally, as commander of the fleet, the *Georgia*, when she joined the Bay Line in 1887. Captain L. B. Eddens also commanded the *Adelaide*.

Two Captains Travers, Thomas and Robert, were successively in charge of the *Westover, Shirley,* and *State Of Maryland*. Captain William Porter commanded the *Louisiana* and later the *Westover* in 1873, and it will be recalled that as a result of his experience in piloting the James River, he was given the *Virginia* when she transferred to the competing route on the James River in 1896. A Captain Dawes had both the *Transit* and *Petersburg* in 1877; Captain Skinner, the *Westover;* and Captain Geoghegan, formerly of the propeller *Empire* on the York River, the *Roanoke* during the same year.

The little freighter *Gaston*, launched in 1881, had a goodly number of masters during her long career with the Bay Line: Jacob Bloodworth, John Mason, Frank Kirby, Jim Foukes, Joseph H. Hall, and James W. Edgar, who retired in 1929 after 51 years of service with the Line, and died in February 1948 at the age of 86. Captain Edgar joined in 1878 and was a son of Captain Thomas Edgar, master of the *Thomas A. Morgan* in Civil War days. His son, the late Howard Edgar, third generation in the Old Bay Line, served many years as chief stevedore at Baltimore.

A well-liked shipmaster who joined the Old Bay Line in 1874 was Wyndham R. Mayo, who married famed Commodore Decatur's daughter. Captain Mayo was a student at the United States Naval Academy when the Civil War started and, on his resignation in 1862, he was commissioned by the Confederate States Navy and served on the Confederate gunboat *Patrick Henry*. After the war, he continued to follow the sea and had commanded Potomac River steamers prior to joining the Bay Line. He was master of the *Louisiana* on her ill-fated voyage and was highly commended for his seamanship during the disaster.

Another popular captain recruited from Bay Line cargo boats was R. H. Smullen. He served on the *Gaston,* and later was taken off as first mate of the *Alabama* to command the new *Raleigh* in 1906. He served as master of the *Florida* and *Alabama* prior to

World War I, when the command of the *Raleigh* fell to Captain Joseph H. Hall, also formerly of the *Gaston*.

Captain Wycliffe J. Bohannon, hailing from Mathews County, Virginia, a veritable breeding ground of splendid seamen, was another well-beloved Old Bay Line shipmaster. Captain Bohannon served on both the *Virginia* and *Carolina* and later commanded the *Georgia* and *Alabama*. He was recalled as a splendid figure, gentle but firm, and had decided inclinations toward the ministry. Many who knew him said he would have made as good a preacher as a skipper. His kinsman, Columbus Bohannon, was also with the Bay Line as mate on the *Alabama*. At present, a nephew, J. S. Bohannon, is a Bay Line engineer and a talented amateur artist.

Another competent mariner, Captain Walter G. Lane, commanded the *Georgia* in 1904 and a few years later was given the new *Virginia*, of which he was master until her sad end in 1919, two years before he retired from the sea.

In more modern times, one of the most celebrated Chesapeake Bay mariners was the late William C. Almy. Captain Almy gained his initial seagoing experience as an officer on the Cape Charles-Norfolk steamers in 1884. A few years later, he joined the Bay Line as master of the *Carolina*, and for forty-four years thereafter, he commanded successively all of the boats that were added to the Line, bringing out the new *Florida* in 1907, the new *State Of Maryland* in 1923, and the *President Warfield* five years later. He retired in 1932, estimating that during his active career on the Chesapeake he had covered two and a half million miles.

In the centennial year of the Old Bay Line, its then oldest active employee, the late Captain R. S. Foster, commanded the *President Warfield* with forty-seven years' service behind him, virtually half of the Company's life up to that time. Captain Foster signed on as seaman in 1893 and had progressively risen in the ranks to become the much respected dean of the Bay Line fleet. He retired at the outbreak of World War II.

Captain Foster's contemporary running mate, the late Captain John L. Marshall, a comparative "youngster" of twenty-five years' service, joined the Line in 1916 as quartermaster and rose through second and first mates until he attained the captaincy of the *State Of Maryland* in 1932 upon Captain Almy's retirement. Captain Marshall served with the Line until 1943.

The three shipmasters of 1961 in the Old Bay Line's employ, commanders of the *City Of Norfolk*, *City Of Richmond*, and the *District Of Columbia*, have amassed an aggregate of 130 years of steamboating on the Chesapeake, as of this writing. Longest in point of service with the Baltimore Steam Packet Company is Captain P. L. Parker, who first went to sea on Government lighthouse-tenders at the age of sixteen and joined the Old Bay Line as

Capt. S. B. Chapman (left) of the *City of Richmond* and Capt. E. H. Eaton of the *District of Columbia*, taken on board the *Richmond* at Old Point, May 27, 1950. (Photo by Robert H. Burgess)

a quartermaster in 1926. Rising in the ranks, Captain Parker received his first command on his thirtieth birthday, when he took over the *State Of Maryland* in 1933 as the youngest man ever to serve as Master of an Old Bay Liner. He then served on various other boats of the Line and, in 1942, was "loaned" to the British Ministry of War Transport to help prepare the *President Warfield* and the *Yorktown* for overseas duty. On December 23, 1943, Captain Parker took command of the *City Of Norfolk* and has been her regular Master ever since. He recalls the phenomenal rescue of Richard Christy as a highlight of forty years' sailing, though the hurricane of 1933, the icy winter of 1936, and many other episodes still stand clearly in his mind.

Captain S. B. Chapman, regular master of the *City Of Richmond*, has been a sailor even longer though he "grew up" in the Chesapeake Line and did not come over into the Old Bay Line until the 1941 merger. A native of Gloucester County, Virginia, Captain Chapman left home at the age of seventeen to take a supposedly two-weeks' job on the old steamer *Atlanta*. Somehow the two weeks stretched out into forty-eight years. He, too, inevitably rose in the ranks and earned his master's ticket when he was only twenty-one years old. Captain Chapman served on all vessels of the Chesapeake Line and has commanded the *City Of Richmond* since 1936.

Old Bay Line steamer *City of Norfolk* at Pier 3 Pratt Street, Baltimore. In the foreground are Captain Patrick L. Parker and Chief Engineer Burton E. Keyser. (Photo by Hans Marx)

Captain E. H. Eaton began a steamboating career as lookout on one of the Norfolk and Washington boats, becoming quartermaster in January of 1918. His service on the Potomac River was uninterrupted from 1923 until 1949. He joined the Old Bay Line when that company took over the services of the Norfolk and Washington Steamboat Company. Captain Eaton has been commander of the *District Of Columbia* from 1942, having received his first master's certificate when only twenty-three years old.

In the hands of these competent mariners, the present fleet sails the Bay.

The Old Bay Line has likewise been fortunate in having long and faithful servants not only in its deck department but also among the engineers, pursers, stewards, and those who man its administrative offices ashore. Particular mention should be made of the many fine colored people who have worked for the Line. Willie T. Harris, whose celebrated trill as he announced "dinnerrr!", had many unsuccessful imitators. Willie was with the Line for four decades and followed in the footsteps of his father, John Page Harris, much beloved bartender on the *Alabama*, who was with the Line for thirty-eight years. Willie developed an uncanny sixth sense which enabled him to spot unerringly any newlyweds among the passengers and to show them the courtly service their new estate warranted.

In the engineering department of early times, only a few names have survived. Albert G. Ramsey was appointed chief on the *Alabama* in 1841, and he was also on the *Medora* on her disastrous trial trip when Duncan Ferguson, chief engineer of the ill-fated boat, was killed. George Ayres was chief on the *Georgia* when the Old Bay Line began operations. Noah Bratt and Thomas James Brownley were on the *North Carolina* and *Adelaide*. The latter had joined the Line in the days of wood-burning steamers, serving on many vessels and, as senior chief engineer, superintended the installation of machinery on the *Carolina* and *Virginia* in the '70's.

Charles Reeder, a member of the illustrious family of steam engine builders who had constructed the first engines used on the Chesapeake, served as chief on the *Thomas Kelso* when she came out in 1866. Martin Rudolph, chief engineer of the *Virginia*, when she was running on the James in 1896, had then been with the Line for thirty-five years. Wallace Hooper, chief on the *Alabama* at the turn of the century, also put in long and faithful service with the Line. Other Bay Line engineers included Erick Lumberson, Harry Spainer, Jim Bitters, and the Deer brothers.

Other former members of the engineering department include G. W. Sadler, 1890-1938; J. A. Berger, 1894-1932; and George G. Webb, 1881-1921. Coming down to more modern times, Chief George M. Johnson was on the Bay Line since he first joined as an oiler in 1913 and Chief W. F. Saunders' record began in 1918. W. A. Miller, Port Engineer, furnished another example of son following father in the Old Bay Line. He died in 1959. His successor was C. M. Walker, with a service of thirty-eight years.

In the purser's department, one finds Messrs. Wilson and David T. Aspirl as "clerks" of the *Alabama* and *Georgia* when the Line began. Walter Ball was also clerk in 1840, becoming treasurer after Thomas Sheppard in 1848, and probably established a record for service in that he had been with the Line for sixty years (fifty as treasurer) when he resigned in 1900. Major Lloyd B. Parks was on the *North Carolina* in 1859 and transferred to the *Adelaide* after the unfortunate loss of the *North Carolina*. George S. Allen was purser of the *Louisiana* in 1860 and Colonel William Boykin was a purser before taking over the Company's agency at Richmond. Later on, we find Walter Doyle and Charles F. Spotswood, pursers of the sidewheel *Virginia*, followed by the *Alabama*. M. T. Thurston and D. S. Cherry served on the screw steamers *Virginia* and *Florida* prior to World War I, and, in 1940, Harry C. Baker was in his twentieth year with the Company as purser on the *President Warfield*.

Among the executives of the organization many names stand out. Of the presidents of the company, John M. Robinson's 26-year tenure of office was the longest, and he succeeded popular Moor N. Falls, who had held this post for 19 years. "Captain" John R. Sherwood, although president for only 11 years, had served just one year short of half a century with the Line. Captain Sherwood signed on as an assistant engineer on the little freighter *New Jersey* just after the Civil War. Although the organization of the Line at that time was made up mainly of those with strong Confederate sympathies, President Robinson having been a former Colonel, the fact that Captain Sherwood had been an engineer in the United States Navy did not hamper his subsequent career. He succeeded Major William C. Smith as Superintendent of the Line in 1874, rising later to the posts of General Manager, Vice-President, and President in 1907, where he was held in high regard by his fellow employees.

Other members of the organization serving the Line after the Civil War included Thomas Kelso, one of the original Directors of the Company in 1840, who died in 1878 at the age of 94. Thomas H. Webb was Norfolk Agent in 1866, followed by William Randall, an ex-purser, twenty years later. Then came P. S. Gornto, who took over at Norfolk in 1919, being succeeded by J. B. Gallagher, the present incumbent with 38 years' service. John Harrison Surratt, a son of unfortunate Mary Surratt, brutally executed for alleged complicity in Lincoln's murder, came to the Line in 1870 with his brother, Isaac Surratt. The former served as Freight Claim Agent and Auditor until, on his death in 1916, he was succeeded by E. P. Hook as General Agent, the post now held by H. J. Schafer with a service of 42 years.

Former officers of long service with the Line, all now deceased, also include: Major Poore, Traffic Manager; Emmet Brown, who retired in 1909 as Treasurer and General Passenger Agent after 40 years' service; his successor, James E. Byrd; Wilbur W. Erdman, who retired in 1918 as General Purchasing Agent after 50 years with the Company; James D. Downes, who retired in 1931 as Treasurer with 32 years' service; P. Byrd Thompson, retiring in

1932 as Traffic Manager with 22 years in the Company, and succeeded by Charles G. Rogers; and Theodore Butler, Traveling Freight Agent.

It would, of course, be manifestly impossible to list all those who have been and are serving faithfully on the Old Bay Line. Added to those whose names have appeared in the preceding pages are the following who rate well-earned though invisible service stripes for longevity with the organization: R. L. Jones, Passenger Traffic Manager, 40 years; P. A. Mattern, General Passenger Agent, 30 years; C. S. Kirwan, Assistant General Passenger Agent, 36 years; W. H. Cox, Traffic Representative, 38 years; C. M. Smyrk, Freight Traffic Manager, 40 years; G. L. Stern, Assistant Freight Traffic Manager, 42 years; R. F. Irwin, Commercial Agent, 36 years; A. H. Bettien, Assistant General Freight Agent, 41 years; G. S. Jenkins, Auditor, 48 years; W. F. Horan, Assistant Auditor, 43 years; W. E. Rice, Purchasing Agent, 22 years, who succeeded G. W. Schuncke, Jr. with a service of 39 years; L. A. Buckley, Office Assistant to Treasurer, 51 years; J. A. Moeller, Agent, 42 years; A. R. Trent, Agent, 39 years; J. F. Thomas, Assistant General Freight Agent, 36 years, and a host of others.

As a family proposition, Mrs. C. E. Clubb's nineteen years' service as Secretary to the President, added to her husband's thirty-eight years as Company Secretary-Treasurer, gives the impressive total of fifty-seven years in the Old Bay Line, as of 1960. President Dunn's long tenure—he came to the Old Bay Line in 1934 from the Seaboard—gets a nine-year boost from his son, R. E. Dunn, Jr., General Freight Agent-Claims, to bring the Dunn family's aggregate years of service to thirty-five.

Length of service in an organization is proof positive of faithful and devoted work. However, it gives an unbalanced picture since junior members of the Company are denied similar evidence of their loyalty. One cannot measure merely in terms of years that intangible quality which has so long contributed to the success and efficiency of the Old Bay Line. There are many present employees who, though they have not yet had time to build up a lengthy service record, are as interested and faithful workers as their seniors in the organization. It is on the shoulders of these men that the success of the Bay Line rests. The Old Bay Line has had good ships, but this would not have been enough without the loyalty of the personnel that has kept the Bay Line at the forefront of American steamship lines well into the second century. The Old Bay Line, beloved by countless travelers the world over, is justly proud of the record it has maintained through the vicissitudes of almost a century and a quarter, and faces the future with the knowledge that future generations are dedicated to maintain the illustrious record of the past.

The Old Bay Line Fleet

The following presents all steamers owned and operated by the Baltimore Steam Packet Company from 1840 to the present time. This roster of ships is compiled from Company records, Baltimore Customs House records, Lists of Merchant Vessels of the United States, and miscellaneous sources. The boats are arranged in order of their acquisition by the Old Bay Line. Owing to changes in the methods of computation, neither tonnage nor horsepower figures are comparable between early and late vessels. Those steamers which were operated by The Baltimore Steam Packet Company on temporary charter are given in parentheses. The full careers of chartered vessels are not cited, however.

The *City of Norfolk* at Seaboard Air Line Wharf, Portsmouth. (Photo by John L. Lochhead)

Pocahontas: Wood, side-wheel, passenger; 428 tons; 138.0′ l. × 30.0′ b. × 11.0′ d. Built at Baltimore, Md., in 1829 by Beacham & Gardiner for the Maryland and Virginia Steam Boat Company. Vertical beam engine by Charles Reeder, 50″ diam. × 78″ stroke, 100 H.P. Acquired by B.S.P. Co. in 1840 for $8,000. Sold in 1845 to the Powhatan Steam Boat Company. The original dimensions of the *Pocahontas* were 116.6′ × 35.5′ × 11.1′. Lost, 1862.

South Carolina: Wood, side-wheel, passenger; 466 tons; 172.0'
l. × 23.0' b. × 12.5' d. Built at Baltimore, Md., in 1835 by
John Robb for Norfolk-Charleston service of the Atlantic Line.
Crosshead engine by Watchman & Bratt, 44" diam. × 102"
stroke, 140 H.P. Acquired by B.S.P. Co. in 1840 for $15,000.
In 1842, the owners resolved either to sell or dismantle the
South Carolina. She was abandoned the same year.

Georgia[I]: (#10039) Wood, side-wheel, passenger; 551
tons; 194.0' l. × 24.0' b. × 12.2' d. Built at Baltimore, Md., in
1836 by John Robb for Norfolk-Charleston service of the
Atlantic Line. Lever-beam engine by Charles Reeder, 46"
diam. × 114" stroke, 140 H.P. Acquired by B.S.P. Co. in 1840
for $32,000. Reported "much damaged" in 1856. Chartered
by U. S. War Department, 1863. Sold by B.S.P. Co. in 1865 to
James A. Hooper. Abandoned, 1878.

Jewess: Wood, side-wheel, passenger; 352 tons; 173.5' l. ×
22.8' b. × 9.1' d. Built at Baltimore, Md., in 1838 by W. & G.
Gardiner for Maryland and Virginia Steam Boat Company.
Lever beam engine by Wells, Miller & Clark, 40" diam. × 132"
stroke, 160 H.P. Acquired by B.S.P. Co. in 1840 for $15,250.
Burned at dock Jan. 11, 1848. Rebuilt and lengthened by
Flannegan & Trimble. Public sale at auction advertised by
B.S.P. Co. for July 1, 1852. Dimensions given 200.0' × 24.0'
× 9.2'. Reported stranded or foundered in 1856.

Alabama[I]: Wood, side-wheel, passenger; 676 tons; 210.0'
l. × 24.7' b. × 13.5' d. Built at Baltimore, Md., in 1838 by
Levin H. Dunkin for Maryland and Virginia Steam Boat Co.
Vertical beam engine by Charles Reeder & Sons, 48" diam. ×
126" stroke, 200 H.P. Acquired (?) by B.S.P. Co. in 1841. Cost
not given. Sold by them to the Havana & New Orleans Steam
Boat Company in 1841 and left for New Orleans Oct. 6, 1841.
Reported lost or stranded in 1852.

(*Norwich:* (#18578) Wood, side-wheel, passenger vessel,
built in 1836 at New York; 346 tons; said to have been on
temporary charter to B.S.P. Co. in 1841. Survived until 1924
as a Hudson River towboat.)

Medora: Wood, side-wheel, passenger; tonnage not given;
180.0' l. × 23.6' b. × 9.6' d. Built at Baltimore, Md., in 1842 by
Brown & Collyer for B.S.P. Co. Lever-beam engine by John
Watchman, 42" diam. × 126" stroke. The *Medora* exploded on
her trial trip on April 15, 1842. Rebuilt as *Herald.*

Herald: (#11936) (ex-*Medora*): Wood, side-wheel, passenger; 329 tons; 184.0' l. × 24.0' b. × 9.6' d. Built at Baltimore,
Md., in 1842 by Brown & Collyer for B.S.P. Co. Vertical beam
engine by John Watchman, 42" diam. × 126" stroke, 250 H.P.
Acquired by B.S.P. Co. in 1842, price not given. Rebuilt and
lengthened in 1849 to 215.0' × 25.0' × 10.0'. In 1867 the

Herald transferred her registry to the Hudson River. Dropped from the Register as "abandoned" in 1885.

Alice: Wood, side-wheel, passenger; 326 tons; 167.6′ l. × 23.4′ b. × 8.8′ d. Built at Brooklyn, N. Y., in 1845 by Divine Burtis. Lever-beam engine, 40″ diam. × 132″. Acquired by B.S.P. Co. a $^{11}/_{32}$ interest for $12,093 in 1845, port of registry is Richmond, Va. The *Alice* was used by the B.S.P. Co. on James River service. Interest sold by B.S.P. Co. in 1848. At New London, Conn., in 1850. Burned on July 22, 1852, at Bridgeport, Conn.

Mount Vernon: (#17009) Iron, side-wheel, passenger; 195.0′ long, 359 tons. Built at Philadelphia, Pa., in 1846 by Birely for Washington & Fredericksburg Steam Boat Co. Vertical beam engine. Acquired by B.S.P. Co. in 1847 for $2,650 and used on Appomattox River service. Sold by B.S.P. Co. in 1852. Sold to U.S. Quartermaster Dept. in 1861; listed as U.S.S. *Mount Washington* April 22, 1861. Redocumented Oct. 18, 1865. Abandoned in 1880.

North Carolina: Wood, side-wheel, passenger; 1,120 gross, 861 net tons; 239.3′ l. × 35.5′ b. × 11.2′ d. Built at Baltimore, Md., in 1852 by Cooper & Butler for B.S.P. Co. Vertical beam engine by Murray and Hazelhurst, 60″ diam. × 132″ stroke. Acquired by B.S.P. Co. in 1852 for $111,272. Burned at sea en route Norfolk, Jan. 29, 1859. Unsuccessful attempts made to salvage her machinery.

Louisiana: (#14539) Wood, side-wheel, passenger; 1,126 gross tons, 266.2′ l. × 36.0′ b. × 122.2′ d. Built at Baltimore, Md., in 1854 by Cooper & Butler for B.S.P. Co. Vertical beam engine by Charles Reeder, 60″ diam. × 132″ stroke, 2,037 H.P. Acquired by B.S.P. Co. in 1854 for $234,197. Rebuilt by William Skinner & Son, Baltimore, in 1871. Rammed and sunk Nov. 14, 1874, by *Falcon*. Hull total loss, machinery salvaged and later used in *Carolina,* 1877.

Adelaide: (#85) Wood, side-wheel, passenger; 972 gross, 734 net tons; 233.0′ l. × 32.1′ b. × 8.8′ d. Built at Greenpoint, L. I., N. Y., in 1854 by Lupton and McDermott for Calais Steamboat Co., Boston-St. John, N. B., service. Vertical beam engine by Guion Boardman & Co., 50″ diam. × 144″ stroke, 1,370 H.P. Acquired to replace *North Carolina* by B.S.P. Co. in 1859 for $91,258. Temporary charter to U.S. Navy in 1861. Rebuilt by Wm. Skinner and Sons, 1871. Sold by B.S.P. Co. in 1879 to Harlan and Hollingsworth, Wilmington, Del. At Long Branch, N. J., steamer was rammed and sunk June 19, 1880, by *Grand Republic* in New York harbor.

Georgeanna: (#10043) Iron, side-wheel, passenger; 738 gross, 501 net tons; 199.1′ l. × 30.0′ b. × 9.6′ d. Built at Wilmington, Del., in 1859 by Harlan and Hollingsworth for G.R.H. Leffler. Vertical beam engine from *Gladiator,* 44″ diam. ×

132" stroke, 1,119 H.P. Acquired by B.S.P. Co. in 1860 for $58,175. April 12, 1864, collision with U.S.S. *Iroquois*. Sold by B.S.P. Co. to Potomac Steamboat Co. in 1869. Transferred registry to New York in 1888 and used as an excursion steamer; renamed *Colonia* on July 12, 1900; scrapped in 1902.

Philadelphia: (#12474) Iron, side-wheel, passenger; 504 tons; 201.0' l. × 29.0' b. × 9.0' d. Built at Philadelphia, Pa., in 1860 by Reanie, Neafie & Co. for Seaboard & Roanoke Railroad. Vertical beam engine by Reanie, Neafie & Co., 45" diam. × 132" stroke, 384 H.P. Acquired B.S.P. Co. in 1860 for $93,000. Sold by B.S.P. Co. in 1861 (?) to Potomac Steamboat Co. Renamed *Ironsides*. Lost on Hog Island Shoals, Aug. 29, 1873.

William Selden: Wood, side-wheel, passenger; 378 tons, 18.0' l. × 24.8' b. × 8.6' d. Built at Washington, D. C., in 1851 by George Page for account of builder. Vertical beam engine. Acquired by B.S.P. Co. in 1860 for $17,465. Expressly burned at dock May 10, 1862, during evacuation of Norfolk by the Confederates.

Thomas A. Morgan: (#24038) Iron, side-wheel, passenger; 681 gross, 520 net tons; 189.3' l. × 28.4' b. × 8.9' d. Built at Wilmington, Del., in 1854 by Harlan & Hollingsworth for Rockhill, Burdon, and Cone. Vertical beam engine by Harlan & Hollingsworth, 44" diam. × 120" stroke, 800 H.P. Acquired by B.S.P. Co. in 1862 for $56,695. 1862, official U. S. War Department mail steamer. 1867, traded for *New Jersey* by B.S.P. Co. Dropped from Register in 1879. (Registers confuse two vessels named *Thomas A. Morgan*, #24038 and #24748).

Eolus: (#7184) Wood, side-wheel, passenger; 731 gross, 275 net tons; 144.0' l. × 25.0' b. × 10.2' d. Built at Newburgh, N. Y., in 1864 by Thomas Marvel. Vertical beam engine by Washington Iron Works, 40" diam. × 96" stroke, 285 H.P. Civil War service. Acquired by B.S.P. Co. in 1865 for $11,314. Used by them on local routes out of Norfolk. 1869, sold to Newport, R. I., and used on Narragansett Bay. Dismantled in 1894 and rebuilt as *Isobel*, Stamford Line.

Thomas Kelso: (#24039) Iron, side-wheel, passenger; 1,430 tons; 236.9' l. × 35.4' b. × 10.4' d. Built at Chester, Pa., in 1865 by Reaney, Son & Co., for B.S.P. Co. Vertical beam engine by Reaney, Son & Co., 53" diam. × 132" stroke, 800 H.P. Acquired by B.S.P. Co. in 1865 for $204,020. December 8, 1866, exploded steam drum off Wolf Trap, towed to Portsmouth for repairs. Sold by B.S.P. Co. in 1869 to Marshall O. Roberts, New York. 1872, home port Providence, R. I. Reported lost at sea Mar. 31, 1884.

George Leary: (#10045) Wood, side-wheel, passenger; 810 gross, 621 net tons; 237.0' l. × 33.0' b. × 10.0' d. Built at Brooklyn, N. Y., in 1864 by Thomas Stack for Leary Bros.

Vertical beam engine by James Murphy & Co., 50" diam. ×
144" stroke, 1,872 H.P. Was on line in opposition to B.S.P. Co.
Acquired by B.S.P. Co. in 1867 for $235,125. Sold by B.S.P.
Co. in 1879 to M. Robinson, Georgetown, D. C., for Potomac
River service. Later a local excursion boat out of Washington.
Last at New York in 1899. Sold to John Roney of Baltimore,
dismantled and converted to lumber barge for Robinson and
Thorington, renamed *Josephine*. Foundered at sea, December
25, 1901 off Winter Quarter Lightship—crew taken off by tug
Ivanhoe which had her in tow.

New Jersey: (#18336) Wood, screw, freighter; 305 tons;
166.5′ l. × 22.6′ b. × 9.0′ d. Built at Baltimore, Md., in 1862.
Simple cylinder reciprocating engine. Acquired by B.S.P. Co.
in 1867 in trade for *Thomas A. Morgan* and $2,000. Total loss
by fire at sea, Feb. 26, 1870.

Transit: (#24368) Wood, screw, freighter; 478 gross, 408
net tons; 149.0′ l. × 25.0′ b. × 9.4′ d. Built at Brooklyn, N. Y.,
in 1864 for Montauk Steam Navigation Co. Simple cylinder
reciprocating engine, 32" diam. × 26" stroke, 500 H.P. Acquired by B.S.P. Co. in 1869 for $32,694. Used on Canton In-
side Freight Line. Sold in 1883 to New York. Renamed *John
Lenox* in 1883; renamed *Reserve* in 1914; abandoned at Cat-
skill, N. Y., in 1938.

Roanoke: (#21986) Iron, screw, freighter; 531 gross, 431
net tons; 168.7′ l. × 27.0′ b. × 9.3′ d. Built at Wilmington,
Del., in 1871 by Harlan & Hollingsworth for B.S.P. Co. Simple
cylinder reciprocating engine by Harlan & Hollingsworth, 34"
diam. × 34" stroke, 713 H.P. Acquired by B.S.P. Co. in 1871
for $64,544. Used on Canton Inside Freight Line. Sold in 1887
to I. H. Panly, Milwaukee, Wis. Dropped from Register 1906
at Tampa, Fla.

Westover: (#80390) Iron, screw, freighter; 577 gross, 416
net tons; 163.0′ l. × 28.0′ b. × 12.4′ d. Built at Wilmington,
Del., in 1873 by Harlan & Hollingsworth for B.S.P. Co. Simple
cylinder reciprocating engine by Harlan & Hollingsworth, 34"
diam. × 34" stroke, 492 H.P. Acquired by B.S.P. Co. in 1873
for $73,214. Used on James River Freight Line. Sold in 1887
to I. H. Panly, Milwaukee, Wis. 1897, home port Chicago.
1901, home port Philadelphia. 1906, renamed *Dover*. Stranded
in St. Johns River, Oct. 2, 1912.

Vesta: (#25863) Iron, side-wheel, tug (?); 219 gross, 147 net
tons; 102.0′ l. × 18.8′ b. × 4.4′ d. Built at Norfolk, Va., in
1870 for Seaboard and Roanoke Railroad. Vertical beam engine, 29 H.P. Acquired by B.S.P. Co. in 1874 for $5,170. One
half interest sold in 1875 by B.S.P. Co. to Wilmington, Weldon
& Seaboard Railroad. Registered at Washington, N. C.
Dropped from Register in 1889.

Shirley: (#115265) Iron, screw, freighter; 576 gross tons; 165.0′ l. × 28.0′ b. × 12.0′ d. Built at Wilmington, Del., in 1874 by Harlan & Hollingsworth for B.S.P. Co. Simple cylinder reciprocating engine by Harlan & Hollingsworth, 34″ diam. × 34″ stroke, 491 H.P. Acquired by B.S.P. Co. in 1874 for $70,538. Used on James River Freight Line. Sold by B.S.P. Co. in 1877 to Baltimore, Chesapeake & Richmond Steam Boat Co. of Baltimore for York River service. Burned Nov. 28, 1880, and rebuilt as *West Point.* Burned again Dec. 26, 1881.

Seaboard: (#115348) Iron, screw, freighter; 662 gross, 563 net tons; 184.5′ l. × 28.7′ b. × 12.3′ d. Built at Wilmington, Del., in 1874 by Harlan & Hollingsworth for B.S.P. Co. Simple cylinder reciprocating engine by Harlan & Hollingsworth, 34″ diam. × 42″ stroke, 693 H.P. Acquired by B.S.P. Co. in 1874 for $78,852. Used on Canton Inside Freight Line. Sold by B.S.P. Co. in 1898 to Hartford & New York Transportation Co. of New York. Used as freighter New York to Bridgeport, Conn. Laid up in 1931-1933. In 1934, hull rebuilt as coastwise tanker by L. D. Pierce. Owned by North Atlantic Trading Co., Providence, R. I.; 450 H.P. Worthington Diesel engine installed. Registered in 1948 by Tanker Seaboard Corp. (N.J.)

Petersburg: (#19542) (ex-*Western World*) Wood, screw, freighter; 675 tons; 178.8′ l. × 34.3′ b. × 8.1′ d. Built at Brooklyn, N. Y., in 1856 by William Collyer for Sherman & Mull. Purchased by U. S. Navy as *Western World,* Sept. 21, 1861. Purchased by H. R. Hazelhurst, June 24, 1865. Purchased by Powhatan Steamboat Co. on Nov. 21, 1865, and renamed *Petersburg.* Purchased by B.S.P. Co. in 1874 for $40,000. Used on Canton Inside Freight Line. Sold by B.S.P. Co. in 1879 to Boston, Mass. Converted to barge in 1880. Tonnage reduced to 497 gross. Reported "lost" Feb. 7, 1895.

State of Virginia[I]: (#22096) (ex-*Northerner*) Wood, sidewheel, passenger; 1,061 tons; 238.2′ l. × 31.1′ b. × 12.5′ d. Built at Ogdenburg, N. Y., in 1849 for Lake Ontario service. Vertical beam engine, 60″ diam. × 132″ stroke, 600 H.P. 1865, purchased by Powhatan Steamboat Co. from U. S. Government after Civil War. Redocumented *State Of Virginia,* Nov. 4, 1865. Purchased by B.S.P. Co. in 1875 for $13,964. Broken up, 1875 and machinery used in *Florida,* 1876.

State Of Maryland[I]: (#22095) (ex-*Atlantic*) Wood, sidewheel, passenger; 774 tons; 186.9′ l. × 33.0′ b. × 11.6′ d. Built at Brooklyn, N. Y., in 1857 by Devine Burtis as East River, New York, ferryboat. Vertical beam engine, 45″ diam. × 132″ stroke, 662 H.P. Purchased in 1863 by U. S. Navy, renamed *Commodore Read,* dimensions and tonnage altered. Purchased by Powhatan Steamboat Co. in 1865, redocumented Sept. 9, 1865, and renamed *State Of Maryland.* Acquired by B.S.P. Co. in 1875 for $7,506. Wrecked Mar. 31, 1876.

Ellie Knight: (#7062) Wood, screw, freighter; 298 gross, 207 net tons; 155.0′ l. × 23.0′ b. × 7.8′ d. Built at Philadelphia, Pa., in 1863 by Birely, Hilman & Co. for New York-Philadelphia Outside Line. Simple cylinder reciprocating engine, 32″ diam. × 30″ stroke, 372 H.P. In 1865 on Peoples Line, Baltimore to Richmond. Acquired by B.S.P. Co. in 1875 for $5,755. Sold by B.S.P. Co. in 1876 to Steamboat Company of Boston for Boston-Gloucester, Mass., service. 1884, home port New Orleans. Dropped from Register in 1886.

Cockade City: (#9050) (ex-*Burnside*, later ex-*Fannie Lehr*) Wood, side-wheel, freighter; 306 tons; 154.9′ l. × 21.6′ b. × 5.3′ d. Built at Baltimore, Md., in 1863 by Norman Wiard for U. S. Government as transport. 1865, sold to Robert Lehr, redocumented Nov. 3, 1865, and renamed *Fannie Lehr.* 1874, rebuilt at Baltimore and renamed *Cockade City.* Purchased by B.S.P. Co. in 1875 for $10,000. Sold by B.S.P. Co. in 1877 to Frank Debelius, Potomac River Barge Co., Baltimore, Md. Converted to unrigged barge, 168 tons, June 14, 1877. Dropped from Register 1884.

Florida[I]: (#120257) Wood, side-wheel, passenger; 1,279 gross, 900 net tons; 259.0′ l. × 36.1′ b. × 13.6′ d. Built at Baltimore, Md., in 1876 by Wm. Skinner & Son for B.S.P. Co. Vertical beam engine from *State Of Virginia*[I], (ex-*Northerner*), installed by James Clark & Co., 60″ diam. × 132″ stroke, 2,513 H.P. Acquired by B.S.P. Co. in 1876 for $231,207. Sold by B.S.P. Co. to James H. Gregory, N. Y., for scrap. Sunk April 28, 1892, while being towed to New York.

Raleigh[I]: (#110136) Wood, screw, freighter; 593 gross, 391 net tons; 169.0′ l. × 30.2′ b. × 16.0′ d. Built at Baltimore, Md., in 1873 by J. S. Beacham & Bro. Oscillating (?) engine, 399 H.P. Acquired by B.S.P. Co. in 1877 for $12,916. Sold by B.S.P. Co. in 1877 to Baltimore. Later owned by Atlantic & Gulf Steam Transportation Co. Dropped from Register, 1897.

Carolina: (#125595) Iron, side-wheel, passenger; 984 gross, 831 net tons; 251.0′ l. × 34.7′ b. × 7.9′ d. Built at Wilmington, Del., in 1877 by Harlan & Hollingsworth for B.S.P. Co. Vertical beam engine from *Louisiana* (Charles Reeder), 60″ diam. × 132″ stroke, 800 H.P. Acquired by B.S.P. Co. in 1877 for $198,963. Sold by B.S.P. Co. in 1893 to Richelieu & Ontario Navigation Co., Toronto, Canada, for St. Lawrence River service. Renamed *Murray Bay* in 1907; renamed *Cape Diamond* in 1921; dropped from Lloyd's in 1933.

Virginia[I]: (#25955) Iron, side-wheel, passenger; 990 gross, 665 net tons; 251.0′ l. × 34.7′ b. × 7.9′ d. Built at Wilmington, Del., in 1879 by Harlan & Hollingsworth for B.S.P. Co. Vertical beam engine Harlan & Hollingsworth, 50″ diam. × 132″ stroke, 800 H.P. Acquired by B.S.P. Co. in 1879 for $211,479.

In 1896, used by B.S.P. Co. on new James River Line. Sold by B.S.P. Co. in 1900 to Joseph R. Wainwright. 1902, ran under charter on Joy Line. 1903, sold to the Richelieu & Ontario Navigation Co., Toronto, Canada, for St. Lawrence River service. Renamed *Tadousac* in 1905. Dropped from Lloyd's in 1927.

Gaston: (#85685) Iron, screw, freighter; 847 gross, 464 net tons; 212.0′ l. × 35.5′ b. × 19.0′ d. Built at Wilmington, Del., in 1881 by Harlan & Hollingsworth for B.S.P. Co. Compound reciprocating engine by Harlan & Hollingsworth, 26″ and 44″ diam. × 36″ stroke, 540 H.P. Acquired by B.S.P. Co. in 1881 for $119,545. Sold by B.S.P. Co. in 1920 to Gulfport (Miss.) Fruit and S. S. Co. Dropped from Register in 1935.

Georgia[II]: (#85961) Iron, screw, passenger; 1,749 gross, 1,188 net tons; 280.1′ l. × 40.0′ b. × 15.0′ d. Built at Wilmington, Del., in 1887 by Harlan & Hollingsworth for B.S.P. Co. Compound reciprocating engine by Harlan & Hollingsworth, 34″ and 64″ diam. × 42″ stroke, 1,950 H.P. Acquired by B.S.P. Co. in 1887 for $252,263. Sold by B.S.P. Co. in 1909 to Hartford & New York Transportation Co. Operated on Providence Line. Became floating night club at New Haven in 1930. Scrapped at Baltimore in 1937.

Alabama[II]: (#106995) Steel, screw, passenger; 1,938 gross, 1,378 net tons; 293.8′ l. × 54.0′ b. × 16.0′ d. Built at Sparrows Point, Md., in 1893 by Maryland Steel Co. for B.S.P. Co. Four-cylinder, triple-expansion reciprocating engine by Maryland Steel Co, 24½″, 40″, & (2) 47″ diam. × 42″ stroke, 3,400 H.P. Acquired by B.S.P. Co. in 1893 for $291,993. Sold by B.S.P. Co. in 1928 to Progress Improvement Co., Seattle, Wash. Converted to oil-burning auto ferry in 1928 and renamed *City Of Victoria*. Used on Edmunds-Victoria route. In 1939, sold to Puget Sound Bridge & Dredging Co. for floating hotel at Sitka, Alaska. Taken into the U.S. Navy as U.S.S. *YHB-24*. Sold to Victoria Salvage Co., burned and scrapped in 1948 at Everett.

Elsie: (#136368) Steel, screw, tug; 39 gross, 19 net tons; 57.6′ l. × 14.8′ b. × 7.2′ d. Built at Baltimore, Md., in 1893 by R. M. Spedden for B.S.P. Co. Compound reciprocating engine, 9″ and 16″ diam. × 18″ stroke, 100 H.P. Acquired by B.S.P. Co. in 1893. Exchanged by B.S.P. Co. in 1923 for tug *Mary O'Riorden* plus $5,000, to Norfolk Lighterage Co. 1939, laid up by Wood Towing Co., Norfolk.

(*Enoch Pratt:* Iron side-wheel, passenger. Built 1878. On temporary charter to B.S.P. Co. in 1896.)

(*Tred-Avon:* Wood, screw, passenger. Built 1884. On temporary charter to B.S.P. Co. in 1896.)

Tennessee: (#145783) Steel, twin-screw, passenger; 1,240 gross, 743 net tons; 245.0′ l. × 38.5′ b. × 15.8′ d. Built at

Wilmington, Del., in 1898 by Harlan & Hollingsworth for B.S.P. Co. Two triple-expansion reciprocating engines by Harlan & Hollingsworth, each 18", 28", & 45" diam. × 30" stroke, 3,200 H.P. Acquired by B.S.P. Co. in 1898 for $158,691. Sold by B.S.P. Co. in 1906 to Joy Steamship Co., N. Y. Used on Long Island Sound until 1930. Renamed *Romance* in 1935 and used by Charles L. Ellis as an excursion steamer. Sunk in Boston Harbor on Sept. 9, 1936, collision with *New York*.

(*City Of Philadelphia:* Wood, screw, freighter. On temporary charter to B.S.P. Co. in 1904.)

Virginia [II] (#202467) Steel, screw, passenger; 2,027 gross, 1,378 net tons; 296.0' l. × 44.1' b. × 15.7' d. Built at Wilmington, Del., in 1905 by Harlan & Hollingsworth for B.S.P. Co. Four-cylinder, triple-expansion reciprocating engine by Harlan & Hollingsworth, 24½", 40", & (2) 47" diam. × 42" stroke, 2,850 H.P. Acquired by B.S.P. Co. in 1905 for $318,318. After gallery added 1909. Burned at sea May 24, 1919, en route Norfolk, total loss, 23 lives lost. Hulk towed to Baltimore by Merritt, Chapman & Scott for scrapping.

Raleigh [II]: (#203422) Steel, screw, freighter; 1,185 gross, 805 net tons; 222.5' l. × 33.0' b. × 21.3' d. Built at Sparrows Point, Md., in 1906 by Maryland Steel Co. for B.S.P. Co. Three-cylinder, triple-expansion reciprocating engine by Maryland Steel Co., 19", 31", & 56" diam. × 30" stroke, 1,200 H.P. Acquired by B.S.P. Co. in 1906 for $132,914. Sold by B.S.P. Co. in 1924 to Saginaw & Bay City S. S. Co., Port Huron, Mich. Acquired by Colonial Navigation Co., N. Y., in 1929 and renamed *Marion.* In 1939, owned by Madrigal & Co., Manila, Philippines. 1942-3, owned by Wallem & Co., Panama. Not listed in 1946-7 Lloyd's Register.

Florida [II]: (#204629) Steel, screw, passenger; 2,185 gross, 1,486 net tons; 298.0' l. × 45.0' b. × 16.1' d. Built at Sparrows Point, Md., in 1907 by Maryland Steel Co. for B.S.P. Co. Four-cylinder, triple-expansion reciprocating engine by Maryland Steel Co., 24½", 40", & (2) 47" diam. × 42" stroke, 2,600 H.P. Acquired by B.S.P. Co. in 1907 for $364,782. Sold by B.S.P. Co. in 1924 to Monticello Steamship Co., San Francisco, Calif., renamed *Calistoga.* Converted to auto ferry in 1927 at *V*allejo. Taken over in 1935 by Southern Pacific Golden Gate Ferries. Withdrawn from service in 1937 and laid up until taken into the U. S. Navy as U.S.S. *YFB-21* and stationed at Mare Island as an "evacuation boat." Sold by Navy after World War II, burned and scrapped in 1948.

(*Benjamin B. Odell:* (#208448) Steel, screw, passenger. Chartered by B.S.P. Co. from Central Hudson Steamboat Co. 1920-1921 during reboiling of *Alabama.* Burned Feb. 22, 1937 at Marlboro, Newport, R. I.)

State Of Maryland[II]: (#222636) Steel, screw, passenger; 1,783 gross, 669 net tons; 320.0' l. × 56.6' b. × 16.9' d. Built at Wilmington, in 1922 by Pusey & Jones Corp. for B.S.P. Co. Four-cylinder, triple-expansion reciprocating engine by Pusey & Jones Corp., 24½", 40", & (2) 47" diam. × 42" stroke, 2,800 H.P. Acquired by B.S.P. Co. in 1923 for $718,778. Converted to oil-burning in 1933. Requisitioned by War Shipping Administrator, April 2, 1942 at Newport News, Va. Converted to transport at Newport News and served during World War II under Army. Laid up after the war and sold Aug. 20, 1950 by U. S. Maritime Commission for scrap. Broken up at Mobile, Ala., in 1951.

State Of Virginia[II]: (#222715) Steel, screw, passenger; 1,783 gross, 674 net tons; 320.0' l. × 56.6' b. × 16.9' d. Built at Wilmington, Del., in 1923 by Pusey & Jones Corp. for B.S.P. Co. Four-cylinder, triple-expansion reciprocating engine by Pusey & Jones Corp., 24½", 40", & (2) 47" diam. × 42" stroke, 2,800 H.P. Acquired by B.S.P. Co. in 1923 for $717,105. Converted to oil-burning in 1939. Requisitioned by War Shipping Administrator, April 1, 1942 at Baltimore. Converted to transport and served in World War II under U. S. Army direction. Laid up after the war and sold by the U. S. Maritime Commission. Broken up at Baltimore in 1952.

Mary O'Riorden: (#10664) (ex-*Glen Iris*) Iron, screw, tug; 64 gross, 34 net tons; 78.7' l. × 16.5' b. × 81' d. Built at Buffalo, N. Y., in 1863 by David Bell. Simple cylinder reciprocating engine, 24" diam. × 22" stroke, 200 H.P. Renamed *Mary O'Riorden* in 1909. Acquired by B.S.P. Co. in 1923 from Norfolk Lighterage Co. in exchange for tug *Elsie* and $5,000. Sold by B.S.P. Co. in 1927 to C. A. Jording, Baltimore, Md. Converted to Diesel, 350 H.P., in 1932. 1939, owned by Capt. T. Nilsson and used on N. Y. State Barge Canal. Listed in 1948 Register as owned by O'Riorden Towing Co., Inc., New York, out of documentation in March 1951.

President Warfield: (#227753) Steel, screw, passenger; 1,814 gross, 706 net tons; 320.0' l. × 56.6' b. × 16.9' d. Built at Wilmington, Del., in 1928 by Pusey & Jones Corp. for B.S.P. Co. Four-cylinder, triple-expansion reciprocating engine by Pusey & Jones Corp., 24½", 40", & (2) 47" diam. × 42" stroke, 2,800 H.P. Acquired by B.S.P. Co. in 1928 for $959,970. Converted to oil-burning in 1933. Requisitioned by War Shipping Administrator, July 12, 1942 at Baltimore. Converted to transport and turned over to British Ministry of War Transport. Sailed from Newfoundland to United Kingdom in Convoy RB-1, Sept. 21, 1942. Returned to U.S. Navy as U.S.S. *President Warfield* (IX-169) in July 1943. Returned to U.S.A. after the war, decommissioned and offered for sale by U. S. Maritime Commission Sept. 19, 1945. Acquired by Haganah, renamed *Exodus 1947*. Seized on July 20, 1947 by British Navy attempting to run blockade into Palestine. Conveyed to Haifa. Laid up after Israel became a nation; burned at Haifa and broken up in 1952.

Alcyone: (#204069) Steel, screw, freighter; 440 gross, 229 net tons; 155.6' l. × 30.0' b. × 17.6' d. Built at South Boston, Mass. in 1907 by George Lawley & Son Corp. for H. W. Putnam, Jr., as private yacht. Steam plant replaced in 1922 by Diesel-electric drive by Winton Eng. Corp., 12 cylinders, 11" diam. × 14" stroke, 450 H.P. Converted from yacht to merchant service, 1935. Acquired by B.S.P. Co. in 1936, for $3,600 plus repairs and alterations. Used as extra freight boat. Sold on Feb. 15, 1941 to W. J. Townsend Transportation Co., Hoboken, N. J. 1945 Register lists her transferred to Honduran Flag; same owners. Listed in 1949-50 Lloyd's.

Marguerite: (#14G160) Wood, screw, launch; 26.6' l. × 9.9' b. × 2.0' d. Built at West Norfolk, Va., in 1936 by W. F. Dunn Marine Railway for B.S.P. Co. Gasoline engine, Chrysler, 53 H.P. Acquired by B.S.P. Co., May 1936 for $1,500. Used by Old Bay Line as ship-to-shore tender at Ocean View on summer houseboat cruises.

City Of Richmond: (#211710) Steel, screw, passenger; 1923 gross, 1127 net; 261.6' l. × 53.1' b. × 14.1' d. Built at Sparrows Point, Md., in 1913 by the Maryland Steel Co. for the Chesapeake Steamship Co. Four-cylinder, triple-expansion reciprocating engine by Maryland Steel Co., 23", 38", & (2) 45" diam. × 36" stroke. 2,500 H.P. Acquired by B.S.P. Co. in 1941 in merger of Old Bay and Chesapeake Lines, June 20. In operation today on Old Bay Line.

City Of Norfolk: (#208414) Steel, screw, passenger; 2379 gross, 1617 net; 297.5' l. × 46.5' b. × 16.2' d. Built at Sparrows Point, Md., in 1911 by the Maryland Steel Co. for the Chesapeake Steamship Co. Four-cylinder, triple-expansion reciprocating engine by Maryland Steel Co., 24", 40", & (2) 47" diam. × 42" stroke. 2,750 H.P. Acquired by B.S.P. Co. in 1941 in merger of Old Bay and Chesapeake Lines, June 20. In operation today on Old Bay Line.

Yorktown: (#227462) Steel, screw, passenger; 1547 gross, 817 net; 269.3' l. × 53.1' b. × 15.8' d. Built at Newport News, Va., in 1928 by the Newport News Shipbuilding and Dry Dock Co. for the Chesapeake Steamship Co. Four-cylinder, triple-expansion reciprocating engine by Newport News Shipbuilding and Dry Dock Co., 23", 39", & (2) 47" diam. × 40" stroke. Acquired by B.S.P. Co. in 1941 in merger of Old Bay and Chesapeake Lines. Requisitioned by War Shipping Administration July 13, 1942 for transfer to British Ministry of War Transport. Converted to transport. Torpedoed by German submarine in convoy en route United Kingdom and sunk on Sept. 27, 1942.

Southern: (#202357) Wood, screw, steam tug. 54 gross, 27 net. 68.0' l. × 17.5' b. × 8.2' d. Built at Baltimore in 1905 by William E. Woodall & Co. for Chesapeake Steamship Co. Single-cylinder reciprocating engine by E. J. Codd Co. 16" diam. × 18" stroke. Acquired by B.S.P. Co. in 1941 in merger of Old Bay and Chesapeake Lines. Owned by Old Bay Line until dismantled and dropped from the Register in 1954.

(*Meteor:* (#127379) (ex-*Chester W. Chapin*) Steel, screw, passenger; 2868 gross, 1822 net; 312' l. × 64' b. × 16.9' d. Built at Sparrows Point, Md., in 1899 by Maryland Steel Co. for Long Island Sound service. Twin-screw, triple-expansion engines, 4,200 H.P. On temporary charter to B.S.P. Co. in 1944 from the U. S. Government. Scrapped in 1948, at Trenton, N. J.)

District Of Columbia: (#224391) Steel, screw, passenger. 2128 gross, 1240 net. 297.8' l. × 51' b. × 16.3' d. Built at Wilmington, Del., in 1925 by Pusey and Jones Corp. for Norfolk and Washington Steamboat Co. Four-cylinder, triple-expansion reciprocating engine by Pusey and Jones Corp. 23½", 37", & (2) 43" diam. × 42" stroke. 2,400 H.P. Acquired by B.S.P. Co. in 1949 at a cost, including improvements, of $287,468. Operated by B.S.P. Co. on Norfolk and Washington service from May 5, 1949 to Sept. 30, 1957. Now serves as spare boat in regular service between Baltimore and Norfolk.

Footnotes

Chapter I, pp. 1-7

[1] Quoted in W. S. Forrest, *Historical Sketches of Norfolk*, 1853, p. 456.
[2] The *American Beacon*, Nov. 21, 1836, quoting from the Baltimore *American*, describes the boat as she was completed.
[3] Baltimore *American*, Nov. 3, 1836.
[4] Richmond *Compiler*, Oct. 24, 1834; *American Beacon*, Feb. 13, 1838.

Chapter II, pp. 8-14

[5] J. H. K. Shannahan, *Steamboat'n Days*, 1930, p. 9.
[6] Norfolk and Portsmouth *Herald*, April 23, 1824.
[7] T. W. Griffith, *Annals of Baltimore*, 1833, p. 248.
[8] *Niles Register*, Aug. 16, 1817, p. 398.
[9] *American Beacon*, Norfolk, July 31, 1817.
[10] Baltimore *American*, Aug. 20, 1817, quoted in E. E. Lantz, *Steamboat on Chesapeake Bay*, Baltimore *Sun*, Jan. 19, 1908.
[11] By a companion, John Stuart Skinner, who discredited the theory that Key was on the cartel *Analostan*.
[12] *Niles Register*, May 22, 1819, p. 233.
[13] *American Beacon*, Norfolk, Aug. 6, 1819.
[14] *Illustrated London News*, May 17, 1845, p. 308.
[15] Norfolk *Herald*, March 16, 1829.

Chapter III, pp. 15-24

[16] *American Beacon*, March 26, 1828.
[17] *Niles Register*, July 26, 1828, p. 351.
[18] New York *Enquirer*, June 14, 1828.
[19] Description of boats in Norfolk and Portsmouth *Herald*, Sept. 1, 1828.
[20] Reprinted from the Baltimore *American* in the Norfolk and Portsmouth *Herald* of Sept. 14, 1829.
[21] T. Power, *Impressions of America*, 1836, Vol. 2, pp. 42-45.
[22] *Ibid.*, pp. 72-74.
[23] London, 1827, pp. 39-40.
[24] Norfolk *Herald*, Nov. 29, 1833.
[25] Petersburg *American Constellation*, Oct. 9, 1838.
[26] Baltimore *American*, June 20, 1840.
[27] Baltimore *American*, Sept. 12, 1840.
[28] Baltimore *American*, Dec. 18, 1840.
[29] Baltimore *American*, Sept. 19, 1840.
[30] Baltimore *American*, Sept. 19, 1840.

Chapter IV, pp. 25-36

[31] Baltimore *American*, Sept. 19, 1840.
[32] Norfolk, *American Beacon*, July 31, 1841.

[33] Baltimore *American*, April 16, 1842.
[34] J. T. Scharf, *Chronicles of Baltimore*, 1874, pp. 505-6.
[35] Dixon's *Letter*, New York, April 14, 1842.
[36] Niles *Register*, April 23, 1842, p. 128.
[37] Charles Dickens, *American Notes*, 1842, Vol. 2, p. 24.
[38] *Ibid.*, pp. 208-9.
[39] T. J. Wertenbaker, *Norfolk—Historic Southern Port*, 1931, p. 197.
[40] *DeBows Commercial Review*, 1852, p. 309.
[41] See R. W. McAdam, *The Old Fall River Line*, 1937.
[42] See *Tales of the Coast* (Merchants & Miners), 1927.
[43] Scharf, pp. 524-5.

Chapter V, pp. 37-47

[44] H. W. Burton, *History of Norfolk*, 1877, p. 19.
[45] W. S. Forrest, *Historical Sketches of Norfolk and Vicinity*, 1853, p. 155.
[46] C. R. Weld, *A Vacation Tour of the U. S. and Canada*, 1855, p. 330.
[47] J. W. Hengiston, "Something of Baltimore, Washington, the Chesapeake and Potomac," in Colburn's *New Monthly Magazine*, London, 1853, pp. 358-373.
[48] T. J. Wertenbaker, *Norfolk—Historic Southern Port*, 1931, pp. 210-216. See also H. W. Burton, *History of Norfolk*, 1877, pp. 19-24.
[49] Mark Gnerro, "Old Bay Line Honors Heroic Nuns of 1855," in *Catholic Review*, Aug. 21, 1959, p. 16.
[50] *Nautical Magazine*, April 1856, p. 63.
[51] H. W. Burton, *History of Norfolk*, 1877, p. 24.
[52] *Ibid.*, pp. 32-33.
[53] R. C. McKay, *South Street*, 1934, pp. 282-4.
[54] H. W. Burton, *History of Norfolk*, 1877, p. 14.
[55] W. A. Wallace, *The* Great Eastern's *Log*, 1860. See also R. H. Burgess, "The World's Largest Ship Called At Old Point A Century Ago." In Newport News, Va., *Daily Press*, July 31, 1960, p. 1D.
[56] Baltimore *Sun*, Aug. 6, 1860.
[57] New Orleans, *Daily Picayune*, Aug. 18, 1860.
[58] H. W. Burton, *History of Norfolk*, 1877, p. 40.

Chapter VI, pp. 48-55

[59] H. W. Burton, *History of Norfolk*, 1877, p. 56-7.
[60] *Official Records of Union and Confederate Navies*, Vol. 4, p. 287.
[61] *Ibid.*, Vol. 4, p. 386.
[62] *Ibid.*, Vol. 8, p. 597.
[63] *Ibid.*, Vol. 8, pp. 35, 38, 39.
[64] *Ibid.*, Vol. 9, p. 611.

Chapter VII, pp. 56-61

[65] Baltimore *Sun*, Sept. 11, 1875, quoted by E. E. Lantz, *Steamboat on Chesapeake Bay*, Baltimore *Sun*, April 12, 1908.

Chapter VIII, pp. 62-78

[66] Wm. and W. F. Robinson, *Our American Tour*, 1871, p. 119.
[67] *Ibid.*, pp. 124-5.
[68] *Illustrated London News*, May 8, 1875, pp. 433-4.
[69] *People's Magazine*, London, Jan. 2, 1871, pp. 34-5.
[70] H. W. Burton, *History of Norfolk*, 1877, p. 168.
[71] *Ibid.*, p. 170.
[72] *Semi-Centennial of the Harlan & Hollingsworth Co.*, 1887, p. 274.

[73] R. W. Lamb, *Our Twin Cities—Norfolk and Portsmouth*, 1887-8, p. 214.

[74] *Seaboard Magazine*, New York, Oct. 6, 1892, p. 815. See also: S. W. Stanton, *American Steam Vessels*, 1895, p. 454-5.

[75] Baltimore *Sun*, April 29, 1892, p. 4.

[76] Richmond *Dispatch*, July 16, 1896, p. 3.

[77] Richmond *Dispatch*, July 21, 1896.

[78] *Manufacturers Record*, Aug. 21, 1896.

[79] R. W. McAdam, *Salts of the Sound*, 1939, p. 192.

[80] *History of Baltimore*, 1902, pp. 123-4.

Chapter IX, pp. 79-87

[81] Baltimore *Sun*, August 28, 1916.

[82] Baltimore *Sun*, Sept. 11, 1907, Baltimore *News*, Sept. 18, 1907.

[83] See: "The fast steamer *Florida*"; in *International Marine Engineering*, New York, April, 1908, pp. 145-8.

[84] Baltimore *Sun*, June 19, June 25, 1909.

[85] See *Old Bay Line Magazine*, Sept. 1912, pp. 1-3.

[86] *Old Bay Line Magazine*, January 1913.

[87] Baltimore *Sun*, May 25, 1919, pp. 16, 6, 7. See also F. J. Fenton, "Tragedy Stalked The Bay When Ship Burned In 1919." In Newport News, Va., *Times-Herald*, April 11, 1960.

Chapter X, pp. 88-96

[88] Baltimore *Sun*, Dec. 28, 1920, p. 16.

[89] *Steamboat Bill of Facts*, June 1948, p. 45.

[90] *Marine Digest*, Seattle, 10, 17 July 1948, 6 Nov. 1948.

[91] Baltimore *Sun*, March 10, 1929, p. 3.

[92] *Daily Press*, Newport News, March 5, 1929, pp. 2, 8.

[93] An Old Bay Line circular issued in 1917 stated: "Automobiles propelled by gasoline will not be received for transportation unless tanks are empty and thoroughly dry."

Chapter XI, pp. 97-101; Chapter XII, pp. 102-115

[94] Newport News, Va., *Times-Herald*, July 10, 1942, p. 2. See also A. C. Brown, "Former Favorite Bay Steamers Battled Nazi Wolf Pack in World War II." In the *Daily Press*, Sept. 25, 1960, p. 1D.

[95] "Ocean Odyssey: 'Skimming Dishes' Atlantic Battle With U-Boat Pack." In *The Shipping World*, June 13, 1945, pp. 663, 665.

[96] "Convoy 'Maniac.'" In *The Log Line*, London, Winter, 1948 (Vol. 3, No. 4), pp. 22-24.

[97] "They Called It The 'Honeymoon Fleet' Convoy" and Captain W. P. Boylan, "Affidavit—Loss of the *Yorktown*." In *Sea Breezes*, May, 1946, pp. 299-301 and 302-304. Recounted in Frank O. Braynard, *Lives of The Liners* (New York, 1947), pp. 188-195; in Roger Williams McAdam, *The Old Fall River Line* (New York, revised edition, 1955), pp. 254-258; and by Robert H. Burgess, "Fightin' Steamboats." In *Shipyard Bulletin* (Newport News Shipbuilding and Dry Dock Company), May, 1946.

[98] Associated Press dispatch, London, May 19, 1945. "Washington Steamer *Southland* Gets 'Probable' In U-Boat War." In the Washington, D.C., *Sunday Star*, May 20, 1945, p. A-6.

[99] A. C. Hardy, "More Reminiscences of the 'Honeymoon Fleet.'" In *Sea Breezes*, December, 1946, pp. 402-405. Also *Steamboat Bill of Facts*, August, 1945, pp. 322-323.

[100] *Steamboat Bill of Facts*, August, 1944, p. 251.

[101] Baltimore *American*, Dec. 5, 1943. Also *Steamboat Bill of Facts*, April, 1944, p. 229.

Chapter XIII, pp. 116-124

[102] A. C. Brown, "*Exodus 1947:* An Interim Report On The Career Of The President *Warfield.*" In *The American Neptune*, April, 1948, pp. 127-131.
[103] *Steamboat Bill Of Facts*, December, 1946, pp. 409-410.
[104] Associated Press dispatch, Baltimore, Aug. 2, 1947.
[105] Harold A. Williams, "From Canton to Canton." In the Baltimore *Sunday Sun Magazine*, Feb. 2, 1947, pp. 6-7.
[106] *Daily Press*, Newport News, Va., Feb. 27, Feb. 28, March 2, 1947.
[107] George Horne, "Palestine-Bound Mystery Ship, Battered By Sea, is Back In Port." *New York Times*, March 7, 1947.
[108] Ruth Gruber, *Destination Palestine: The Story of the Hagana Ship Exodus 1947.* New York, 1948, p. 17.
[109] H. C. Timewell, "*Exodus 1947* Takes On Her Cargo." In *The American Neptune*, October, 1949, pp. 300-301.
[110] Stanley Ritzer, " 'I Ran The Blockade To Palestine': The True Story Of The *Exodus.*" In *Argosy*, February, 1960, p. 78-79.
[111] Ruth Gruber.
[112] *Life*, Sept. 22, 1947, p. 33.
[113] Leon Uris, *Exodus*, Garden City, 1958 (Bantam Books, 1959), p. 148.
[114] Warner Twyford, "[Abbott] Lutz, Veteran of the *Exodus* Is Home Again." In Norfolk *Virginian-Pilot*, Nov. 18, 1947.
[115] Anon. "*Warfield's* Epic Cruise: Passenger Narrates Odyssey Of Jewish Ship." In the Baltimore *Sun*, Sunday, Sept. 7, 1947.
[116] *Life*, Sept. 22, 1947, p. 33; *Illustrated London News*, July 26, 1947, p. 95.
[117] *Syren and Shipping*, Jan. 21, 1948, p. 191.
[118] Ruth Gruber, p. 25.
[119] Information from W. C. McDonnell of Hagerstown, a "self-appointed 'Foreign Correspondent' of the Old Bay Line."

Chapter XIV, pp. 125-141

[120] Annual Report of the President of the Baltimore Steam Packet Co. to the Directors, 1950.
[121] Annual Reports, 1955, 1956. Press accounts in Norfolk *Virginian-Pilot*, Oct. 26, 1955, Nov. 9, 1955, March 9, 1956, Oct. 14, 1957; Newport News *Daily Press*, editorial Oct. 13, 1955, Oct. 14, 1955, letter to the editor Oct. 19, 1955, Oct. 26, 1955, Dec. 11, 1956.
[122] See Chapter I.
[123] Annual Reports, 1949, 1957.
[124] Norfolk *Virginian-Pilot*, Jan. 17, 1950. Company memorandum April 26, 1951. Annual Reports 1949, 1957.
[125] Letter to the company, dated Sept. 6, 1948. Norfolk *Virginian-Pilot*, Sept. 2, 1948. Service record Capt. P. L. Parker.
[126] Newport News *Daily Press*, Dec. 29, 1948; Norfolk *Virginian-Pilot* editorial, Jan. 2, 1949; Frank J. Fenton, "From the Files—Fog Bound Collision. . . ." In Newport News *Times-Herald*, Aug. 31, 1959.
[127] Newport News *Daily Press*, March 1, 1949; Newport News *Times-Herald* editorial May 7, 1949; Norfolk *Virginian-Pilot*. May 15, 1949; Annual Report 1949.
[128] Washington *Star*, Dec. 15, 1957; Newport News *Times-Herald*, Dec. 17.
[129] Newport News *Times-Herald*, Nov. 18, 1953.
[130] President's "Memorandum with Respect to Traffic Handled over Old Point Comfort Pier by Baltimore Steam Packet Co." April 5, 1955.

[181] Norfolk *Virginian-Pilot*, Sept. 27, 1956.

[132] Newport News *Daily Press*, Nov. 13, 1959 and editorial Nov. 18, 1959.

[133] Newport News *Daily Press*, Dec. 31, 1959; A. C. Brown, "Steam Packet Bids Melancholy Farewell." In *Daily Press*, Jan. 3, 1960, reprinted in *Steamboat Bill of Facts*, Winter, 1959, pp. 110-11.

[134] Letter to the author from W. M. Whitehill, June 2, 1947.

[185] Norfolk *Virginian-Pilot*, April 27, 1957.

[136] Norfolk *Virginian-Pilot*, Aug. 13, 1955.

Appendix, p. 152

[187] Quoted by Jacob Hay in *Holiday*, July 1957, pp. 90, 92, from *Rivers of The Eastern Shore*, by Hulbert Footner.

Bibliography

INCLUDING BOOKS, PAMPHLETS, SPECIAL ARTICLES
AND MANUSCRIPTS

PRINTED MATERIAL ESPECIALLY PERTAINING TO THE OLD BAY
LINE, OR TO ITS SHIPS

ANON.: "Convoy 'Maniac,' " in *The Log Line*, Winter, 1948, pp. 22-24.
————: "The 114-Year-Old Bay Line," in *Plymouth Rope Walk*, Fall, 1954.
————: *The Marvelous Adventure of Captain John Smith—A Voyage to the Virginia Peninsulas*, Baltimore: Old Bay Line, 1935.
————: "The Steamboat Plies the Potomac Again," in Norfolk *Virginian-Pilot*, Sunday, May 15, 1949, Sect. 5, p. 1.
————: "Ocean Odyssey: 'Skimming Dishes' Atlantic Battle with U-Boat Pack," in *The Shipping World*, June 13, 1945, pp. 663-665.
————: "Old Bay Line," in the *Esso Marketer*, August, 1957, pp. 8-10.
————: "The *President Warfield*," in *Municipal Journal*, Baltimore, July 28, 1928.
————: "They Called it the 'Honeymoon Fleet' Convoy," in *Sea Breezes*, May, 1946, pp. 299-301.
————: *Via Old Bay Line*, Baltimore: King Printing Co., 1923 (Pamphlet).
————: "*Warfield's* Epic Cruise: Passenger Narrates Odyssey of Jewish Refugee Ship," in the Baltimore *Sun*, Sunday, September 7, 1947.
BALTIMORE STEAM PACKET COMPANY: *An Act to Incorporate the Baltimore Steam Packet Company, passed 1839-40. Also acts of the General Assembly of Maryland supplementary thereto. Also the Act of 1922, By-Laws, April 4, 1930.* Baltimore: The Company, 1930. (Pamphlet.)
Bay Line News, The: Baltimore, Weekly Newspaper published by the Company, May 15, 1926-May 21, 1927.
BOOTH, ED.: "Steamboat Up the Bay to Baltimore," in Richmond *News Leader*, Sept. 19, 1959, p. 3.
BOYLAN, CAPTAIN W. P.: "Affidavit—Loss of the *Yorktown*," in *Sea Breezes*, May, 1947, pp. 302-304.
BRAYNARD, FRANK O.: "An Ocean Odyssey,' in *Lives of the Liners*, New York: Cornell Maritime Press, 1947, pp. 188-195.
BROWN, ALEXANDER CROSBY: "The Old Bay Line of the Chesapeake, A Sketch of a Hundred Years of Steamboat Operation," in the *William and Mary Quarterly Magazine*, Williamsburg, Va., October, 1938, pp. 389-405. (Reprinted as Mariners Museum, Newport News, Va., Pub. No. 6).
————: "*Exodus 1947*: An Interim Report on the Career of the Steamer President Warfield, in *The American Neptune*, April, 1948, pp. 127-131. (Reprinted by The Baltimore Steam Packet Company).
————: "Odyssey of Frustration Began 5 Years Ago With Ship Leaving Here," in Newport News *Daily Press*, Sunday, Feb. 24, 1952, p. D3. (*President Warfield* as *Exodus 1947*).
————: "The Old Bay Line," in *Baltimore Magazine*, July, 1954, pp. 30-34.

————: "Steam Packet Bids Melancholy Farewell," in *Steamboat Bill of Facts*, Winter, 1959, pp. 110-111. (Reprinted from Newport News *Daily Press*, Jan. 3, 1960. Last call at Old Point Comfort of *City Of Richmond*.)

————: "Steamers of Old Bay Line Have Sailed the Chesapeake for 112 Years," in Newport News *Daily Press*, Sun., Sept. 7, 1952, pp. D1, D6.

————: "Former Favorite Bay Steamers Battled Nazi Wolf Pack in World War II," in Newport News *Daily Press*, Sunday, Sept. 25, 1960, p. 1D.

————, and SOLITO, DICK: "Dock at Old Point Once Witnessed Hey-Day of Steamboating," in Newport News *Daily Press*, Sunday, July 19, 1953, p. D1.

BURGESS, ROBERT H.: "Fightin' Steamboats", in *Shipyard Bulletin*, Newport News, May, 1946.

————: "Steamboat 'Round the Bend,' " in *The Chesapeake Skipper*, March, 1955, pp. 20-21, 37-39.

————: "Steamboating on the Old Bay Line," in *Commonwealth*, Richmond, July, 1959, pp. 11-13, 48-49.

FENTON, FRANK J.: "Tragedy Stalked the Bay When Ship Burned in 1919," in Newport News *Times-Herald*, April 11, 1960. (Loss of Old Bay Liner *Virginia*.)

GNERRO, MARK: "Yellow Fever Epidemic—Old Bay Line Honors Heroic Nuns of 1855," in *Catholic Review*, Aug. 21, 1959, p. 16.

GROH, LYNN: "115 Years and Still Going Strong," in *Ships and the Sea*, Spring, 1955, pp. 8-11, 52-58.

GRUBER, RUTH: *Destination Palestine: The Story of the Hagana Ship* Exodus 1947, New York: A. A. Wyn, 1948.

HARDY, A. C.: "More Reminiscences of the 'Honeymoon Fleet,' ", in *Sea Breezes*, December, 1946, pp. 402-405.

HART, ALFRED I. (Editor): *The Old Bay Line Magazine*, Baltimore, monthly magazine published by the Company, 1910-1918.

HAY, JACOB: "The Chesapeake's Old Bay Line," in *Holiday*, July, 1957, pp. 72-73, 90, 92-93.

HESS, JEAN B.: "Last Of Their Kind," in *The Sea Breeze* (Boston Seaman's Friend Society), July, 1961, pp. 8-13.

HILL, DON: "After 120 Years, Old Bay Line Still Steaming," in Norfolk *Virginian-Pilot*, Lighthouse Section with photos by Neal V. Clark, Jr. Sunday, Sept. 18, 1960.

HORNE, GEORGE: "Palestine-Bound Mystery Ship, Battered by Sea, is Back in Port," in the *New York Times*, March 7, 1947.

JENKINS, GEORGE, and WOODRUFF, A. E.: "The Fast Steamer *Florida*," in *International Marine Engineering*, April, 1908, pp. 145-148.

KILBURN, HENRY: "Time for a Stew," in *The Skipper*, August, 1961, pp. 19-21, 38. (Photographs of steamer *City Of Richmond* by Robert de Gast.)

KIME, LOLINE W.: " 'Steamboat 'Round the Bend' on the Chesapeake Bay: A Trip on Baltimore's Old Bay Line, America's Oldest Steamship Company Linking Maryland and Virginia for 120 Years, is a Rendezvous with History," in Chesapeake and Potomac Telephone Co. *The Transmitter*, May–June, 1960, pp. 4-7.

LANTZ, EMILY EMERSON: "History of the Steamboat on the Chesapeake," in Baltimore *Sunday Sun*, various dates, 1908. (Particularly Article XII, "The Baltimore Steam Packet Company", March 29, 1908, p. 15.)

MEEKINS, LYNN R.: "Down the Bay to Norfolk," in Baltimore *American*, April 2, 1922, p. 4D.

NELSON, JIM: "Night Trips by Water—Chesapeake Ships Recall Colorful Travel Era," in *New York Times*, Sunday, June 29, 1952.

"Powell, Legh R., Jr.": in *Railway Age*, New York, Nov. 26, 1927, pp. 1053-54.
RAMAGE, ROBERT C.: "Ferry to Palestine—20th Century Exodus," in Norfolk
    Virginian-Pilot, Sunday, April 17, 1960, p. 1B.
RITZER, STANLEY, as told to MICHELMORE, PETER: "I Ran the Blockade to
    Palestine: The True Story of the *Exodus*," in *Argosy*, February, 1960,
    pp. 19-21, 78-80.
SHANER, J. JEAN: "Old Bay Line Gets Up Steam," in Baltimore Evening *Sun*,
    Feb. 19, 1940, p. 21.
STANTON, SAMUEL WARD: "Baltimore and Norfolk Boats from the Early Days
    to the Present," in *Seaboard Magazine*, June 16, 1892. (Reprint No. 4
    of Steamship Historical Society of America, 1947, pp. 23-26.)
TIMEWELL, H. C.: "*Exodus 1947* Takes on Her Cargo," in *The American Nep-
    tune*, October, 1949, pp. 300-301.
TWYFORD, WARNER: "[Abbott] Lutz, Veteran of the *Exodus*, is Home Again,"
    in Norfolk *Virginian-Pilot*, November 18, 1947.
"Warfield, S. Davies," in *Railway Age*, New York, Oct. 29, 1927, pp. 853-854.
WILLIAMS, HAROLD A.: "From Canton to Canton," in Baltimore *Sunday Sun
    Magazine*, Feb. 2, 1947, pp. 6-7.
Miscellaneous Company circulars, leaflets, and other advertising and promo-
    tional material.

PRINTED MATTER ON AMERICAN STEAMBOAT NAVIGATION IN
    GENERAL

ANON.: *Narrative of the Loss of the Steam-Packet* Pulaski, Providence:
    H. H. Brown, 1839 (Pamphlet).
BRADLEE, FRANCIS G. B.: *Steam Navigation in New England*, Salem: Essex
    Institute, 1920.
COLCORD, JOANNA C.: *Songs of American Sailormen*, New York: W. W.
    Norton, 1939.
DAYTON, FRED ERVING: *Steamboat Days*, New York: Stokes, 1925.
DUNBAR, SEYMOUR: *A History of Travel in America*, Indianapolis: Bobbs-
    Merrill, 1915, 4 vols.
EMMERSON, JOHN C., JR.: *The Steamboat Comes to Norfolk Harbor, and the
    Log of the First Ten Years, 1815-1825*, Portsmouth: The Author, 1949.
————: *Steam Navigation in Virginia and Northeastern North Carolina
    Waters, 1826-1836*, Portsmouth: The Author, 1949.
FENTON, FRANK J.: "Fog-Bound Collision Cost Life of Woman Passenger,"
    in Newport News *Times-Herald*, Aug. 31, 1959, pp. 11, 12. (Washington
    Line boat *District of Columbia*.)
HARDING, GARDNER: "Save the Steamboat," in the *Atlantic Monthly*, January,
    1938.
HARDY, A. C.: *American Ship Types*, New York: Van Nostrand, 1927.
HARLAN AND HOLLINGSWORTH CORP.: *Semi-Centennial Memoire of the Harlan
    and Hollingsworth Company, 1836-1886*, Wilmington: The Company,
    1886.
ISHERWOOD, J. B.: *Experimental Researches in Steam Engineering*, Philadel-
    phia: Franklin Institute, 1863-1865. Two vols.
KELLEY, WILLIAM J.: "Baltimore Steamboats in the Civil War," in *Maryland
    Historical Magazine*, March, 1942, pp. 42-52.
LANE, CARL D.: *American Paddle Steamboats*, New York: Coward-McCann,
    1943.
MCADAM, ROGER WILLIAMS: *The Old Fall River Line*, Brattleboro: Stephen
    Daye, 1937, revised edition, New York, 1955.
————: "On the Old Fall River Line," in *Travel*, July, 1938, pp. 30-33, 47.
————: *Salts of the Sound*, Brattleboro: Stephen Daye, 1939, revised edition,
    New York, 1957.

MACGREGOR, JOHN: *Progress of America from the Discovery by Columbus to the Year 1846*. London, 1847, two vols. (Vol. II)

MARESTIER, J. B.: *Memoire sur les Bateaux à Vapeur des Etats-Unis*, Paris, 1824, two vols., text and plates.

MERCHANTS AND MINERS TRANSPORTATION COMPANY: *Tales of the Coast, a Brief History of the Company, 1852-1927*, Baltimore: Read-Taylor Press, 1927.

MORRISON, JOHN H.: *History of American Steam Navigation*, New York: W. F. Sametz, 1903.

PARKER, CAPT. HARRY, and BOWEN, FRANK C.: *Mail and Passenger Steamships of the 19th Century*, Philadelphia: Lippincott, 1925.

RINGWALT, J. L.: *Transportation Systems in the United States*, Philadelphia, 1888.

ROSS, MAJOR ODGEN J.: *The Steamboats of Lake Champlain*, Champlain Transportation Co., 1930.

————: *The Steamboats of Lake George*, Lake George Steamboat Co., 1932.

SHANNAHAN, JOHN H. K.: *Steamboat'n' Days*, Baltimore: Norman Publishing Co., 1930.

STANTON, SAMUEL WARD: *American Steam Vessels*, New York: Smith and Stanton, 1895.

Steamboat Bill of Facts, Journal of the Steamship Historical Society of America, Inc., 1940-1960.

U. S. NAVY DEPARTMENT: *Official Records of the Union and Confederate Navies in the War of the Rebellion*, Washington: Government Printing Office, 1894-1927. Series I, Vols. 1-27; Series II, Vols. 1-3; Index.

WALLACE, W. A.: *The Great Eastern's Log*, London: Bradbury and Evans, 1860.

WHALL, CAPT. W. B.: *Sea Songs and Shanties*, Glasgow: Brown, Son and Ferguson, 1910.

WOOD, H. GRAHAM: "A Room With a View," in *Steamboat Bill of Facts*, April, 1946, pp. 362-364.

PRINTED MATERIAL ON THE LOCAL HISTORY OF THE CHESAPEAKE BAY AREA

ANON.: "Activities of the Port of Baltimore," in *Municipal Journal*, Baltimore, March 25, 1925.

————: "The Steamship Lines of Chesapeake Bay," in *Municipal Journal*, Baltimore, Oct. 5, 1923.

ARTHUR, ROBERT: *History of Fort Monroe*, Fort Monroe: Coast Artillery School, 1930.

BALTIMORE AMERICAN: *A History of the City of Baltimore, Its Men and Its Institutions*, Baltimore: The *American*, 1902.

BORUM, SAMUEL R.: *Norfolk Port and City*, Norfolk, 1893.

BREWINGTON, M. V.: *Chesapeake Bay: A Pictorial Maritime History*, Cambridge: Cornell Maritime Press, 1953.

BURGESS, ROBERT H.: "The World's Largest Ship Called At Old Point A Century Ago," in Newport News *Daily Press*, Sunday, July 31, 1960, p. 1D. (*Great Eastern's* visit).

BURTON, H. W.: *The History of Norfolk, Virginia*, Norfolk, 1877.

City Directories of Baltimore and Norfolk. Various dates and publishers, including W. S. Forrest, Chataigne, Woods, John Murphy, etc.

ENOCH PRATT FREE LIBRARY: *The Cator Collection of Baltimore Views, A Catalogue*, Baltimore: The Library, 1933 (Pamphlet).

FORREST, WILLIAM S.: *Historical and Descriptive Sketches of Norfolk and Vicinity*, Philadelphia: Lindsay and Blakiston, 1853.

GILFILLAN, S. COLOM: "Early Steamboats of the Chesapeake," in Baltimore *Sunday Sun Magazine*, May 17, 1931, pp. 10-11.
GRIFFITH, T. W.: *The Annals of Baltimore*, Baltimore, 1833.
HAIN, JOHN A.: *Side Wheel Steamers of the Chesapeake Bay, 1880-1947*, Glen Burnie: Glendale Press, 1947.
HOWARD, GEORGE W.: *The Monumental City*, Baltimore, 1873.
JONES, CARY W.: *Norfolk as a Business Centre*, Norfolk.
LAMB, ROBERT W.: *Our Twin Cities of the 19th Century, Norfolk and Portsmouth*, Norfolk: Barcroft, 1887-1888.
LOSSING, BENSON J.: *The Pictorial Field Book of the Revolution*, New York: Harper and Bros., 1851-1852.
MORDECAI, JOHN BROOKE: "Travel and Communications," Chapter XIV in *Richmond, Capital of Virginia, Approaches to its History*, Richmond: Whittet and Shepperson, 1938.
————: *A Brief History of the Richmond, Fredericksburg, and Potomac Railroad Company*, Richmond, 1940.
NORFOLK ADVERTISING BOARD: *Through the Years at Norfolk*, Norfolk: The Board, 1936.
NOWITZKI, GEORGE I.: *Norfolk*, Norfolk, 1888.
PEALE MUSEUM: *Harbor 1854-1955: A Century of Photographs of the Port of Baltimore*, Baltimore: Municipal Museum Pamphlet Historical Series No. 11, 1955.
POLLOCK, EDW.: *Sketch Book of Portsmouth, Va*, Portsmouth, 1886.
PORTER, JOHN W. H.: *A Record of Events in Norfolk County, Va., from April 19, 1861, to May 10, 1862*, Portsmouth: W. A. Fiske, 1892.
SCHARF, COL. J. THOMAS: *The Chronicles of Baltimore, Being a Complete History of Baltimore Town and Baltimore City*, Baltimore: Turnbull Bros., 1874.
————: *The History of Baltimore City and County*, Philadelphia, 1881.
STEINER, BERNARD C.: *Descriptions of Maryland*, Baltimore: The Johns Hopkins Press, 1904.
————: *Men of Mark in Maryland*, Washington, 1907.
STEWART, WILLIAM H.: *History of Norfolk County, Virginia*, Chicago, 1902.
WERTENBAKER, THOMAS JEFFERSON: *Norfolk—Historic Southern Port*, Durham: Duke University Press, 1931.
WOOD, H. GRAHAM: "Steamers Operating out of the Port of Baltimore," in *Marine News*, February, 1947.

PUBLISHED TRAVELERS' IMPRESSIONS, GUIDES, ETC.

APPLETON: *Appleton's Illustrated Hand-Book of American Travel*, New York, 1857.
CRAM, MILDRED: *Old Seaport Towns of the South*, New York: Dodd, Mead & Co., 1917 (pp. 51-53).
DEROOS, F. F.: *Personal Narrative of Travels in the United States in 1826*. London, 1827.
DICKENS, CHARLES: *American Notes For General Circulation*. London, 1842, two vols. (Vol. II).
DUNLAP, WILLIAM: *Diary of William Dunlap, 1776-1839*, New York: New York Historical Society, 1931, three vols. (Vol. II).
HENGISTON, J. W.: "Something of Baltimore, Washington, the Chesapeake and Potomac," in *Colburn's New Monthly Magazine*, London, 1853 (Vol. 97, pp. 358-373).
JONES, CHARLES H. (Compiler): *Appleton's Hand-Book of American Travel— Southern Tour*, New York: Appleton, 1874.
LLOYD, W. ALVIN: *Steamboat and Railroad Guide*, New Orleans, 1857.

Official Guide of the Railways and Steam Navigation Lines of the United States, Puerto Rico, Canada, Mexico, and Cuba, New York: National Railway Publication Co. (72nd year, No. 10, edition of March, 1940, published monthly).

POWER, TYRONE: *Impressions of America During the Years 1833, 1834, 1835,* London, 1836, two vols. (Vol. II).

ROBERTSON, WILLIAM, and ROBERTSON, W. F.: *Our American Tour: Being a Run of 10,000 Miles from the Atlantic to the Golden Gate in the Autumn of 1869,* Edinburgh: Privately Printed, 1871.

WELD, CHARLES RICHARD: *A Vacation Tour of the United States and Canada,* London, 1855.

SHIP REGISTERS AND OFFICIAL LISTS

List of the Merchant Vessels of the United States, Washington: Government Printing Office, Annual Reports, 1868-1960.

Lloyd's Register of Shipping, Annual Reports, -1960.

LYTLE, WILLIAM M.: *Merchant Steam Vessels of the United States, 1807-1858* —"The Lytle List," Mystic: Steamship Historical Society of America, 1952 (Publication No. 6).

New York Marine Register, A Standard Classification of American Vessels, New York: Root, Anthony and Co., 1857.

ROGERS AND BLACK: *Marine Roll or List of Names Comprising the Mercantile Marine of the United States,* Baltimore: F. Lucas, Jr., 1847.

NEWSPAPERS

BALTIMORE
    American and Commercial Daily Advertiser
    News
    News-Post
    Sun
NEW YORK
    Dixon's Letter (Supplement, 1842)
    Times
NEWPORT NEWS
    Daily Press
    The Times-Herald
NORFOLK
    American Beacon
    Argus
    Herald
    Virginian-Pilot
PETERSBURG
    American Constellation
PORTSMOUTH
    Advertiser
    Star
    Times and Commercial Advertiser
RICHMOND
    Commercial Compiler
    Dispatch
    Enquirer
    Times-Dispatch
    Whig
Miscellaneous unidentified newspaper clippings owned by the Baltimore Steam Packet Co.

MANUSCRIPT SOURCES

BALTIMORE CUSTOMS HOUSE, Enrollment Books.
BALTIMORE STEAM PACKET COMPANY, Manuscripts—
    Extracts of Minutes of the Board of Directors, 1840-
    Contracts entered into by the Company
    Agreement of January 11, 1877 between the Company and the Richmond
      Steamboat Company
    Miscellaneous correspondence
    Memorandum with respect to traffic handled over Old Point Comfort
      Pier, April 5, 1955.
BUREAU OF MARINE INSPECTION AND NAVIGATION, Early Records. Collection
    of the National Archives, Washington, D. C.
HARLAN AND HOLLINGSWORTH COMPANY,
    Four portfolios of plans of vessels, hull and machinery, constructed by
    H & H, Wilmington, Del., 1849-1896. Collection of the Mariners Museum,
    Newport News, Va.
NORFOLK, VIRGINIA, NEWSPAPER ITEMS
    Transcripts of articles pertaining to shipping and steamboats appear-
    ing in various Norfolk newspapers as compiled by John C. Emmerson,
    of Portsmouth. A: Steamboats 1837-1860; B: Steamboats 1866-1878.
    Collection of the Mariners Museum, Newport News, Va.
POSTAL CONTRACTS,
    Memoranda covering records of postal contracts awarded the Baltimore
    Steam Packet Co. In the Post Office Department Library, Washington,
    D. C.

Key to abbreviations in this index:

aux.—auxiliary
barr.—barracks
bg.—barge
Brit.—British
bt.—boat
Chin.—Chinese
csr.—cruiser
Conf.—Confederate
dstr.—destroyer
fght.—freight
fghtr.—freighter
fy.—ferry
gbt.—gunboat
Hond.—Honduras
iron.—ironclad
Ital.—Italian
lch.—launch
lcm.—locomotive

mtr.—motor
pass.—passenger
rdr.—raider
s.—screw
sbt.—steamboat
sch.—schooner
shbt.—showboat
ss.—steamship
stm.—steam
stmr.—steamer
s. tug—screw tug
Swed.—Swedish
sw.—side-wheeler
tkr.—tanker
trspt.—transport
t. s.—twin screw
U.S.S.—United States Ship

General Index

Index to Ships' Names

Vessels With Compound Names, Arranged Alphabetically by Last Names

ALEXANDER CROSBY BROWN, a lifetime resident of Newport News, Virginia, graduated from Yale University and received his master's degree in history from the College of William and Mary. He is a prolific writer with a special fondness for maritime history, and is the former literary editor of the *Newport News Daily Press*. For many years he was associate editor of the *American Neptune*, a quarterly journal of maritime history. He is also a retired Commander in the United States Naval Reserve and the recipient of many distinguished awards and prizes. Mr. Brown is the author or more than twenty books on a variety of subjects ranging from stories written for children to scholarly monographs on affairs of the sea.

CPSIA information can be obtained
at www.ICGtesting.com
Printed in the USA
LVOW13s1506060518
576188LV00038B/955/P